ERIC OWEN MOSS ARCHITECTS

For A

For M

I'm looking for that stress. Only that tension between possibilities accurately represents our culture to itself.

– Eric Owen Moss

ERIC OWEN MOSS ARCHITECTS

images
Publishing

Published in Australia in 2017 by
The Images Publishing Group Pty Ltd
ABN 89 059 734 431
6 Bastow Place, Mulgrave, Victoria 3170, Australia
Tel: +61 3 9561 5544 Fax: +61 3 9561 4860
books@imagespublishing.com
www.imagespublishing.com

The Images Publishing Group Reference Number: 1300

National Library of Australia Cataloguing-in-Publication entry

Title: Eric Owen Moss Architects / Eric Owen Moss Architects.
ISBN: 9781864707137 (hardback)
Series: Leading Architects of the World.
Subjects: Eric Owen Moss Architects.
Architecture, Modern—20th century.
Architecture, Modern—21st century.
Architectural practice, International.
Architectural design.

Production manager: Rod Gilbert
Senior editor: Gina Tsarouhas
Assisting editor: Sue Bennett
Graphic designer: Steve Farrow

Printed on 140gsm GoldEast Matt Art paper by Everbest Printing Co. Ltd., in Hong Kong/China

CONTENTS

SAMITAUR

THE ARCHITECT'S LESSON

If it ain't broke,
Don't fix it.

Sound familiar?
Maybe.

But you'll never bump into that banality in the corridors of Eric Owen Moss Architects.

Occasionally architecture subsumes time—freezes it;
And I want to assure you, very few human endeavors share that capacity.

Now some of you may think of EOMA as academic.
And it is.

And some of you may think of EOMA as a Los Angeles venue. And it is.

And some of you may even think of EOMA as a bastion of rebellion. And sometimes it is.

But there is something else.
More elusive.
Deeper.

Not limited to place.
Not defined by time.

We are idealists.
Nominally, of course, our subject is building and buildings, but in the broadest sense, (W)rapper is a pursuit of freedom and imagination.

Pursuit, I said, with no warranty that the pursuit is requited.
Remember, no one owns freedom and imagination.
It alights for a moment, then dissipates, and disappears.
Perhaps we are now in the midst of one of those moments.
But we don't hang on by holding tight.

Only a world of invention and discovery sustains a world of freedom and imagination.

That means architecture at its best is intrinsically at risk.
Architecture and risk are synonyms.
No risk?
No freedom.

Sometimes I hear people say that we are naive.
Sometimes I hear people say that we are unsophisticated.
Could be—but we know naive and unsophisticated as assets, not liabilities.

Architecture is a hypothesis about how to live.

'Who am I?' asked the little boy.

Architecture is not only what you do.
Architecture is why you do what you do.

We imagine it.
We produce it.

And special moments like today won't end when the day ends.

The so-called history of architecture is a retrospective of invented moments.
But (W)rapper is less concerned with history as a study of what's past.
And more concerned with the history we will make in the future.

We have listened to what has been said.

We have learned what can be taught.

Now our job is to tell architecture what has been left out.
What was missed.

Build what is missing if we can.
That is the challenge.

Because I guarantee there's always something missing.

The world gets different.
Architecture gets different.
I didn't say it gets better.
I didn't say it gets worse.

We study what has been done.
We learn the hypotheses.
We scrutinize the tactics.
We analyze the results.

But we don't know what 'rough beast' is coming next.

There's a profound tension, even anxiety, located between past and future.

It's inevitable.
Learn to cultivate that anxiety.
The past demands allegiance to what it did.
Won't willingly release its grip.
Apprehensive, the future will undo it.

And the future will.

Sooner or later…

Do you know the tale of the Gordian knot?
All the notorious characters who labored for years to develop a theory for unraveling that intricate coagulation of ropes. Until Alexander the Great showed up, pulled out his sword, and sliced the knot in half.

Just like that.

Cut the knot.

Sever the past from the present, and build the future.

Contemporary psychologists preach the avoidance of tension.
Architecture, on the other hand, chases that tension.
Looks for it—somewhere between where we have been and where we are going.

Get comfortable being permanently uncomfortable because the architecture adventure is enduring.

That's a lot to ask.
I know.
Expectations are high.

Did you happen to glance at the *New York Times* today?

'Who are we?' asked the little girl.

There is love in the afternoon; there is politics and art and culture and numberless events and experiences on the land, on the sea, in the sky…introverted and extroverted… named and nameless…things and fragments of things… on and on and on.

How do we navigate that multifaceted, multitudinous conflagration?

I'm convinced architecture can narrate that story, and discover its meanings.

I believe that.

Architecture can build the culture.
Meaning, architecture builds and rebuilds meaning.

That's our job.

Architecture reports on the culture:
Who we aspire to be.
What we love.
What we hate.

Architecture affirms us.
Architecture dissects us.
Architecture denigrates us.

And architecture sustains the story for those who aren't born yet.
Architecture bestrides time.

Architecture the way in.
Architecture the way up.
Architecture the way out.
Architecture the way down.

Here's the (W)rapper coda, a text by Thomas Wolf, an old friend, discovered in the 1930s written on a subway wall at 59th and Lexington in New York City:

'I cannot yet tell him how to design; I cannot yet attempt to give rules whereby she will be enabled to build. I am becoming an architect, discovering the line, the structure, and the articulation of the language which I must discover if I am to do the work I want to do. It is for just this reason, because I sometimes stumble, because my energy and talent is still involved in this process of discovery, that I am speaking as I speak here. Starting today this is a story of a contest, with focus and sweat, with successes and defeats, and in the end, achievement. I don't know how to design and build just yet. But I'm on my way. I have learned something essential about myself and about the work of architecture, and I'm committed to continuing that story.'

Architecture is an eternal river flowing from past to future.
Drop in your offering.
See if it floats.
We think it will.

Talk to your peers;
Talk to your culture;
Talk to yourself;
Talk to those who aren't born yet.

Write us a chapter.
No one writes the whole story.
Architecture's the unfinished symphony.
Keep the music playing.

If it ain't broke,
Break it.

If it ain't broke,
Fix it.

Make it new.

That's the architect's lesson.

Welcome to the (W)rapper.

Eric Owen Moss
Speech written for the opening of (W)rapper

EOMA: PHILOSOPHY

'Build Your Cities on the Slopes of Vesuvius!' —Frederick Nietzsche

Contemporary builders don't master plan the slopes of the world's volcanoes. What the quote proposes is an aspiration to risk, in one's life, and in one's architecture. What is risk?

Skepticism of any governing rules as presently constituted. Building on Vesuvius suggests that the pedagogical environment is premised on an enduring dissatisfaction with the world as we find it. If that dissatisfaction quotient is missing, there is no motivation to challenge conditions in the world as we find them. The world changes; emphases, priorities, capacities move. Perhaps the world gets better, perhaps worse, perhaps better and worse simultaneously. We can debate those possibilities.

What I'm interested in is that the architect has the courage to speculate on what the content of that change could be, to orchestrate that change, and to critique that change including building on the slopes of a volcano.

Medusa Column Capital Inverted, Roman Cistern, Istanbul

Across the street from Hagia Sophia (before there was a Hagia Sophia), down a dank, dark stair several levels beneath the street, stands Istanbul's 2000-year-old Roman cistern. Sitting in the collected water, perhaps three feet (a meter) deep, are two inverted Medusa-headed columns with their erstwhile capitals partially submerged. The Romans constructed the cistern using columns from a dismantled Greek temple. The inverted columns support the cistern's roof at street level, and two Medusa-headed column capitals reside upside down in the water.

Recall that for the Greeks, one look at the snake-covered Medusa head turned the viewer to stone. So the Romans positioned the Greek religion underwater.

A culture sometimes explains itself to itself with respect to a rivalry with an antecedent culture. The present and the past are rivals for ownership of the future. How that contest transpires is our subject. There's a lot of talk today, particularly in conservationist circles, about the gradual evolution of ideas over time. And they call that progress.

The upside-down Medusa suggests the opposite, the prospect of a radical discontinuity of ideas over time, and it is essential that young architects see evidence that an attack on the cultural past and an aggressive posture going forward are what suddenly creates a new design vocabulary. Not a gradual cultural evolution, but an instant adversary position, culture versus culture, old versus new.

The Romans confront their cultural nemesis—the Greeks. Whatever the complexities of that historic exchange, the Greeks own a poetic content that never belonged to the Romans. The Romans own organization, utility, and scale, but the Greeks own Phidias and Aeschylus.

According to my psycho-therapeutic rendition of this cultural confrontation, the Romans attack an antecedent ethos, the Greek vision, in order to validate their own. The Romans roll through Central Asia. What do they find? A Greek temple near Constantine's city. They dismantle the temple, and build a cistern with the used parts. The temple is small and religious. The cistern is gargantuan and utilitarian. The Romans collect the water and support the structure above on the old Greek columns. To emphasize the new priorities the Romans invert the capitals and place them in the water.

Architecture ratifies the arrival of a new cultural vision in Constantinople. The old is bulldozed by the new. The Romans invert the content, and debase its original meaning. The spirit of that impetus to invert, the energy and the ferocity of the 'out with the old' modus, is the capacity we're interested in engendering.

Trajan's Baths over Nero's House

In the area that (today) overlooks the (not yet constructed) Coliseum in Rome, Nero built the Domus Aurea. Nero departs, Trajan arrives, and Trajan builds his baths. Trajan's design strategy is to aggressively impose the new baths on top of Nero's house.

What do you think is the design intent of 'mine over yours'?

Today you can still see the violent intersection of two very different spatial conceptions. Trajan has no interest in preserving Nero qua Nero. His project is an intersection of two sources of political power, one old, one new, and the primacy of new over old. Strangely, Trajan is unable to demolish his predecessor. History is like that. We can alter its contemporary presence, but it is difficult to entirely eradicate.

Exchange between Kublai Khan and Marco Polo

Kublai: *Marco, when you return to the west, will you repeat to your people the same tales you tell to me?*

Marco: *I speak and speak, but the listener retains only the words he is expecting.*

An essential learning principle: can you imagine the contemporary world in a form different from the one you have come to understand? Can the world become other than it is?

The exchange between Marco Polo and Kublai Khan suggests a capacity that few of us actually practice. It's an intellectual challenge: can you hear what you haven't listened for? Can you imagine what you've never seen? Or do you only hear yourself coming back to yourself, the version you have learned, and learned to repeat. The objective is to be able to open your skull and pour in something new; the objective is to find a capacity to imagine what you don't yet recognize.

In this dialogue between Kublai Khan and Marco Polo, Marco's answer to Kublai's question is pessimistic.

Marco Polo says he may talk endlessly about his adventures in astonishing, unprecedented Cathay, but he knows his Venetian audience will only authenticate what they already know.

Marco's response is antithetical to what we would like to see educationally. Can we learn to anticipate what we haven't anticipated?

Overgrown Angkor Wat

We are conventionally told that buildings endure over long stretches of time. Buildings transcend time. Is that so? Or are buildings both durable and fragile simultaneously? Rarely does one imagine a building that changes form and meaning over time. But buildings, if they last, often outlast the cultural meanings in which they originated. That is what has happened in Angkor Wat. Domes collapse. Walls fall. The human content, the cultural ethos that drove this colossal construction, is gone.

Trees grow out of the roof. Did the original builders anticipate a time when trees would originate from that enormous roof structure? Did they imagine the structure as an historic voice commenting on Angkor's lost culture to ages yet unborn? Architecture here is a spatial purveyor of cultures long gone. It happens. And that implicates our buildings too. And we can't anticipate what will endure and what won't.

Do you doubt that? Walk through Teotihuacan, Stonehenge, Angkor Wat, and the Roman Forum.

Two vantage points on the durability of architecture: there is forever an impetus to make it new, and forever a limit on the lifespan of the new. Architecture belongs to time, and, on occasion, exists outside time. We build time into architecture. It is impossible to avoid that conjunction.

Walk around Shanghai or Beijing now and see what is going up. Then go to Xian and see the terra cotta warriors buried in the mud.

How durable are architecture's meanings and how fragile?

Amerigo Vespucci's Fifteenth-Century Map of the World

Mapmaking, in the broadest conceptual sense, orders and re-orders our conception of the planet. How dependable is our map if we are aware that another re-ordering is coming?

I collect maps. It is fascinating to see, over thousands of years, how the conception of the world's geography and the definition of nation-states change. We often think of maps as enduring in geographical and topographical content. But national boundaries change, sometimes quickly, as do both the topography and our capacity to technically represent that topography. The technical knowledge that allows us to describe the configuration of land and water also continues to evolve. We consistently behave as if all the tools are there, and the final information is in, so the era of changing maps is over. Until we realize that each age thinks the very same thing.

Psychologically we want to feel assured that the form of the land we're walking on or flying over and our capacity to measure it are constants. But the 2011 Sendai earthquake moved the earth's axis 4 inches (10 centimeters), and the famous and heretofore non-existent Northwest Passage has now opened up as the ice cap continues to melt.

The human need to lay out a route or a rule in order to proceed remains. So our maps are integral to our purpose, and simultaneously subject to revision. Every map is provisional. The necessity to map and the intrinsic limits of mapping are our subject. How to follow a map that we know to be provisional?

Oppenheimer at Alamogordo

It is not the discovery of the means to split the atom, per se, nor an intrinsic interest in investigating the atomic structure of matter that is the issue here. Rather it is the purpose to which abstract science is applied that is the subject.

The original 'what is an atom?' subject goes back to Democritus. Beneath appearances, what is everything made of? But the applied application of the split-the-atom investigation belongs to the era of Tojo and Hitler.

The capacity of applied science to re-make our conception of the world is on display at Hiroshima and Nagasaki. This is not intended to demean the capacity for Oppenheimer's team to think profoundly. Rather the question is why they were asked to think about this particular application of atomic science? On what human premise is their work sitting? Someone could equally have assigned the Oppenheimer team a plane, a boat, a housing project, or an alternative energy plant to design where the same commitment and intelligence could have been applied.

However internally logical and systematic were the thinking processes that led to the making of the atomic bomb, the choice to make it was external to Oppenheimer's problem-solving logic.

Purposeful, scientifically derived solutions always sit on other-than-scientific premises. The decision to assemble those intellectual talents at Alamogordo in 1944 in the service of bomb design rests on a different human intention that should be evaluated as a positive or negative decision regardless of the success of the technical results. The bomb making was clearly a debatable assignment, and its consequences can't be measured using the same intellectual tools as were used to achieve the goal. What was done with applied atomic energy at Alamogordo could have been done elsewhere, for different reasons, and taken a very different form.

We moved history in one direction.

We could have moved it in another.

Back Up the Dump Truck

A caricature of contemporary LA: a city constantly remodeling itself and its own self-conception. Los Angeles, unlike most large cities, has not yet determined its course and discourse. The city's future is in the future. We're making that future now.

Walk down Michigan Avenue: granite, concrete, and steel. Meanwhile in Los Angeles, it is sticks and plaster. Los Angeles is the ephemeral city. New building opportunities are readily available, and old manifestations have a predictably abbreviated life. Los Angeles is the adolescent's city, continuing to experiment, without (as yet) any long-term planning and building convictions. The production of architecture in Los Angeles runs on a different clock than other cities. Durability of purpose is, so far, antithetical to the planning conception of the city.

The Cycle of Urban Design

A hypothetical chronology of the history of urban development. We examine a sequence of urban ordering tactics.

Step one: what is a city? We don't yet know. This is the discovery stage. The city originates: imaginative, inconsistent, unpredictable, happenstance. The add and subtract, multiply and divide city. No firm postulates. We will call this the City as Instinct.

Step two: gradually a more predictable ordering mechanism takes shape; the beginning of planning patterns, the growth of precedents. We begin to understand the problems we are solving. What are the problems we can anticipate? Organizational prototypes develop. This is the city of burgeoning tactics: the cerebral city. We will call this the City as Method.

Step Three: the problems, in the mind of the problem solvers, are now solved. We now know what our city is. We know the rules that govern its making and its extensions. We understand what the city should look like. Continuity of implementation is the primary concern. Precedents are confirmed. The question of conceptual content no longer needs to be asked. The invention of step one and the pattern-making dexterity of step two disappear from the lexicon, and a repeatable rule system remains. We will call this the City as Redundancy.

The City as Instinct is the before-the-city city: planning where no plans yet exist. It is not formulaic; it is not systematic; it is not methodological.

It grows by accretion and experiment. It tolerates errors because there is as yet no correct solution.

The City as Method is also useful. That is the cerebral city—a strategic discussion of policy options and organizational opportunities and their consequences to realize the city.

It is the third city, Redundancy, that is anathema for us. 'No' to the city by rote, that no longer facilitates human vitality. The Redundant City is the end of learning.

And, of course, there may be a different chronology: historically they are a sequence, but the three are often found side by side in the contemporary city.

Hispanics March on City Hall, Los Angeles

This is a fascinating example of the burgeoning sociological prospects for Los Angeles. There is a large and growing

Hispanic population in LA, which will inevitably impact the political and organizational structure of the city, and ultimately its architecture. The potency of that Hispanic presence on a Saturday morning protest march to City Hall filled the downtown streets for ten blocks—perhaps 300,000 marchers.

What are the urban consequences of significant population change and the prospect of deep racial divisions for the study of architecture in Los Angeles? The Los Angeles riots of the 1960s and 1990s in what remains largely a racially segregated city are important reminders of the consequences.

I was briefly surrounded in my car among the marchers, unable to move. I could feel the tensions and the demographic intricacy of the intersection of rich, poor, black, white, and Hispanic; affluence and poverty bumping into one another in cars, on buses and on foot.

The form of the future city is largely ahead of us. It is open, meaning there are a number of alternative planning options that could re-direct the city's racial divides. And that future form is largely a question. That open future, the opportunity to imagine a very different Los Angeles, is important for students to understand. The city's not complete; not built and zoned, organized and understood. That urban re-imagining is ahead of us.

US–Mexican Border, *The New York Times* Foreign Affairs

My office produced a concept strategy for the redesign of the US–Mexican border at the request of *The New York Times*. The Foreign Affairs Editor asked us to suggest a border strategy that would alleviate the current social and political tensions. What should the border look like?

Can architecture convey public policy?

What policy issues are manifest in the redesign of the zone between the two nations? The project connects a landscape design concept with the policy issues that divide Mexico and the United States. In a broader sense, the proposal is a speculation on whether that sort of policy question is a legitimate subject for architecture.

How to address the admixture of two different cultures? Other than the predictable walls and fences—is there a form language for national border security? What are the connotations of a 'walled' versus an 'open' border? What should be shared between two nations, and what should remain discrete?

The solution here involves the construction of a 2000-mile-long earth mound, a multicultural promenade on raised earth, positioned on the border itself, with traffic over the border directed through a series of Siqueiros' murals on the walls of the tunnels to be excavated under the border/mound. Vertical glass tubes, a 'glass forest,' are positioned on the mounds, bringing light to the under-border tunnels, and orchestrating the parallel to the border walk along the mound. This is the architecture of open borders and cultural exchange, forgoing the conventional manifestations of nation-to-nation insecurity.

Bridge Collapse in Minneapolis

Infrastructure ties the country together operationally, so what does a systematically neglected infrastructure tell us about America's future purpose and will. We live here. What is America today? To what subjects are we paying attention? How durable is our current attention span?

What does that tell us about who we are? How do we define the operational coherence of our cities? How do we interconnect our cities, or do we? What's the prognosis for the future of American urbanism? How might it compare to that prognosis in Western Europe or East Asia?

Headline: Los Angeles' Subway to the Sea to be Complete in 2032

A subway planned for Wilshire Boulevard in Los Angeles to be completed, says the mayor, in 2032, means, in practical terms, there is no serious commitment to the subway construction at all. Paradoxically the capacity of a few architects to make projects in the last 20 years or so that identified Los Angeles as the quintessential venue for experimental architecture, identifies the incapacity of the same city to make comprehensive and imaginative long-term planning decisions. This happenstance, multi-city-city—Beverly Hills, Culver City, Santa Monica, Burbank, West Hollywood—with liberal instincts and a generous combination of tolerance and inattention, makes unique architecture a possibility. The architecture requires a personal vantage point, and a will to implement it. The context of the city, this city, unlike others, won't guide your architecture. Acts of imagination sporadically pop up on this happenstance landscape. But to discipline the multi-city-city, to collectively acknowledge a supra-city organizational necessity, à la the Wilshire train, requires both the political apparatus to implement, and a capacity to see and to plan on a city scale what we do not yet see and have not yet planned. Los Angeles at its best is a city in the process of becoming, building by building. So the city has a demonstrated capacity to define itself building by building, but as yet, little capacity to orchestrate its future with supra-building conceptions.

The Yellow River, China. The Mississippi Delta, Louisiana, United States. The Gotthard Base Tunnel, Switzerland. Han/Nakdong Rivers, South Korea

Architecture is changing its scale. Here are examples of that burgeoning capacity to make new environmental, social, political, and economic landscapes. The discussion is more complex.

The constituency is broader. And the vision is no longer limited to single buildings. Instead, colossal components of infrastructure in combination with large building complexes have the potential to redefine the purposes of cities and the content of nations.

Architecture can do this.

Today.

Northern China is historically short of water. The thirsty population grows. How to accommodate that growth? Relocate the Yellow River, 'China's sorrow.' And they're doing just that: an act of will, an act of purpose.

We can make the world other than it is.

Architecture can make the world different.

Beware the, 'Should we do it?' quotient. 'Should we do it?' is not a surrogate for 'Let's debate endlessly,' which so often in America now translates to, 'We'll never do it.'

Recall Hurricane Katrina. The environmental damage at the point of connection between the Mississippi and the Gulf of Mexico can be reconstituted. Adjust the position of the river and reorganize the delta. Extend the viable life of New Orleans. That is what this project proposes.

This is a regional project, remaking landforms, water, wetlands, levies, and the concomitant organization of buildings.

These projects are coming.

These projects are plausible.

It is our job to direct that advocacy.

Fantastic is not fantasy.

The Gotthard Base Tunnel, 35.4 miles (57 kilometers) through the Swiss Alps, is the longest tunnel ever built, a colossal act of design and engineering, facilitating transit over the Alps, heretofore a hardship for 2000 years.

There are two large rivers in South Korea: the Han, and the Nakdong. They originate in the mountains, and flow down to the sea, and there is an open land area separating the two, which is largely wild. A candidate for President proposed, as part of his program for a renewed South Korea, that the two rivers be connected. The idea is to enable sailing from Japan, through South Korea, to China, and back. A new linear, river-based city. A new commercial route. A new recreational route. This proposal would transform South Korea and its associations with adjacent nations. A quintessential river-city nation. That prospect is fascinating. It is controversial, of course, with environmentalists, politicos and so on, but the audacity of it is intriguing, and the willingness to consider radically modifying that mountainous environment, to recognize the potential and the capacity to do it, is the essential point.

Rock as Building; Building as Rock

What conceptual limits are there on what form a building might take? How should a building appear? A traditionalist says, 'This is a wall, a floor, a window, a door, a ceiling, a roof.' That is, a building is made of a predictable assembly of components, which we recognize a priori. The components have a history. Precedents. Should new building confirm the old history? If you do not acknowledge the dictionary definition of those conventional building parts, and the known strategies for assembling, then the question becomes, 'What is a wall, a floor, a window, a door, a ceiling, a roof?' How do we organize the components when the component definitions are indeterminate?

That is an interrogatory for contemporary architecture.

Mondrian, *Broadway Boogie Woogie*

Mondrian's *Broadway Boogie Woogie*: contemporary art as a belief system.

Mondrian painted his case for essence as austerity. If, beneath appearance, what is real, what is so, is what is simple, orderly, and logical, then we should get rid of all the surface fluff and reveal that simple underlying essence. In other words, what we see (understand) is not what we see (view). We have to see under what we see. The artist makes his conceptual argument using the primary colors: red, blue, and yellow, and black, white, and gray, and straight lines and right angles. But the results of the paint applied on canvas do not confirm the theoretical essence, as the painted details illustrate.

Imagine I am the art history teacher, and I am leading a class discussion: 'Tell me class, what conceptual message does *Broadway Boogie Woogie* deliver?' And you give me back the conventionally rehearsed exegesis, 'primary colors and right angle synopsis,' and we are finished, or are we? Take a careful look at the actual painting detail. The straight lines, if we examine them closely, are not straight. Some are made of tape, and the tape hangs off the painting. The colors are not smooth and homogeneous. Instead, a precise empirical review shows a bumpy, irregular painted surface. The colors are fading, and fading unevenly, and the right angles are never precisely right angles. It is important to see the physical reality of the painting, with the tape hanging off. It is not pristine and pure and straight and orderly and rectilinear and consistent.

The painting's physical presence doesn't ratify its implied ideology. Why should we subscribe to an aesthetic theory that the aesthetic does not substantiate?

Magazine Covers: *Dwell*, 2009, and *House Beautiful*, 1953

The *House Beautiful* article was once well known. It is a period piece evaluating the threat of modern architecture as the editors saw it. The traditionalist's country house was the American ideal in 1953, say the editors. Sixty years later that ideal is gone and the erstwhile modern enemy has become a friend on the cover of *Dwell* magazine.

What was once feared (the advent of 'dictatorial' modernism) becomes a feckless friend (*Dwell* modernism as the new architectural standard). The *House Beautiful* article explains the apprehensions of the Hearst Corporation, owners of *House Beautiful*, at mid-century, with respect to the perceived threat of modern architecture to the traditional American way of building homes. Taken to its logical political conclusion, modern architecture was a threat to the Hearst Corporation itself. Modern architecture, European and leftist in origin in *House Beautiful*'s editorial view, was the political and stylistic adversary of the indigenous American country style. Modern architecture was the enemy creed.

Polemical architecture engenders enemies. Polemical content is ipso facto dissatisfied with the current conditions in the world, suggests modifications to those conditions, and threatens the status quo. *House Beautiful* was the 1950s' voice for status quo architecture in America.

Now, on the checkout stand in Gelson's, that once polemical adversary becomes today's country house. Modernism, absent its leftist political affiliations, is today the style of choice, the cool guy's pad.

But the *Dwell* cover article is really a reflection of the dissipation of modernism's potency. The fear is gone. Polemical work generates adversaries. To build a modern building today is a different proposition. In 1953 modern building was confrontational in its aesthetic content, and aspired to a new lexicon to describe a new worldview. Modern in today's *Dwell* is not modern at all.

Over the last 100 years of architectural discourse, architecture has been a chronic borrower, expropriating the content drawn from a variety of avant-garde venues, to architecture itself. The aim is always to associate architecture with progressive thinking in other fields, suggesting that avant-garde thinking is contagious. Architecture's appliqué of a foreign subject matter to itself over the last 100 years is an attempt to validate its experimental qualifications.

Juan Gris and Le Corbusier

Architecture becomes cubism. Cubist art provides a pedigree for 'cubist' architecture. Look at the form languages of the two. A virtual identity. Radical art as a credentialed pedigree for radical architecture.

Architecture is cubism.

1920s, the Ford Assembly Line and the Bauhaus

The Ford assembly line, mid-1920s to early 1930s. Hannes Meyer, leader of the Bauhaus School of Design, tells the world, 'Industry now produces cars in a sequential line, let's make houses that way too.' Le Corbusier agrees. The linear assembly process for making automobiles should be replicated as the means to construct modern houses, the architectural avant-garde argues.

Successful industrial techniques should set the precedent for new building construction and for the form language of new architecture. The machine product from an assembly line, becomes the lexicon for the Bauhaus building.

Today, 80 years later, that machine-image advocacy is a design vocabulary of choice, associated with an industrially progressive vision of architecture. Pipes, ducts, the machines that operate building equipment, and the columns and beams that support the structures, become, by analogy, an expression of technical requirements. Houses are analogue industrial tools. As the tools evolve so do the images, but the operational principle linking new architecture with the expression of technical capacity is unchanged. The application of the image of technology to building is an attempt to associate architecture with the connotations of technical inventiveness.

The assembly line changed the world of fabrication. Good enough for cars, so why not for buildings?

Architecture is industry.

Human Metabolism Diagram and Kenzō Tange's Plan for Tokyo Bay, 1972

Kenzō Tange's scheme for expanding the city of Tokyo into the Bay. Another instance of architecture's continuing efforts to associate new architecture with a highly pedigreed, experimental science, in this case, physiology–human metabolism. An important group of Japanese architects in the 1960s, and 1970s—Kikutake, Tange, Kurokawa, and others—developed the 'metabolist school,' borrowing their exegesis of building and urban form from the innovative discourse in medicine, biology, and physiology. Bodily functions take on the names, and are explained, by analogy, with the processes of organizing cities and constructing buildings. Again, an example of the continuing need for architecture's pedigreed discourse to associate imaginative discoveries in science or the arts with innovative architecture.

Architecture is physiology.

Book of Essays by Paul de Man, and Peter Eisenman's Wexner Center in Columbus, Ohio

Paul de Man, the author, has a complicated personal history. He worked for the Nazis in occupied Belgium during the Second World War, writing for a right-wing, French-language newspaper called *Le Soir*. He had a wife and kids whom he apparently deserted somewhere in the midst of his journey, and finally found himself teaching at Yale. De Man is known as the inventor of the term 'deconstruction,' the name of a literary movement that purports to explain variable readings of written texts, rather than any single interpretations.

For instance, Melville writes the novel *Moby Dick*. But for de Man there is no single interpretation of that text. Rather there are multiple Mobys and Dicks, each conceivably the property of a different reader, or perhaps even of a different time for the same reader. For de Man, Moby Dick is a plural.

An implicit critique of the deconstruction hypothesis by those not fond of the concept was that de Man had invented an intellectual tool he could use to expunge his own personal history. The argument ran that de Man made his history (and ours) an infinite series of options or interpretative readings rather than an empirical, evidentiary based, single reading of his life. Multiple (and presumably exculpatory) interpretations were plausible. Whether or not that explanation accounts for the essential meaning of deconstruction (and I am convinced it does not), architecture again makes the predictable effort to align its content with an esoteric discourse outside itself, the intricate conceptual exegesis of literature.

Neither cubism, nor metabolism, nor the Ford assembly line belongs intrinsically to architecture. Along comes architect Peter Eisenman at the Wexner Center in Columbus, Ohio, and designs the quintessentially deconstructed building.

Architecture is deconstruction.

The Matrix and Jason Payne's House

Now the digital coding label for new architecture arrives—another effort to associate with an emerging speculative exploration. The film *The Matrix* exemplifies the application of new digital animating tools to cinema. The house by UCLA architect Jason Payne is assigned to that digital lexicon, both because of the use of multiple software tools in the design process, and the distinctly legible image of the application of those tools to building form. Architecture is digital.

In the discourse over the last 100 years, architecture's meanings have never belonged to internal, self-justifying processes. Instead, architecture assigns conceptual meanings to its content by associating architecture with experimental topics outside itself. In this discourse the ultimate meanings are extrinsic to architecture, though the critics have rarely acknowledged that circumstance.

Architecture is labeled art; architecture is industry; architecture is metabolism; architecture is literary criticism; and architecture is digital coding.

For 100 years architecture has utilized these associations to validate its contents and justify its form language.

The Wind, Directed by Victor Sjöström

The Wind is a 1928 silent film made by the Swedish director Victor Sjöström. The capacity to give the wind an allegorical form is what is fascinating here. What is wind? How to embody the physical and spiritual qualities of wind?

The imaginative act by Sjöström is to find a physical metaphor that suggests the wind's transparent effects.

How do you give form to a formless cause?

Not unlike the task for architecture. Architecture at its best imagines a spatial effect, and by building, communicates a cause. According to the Indian legend in the film, when the wind comes up, it appears as a galloping horse in the sky. The absence of sound in the film (subtitles only) focuses our visual attention on the horse galloping through the clouds.

The wind is an insurmountable force/horse in the sky.

Let's build that sky horse.

Charlie Chaplin, *The Gears of the Machine*

This is Chaplin mocking the conventionally accepted prowess of the machine. Architects certainly number among the machine's acolytes. The film image is a critique of the largely unfettered adulation of technology, and of the architects' favorite—the image of those technical tools. As in Alamogordo, the questions are, 'Who rules the rules of the machine? What's the human pro forma?' Otherwise the monstrous capacity and size of the machine, rolling and grinding, building our lives, is guided only by its technical logic. Metaphorically, we build the machine and then our machine builds us. Chaplin objects.

I would like the machine to be interrogated, examined, and evaluated. 'Throw your body on the gears,' he says. 'Slow it, interrupt it, stop it so we can scrutinize it.' It is the machine, yes and no rather than the machine exclusively as yes.

Staatsgalerie, Stuttgart, James Stirling. Carpenter Center, Harvard, Le Corbusier

These two projects interrelate goals for the use of public space with the objectives of private architecture. Both suggest an integration of private program components with a conception of public pedestrian circulation. Stirling and Le Corbusier show us how to unify those often contradictory purposes. Both are small projects that suggest a larger, strategic relationship between single buildings and the public circulation that conventionally bypasses the operational interiors of those buildings.

The Carpenter Center is on the campus at Harvard, designed by Le Corbusier. It houses classrooms and galleries for the arts, sculpture, and graphic design. The focus of the design is an open-air ramp connecting parallel streets on either side of the building by marching the pedestrian public through the building. Suppose students on the way from Physics to English shortcut the usual routes by heading up the ramp, through the Carpenter Center, viewing, by-the-way/on-the-way, a variety of the arts on exhibit, on down the ramp, and off to class. The building makes art accessible to an audience, which is not looking for art, just for a shortcut. So art becomes an integral component of a public walking process. What Le Corbusier has done is to conceive a street that includes a building interior normally reserved only for those whose interest is expressly to visit that interior.

Stirling's Staatsgalerie takes a similar organization tack. Stirling knows the Carpenter Center well, and replicates its urban message. Begin at your apartment at the top of the hill, cross the street and walk down the hill, through the museum courtyards surrounded by gallery art, on to the base of the hill. Arrive at the bus stop, and off you go. Again, the architect integrates directed pedestrian movement, here between a residential neighborhood and a public transit stop, now conducive to an unanticipated viewing of art on the way to the bus.

The single-minded urban journey now promises a more complex cultural event.

Brazil and Argentina

Soccer, the beautiful game. Why?

A game of instinct, imagination, happenstance, and will. A contest where there is forever a divergence between what is practiced, and the actual event.

Practice cannot replicate the game itself. So can we learn to anticipate what we cannot anticipate? That is a conceptual issue for architecture.

Learning involves practice, and practice involves repeating conceptual patterns we have been taught and learned. And then the match begins, and, to be uniquely successful, instinct replaces the learned response.

Architecture cannot be delivered according to an a priori rule system. Like architecture, each participant brings a different repertoire to the field. Architecture is personal and it is the deviant behavior, the departure from the practiced norm that sometimes delivers the unprecedented goal.

Architecture is fútbol.

Jacket of *Foucault's Pendulum*, Umberto Eco

Today, unlike in previous periods in human history, information on every cultural precedent, on every civilization's way of seeing, thinking, understanding, and building is available to us in some detail. When multitudinous cultural vantage points are accessible we face a very different problem than in those eras where cultures were discrete, remote from one another, and citizens were generally receptive to the single, local belief system.

Multitudinous cultural and belief options are available. So which one(s) prevail? What to choose? How to choose? What to disregard? Why? That is also a substantial issue for architecture when cultural content is associated with building content. For international architecture, which cultural context is applicable?

This cultural mélange is Umberto's Eco's subject. Every prospect is a prospect, but there are no clear critical intellectual means of discerning which choice(s) to make. That suggests the possibility of an unreadable cultural chaos surrounding contemporary architecture. Recent efforts to associate architecture with the arts, technologies, the medical sciences, literary criticism, and digital tools are examples. Intellectually we are engaged everywhere and resolved nowhere.

Should the 'Masters of the World' have a say, or the Comte de Saint-Germain make a comment? Should the Great Pyramid fulfill a role, or the Rosicrucian's form a plan? The Knights of the Temple and Brazilian Voodoo, what part should they play? Across time, and across the planet, vestigial hypotheses, theories, mysteries, solutions and problems are all simultaneously available.

How to sort it all out? Eco suggests we find a solution by dumping the diverse data into the cabalistic, Jewish computer (Foucault's facetious play on our increasing reliance on the ubiquitous computer as arbiter and judge of content), and allowing the computer to provide the priorities to those who originally gave the computer its operational priorities:

'I will tell you who you are so you can tell me who I am based on what I told you.'

Don Quixote and the Windmills

For students of architecture, the depiction of Quixote's famous windmill battle is a 'self-confidence' allegory. It is a case for insisting on the correctness of your case, in spite of prevailing opinions.

Have you considered the possibility that everyone misreads the windmills/monsters and Don Quixote alone is correct? Yes, they are giants, not windmills. Whatever you make of that interpretation, the interest I have is in creating an independent, poetic self-sufficiency in a student. So a student could look at their world, and say to me, 'This is what you see, but it's not so, actually. This is what's really there.' A student by student independence quotient, as opposed to a student allegiance to conclusions developed by consensus.

Lucian Freud, Self-Portrait

The British painter Lucian Freud insists that every genuine work of art is a self-portrait. Freud argues that the sole subject one might master is one's own autobiography. From Freud's vantage point, only genuine autobiography is genuine art.

Is architecture a corollary to Freud's premise? New perspectives in architecture (as in art) are likely to originate from individual insights rather than from more readily available generic conceptions.

Architecture is personal, one architect at a time.

HOW THE PERMANENT REVOLUTION ENDED

Once there was an architect malcontent.
His name was _________.

Some called him rebellious.
His peers labeled him immature.
Others said he was an angry young man,
and a dangerous misfit.

The misfit argued the world should be other than it is,
and architecture might make that world so.
He claimed each new building must be a critique of
all previous building.

The rebel architect had no interest in establishing
design precedents.
He never intended that his lesson be taught.
He never sought public approval.
He never built for an audience.

Then, almost imperceptibly, a surprising thing happened.

The malcontent became a new behavioral model.
The community that once shunned his work now
welcomed him.
Prizes were awarded to the biggest malcontent.
Critics taught we should all be rebels, and told us
how to become one.

Wanna be a dangerous architect, young man?
Just follow these steps...

No one realized the rebel's essence was personal.
No one realized the rebel's essence was not transferable.
And so rebellion became architecture's accepted proforma.

The malcontent architect became a brand.

The rebel's home was called 'outside the box.'
But no one noticed there was yet another box just
outside the outside of the original box.

So, astonishingly, [or perhaps, not so astonishingly after all]
a misfit and a contrarian, became a hero in a land called
popular culture.
But the image of rebellion remained, in fact,
a disingenuous advocacy.
The one-time malcontent was now the logo for a happy
and reassured constituency of peers and pals.

The danger was over.

The iconoclast had become the icon.
And the icon now declared he had matured,
and the rebellion had ended.

Once again there was an architect malcontent...
Her name was _________.

PROJECTS

MORGENSTERN WAREHOUSE

Location Los Angeles, California, United States
Client Arthur Morgenstern
Size 15,000 ft^2 (1393.5 m^2)
Date 1978

The essence of the area was introverted, protective, defensive—a response to the after-hours crime level of a minority neighborhood, and the predictable merchants' strategy to protect goods and lives with walls and bars. A fundamental design intention was that the warehouse should formally challenge this security-conscious climate, and at the same time acknowledge a level of enthusiasm for the city and the street.

The perimeter walls and two interior shear walls are concrete block. The block is finished in two ways: left as is, with a raked joint, or painted, with a flush joint. The intention of the first is to illustrate the nature of the material, but the intention of the second is to throw into question the attitude of the first.

The use of the four pre-cast concrete sewer pipes as signs, as oversized street bollards, intentionally contradicts the ideology that sought to relate configuration to utility. Recognizable as sewer pipes, the cylinders have only a minor plumbing function. The possibility of holding hot water heaters inside was once considered, but the idea of a resurrected sewer pipe come barber shop pole was always the governing notion.

The roof profile relates to functional purpose. Low roof—entry; sloping roof—office; high roof—warehouse. These decisions signify intended compromise with the notion of building as minimum shed with maximum interior flexibility, since the interior heights in office areas are spatially prescriptive, thereby excluding warehousing functions.

Colors play an intentionally ambiguous role. Ideologically the intent was not to matriculate with either the 'school of primary colors' or the 'pastel academy.' Colors identify each of the four tenant units, and distinguish office from warehouse on the front elevation. Color partially dismembers the form of the cylinders, rendering their identification as simple objects more difficult.

The roof graphics are a map, a means to locate additional mechanical equipment (space heater vents, heating/air-conditioning units). The roof colors also serve as a continuation of the graphic ribbons from the elevations. It is interesting to note that the roof graphics solicit reaction from those who inhabit the office towers that overlook the building. Workers in the nearby Occidental Towers have labeled the roof the 'Italian Board Game.'

AERIAL VIEW

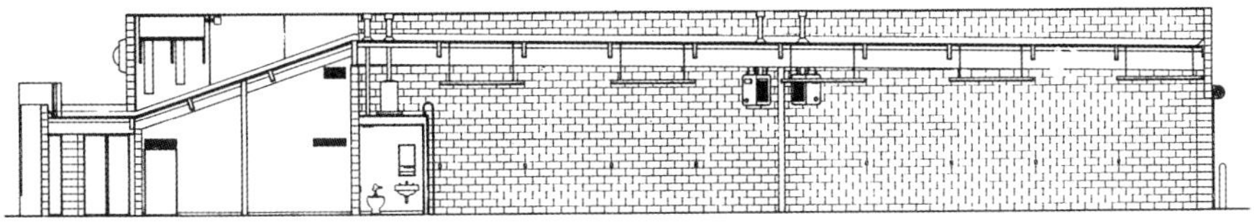

SIDE ELEVATION

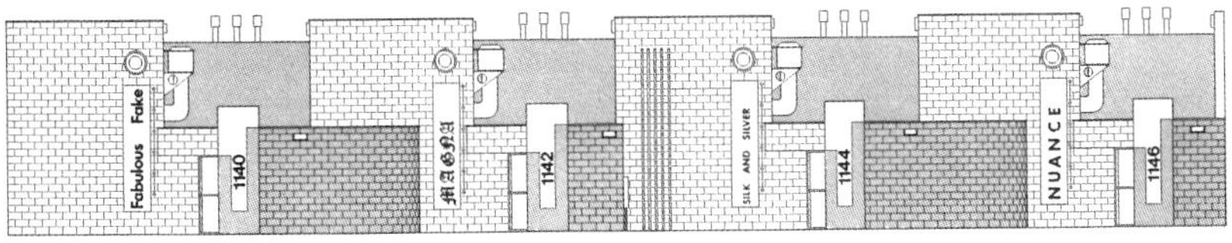

FRONT ELEVATION

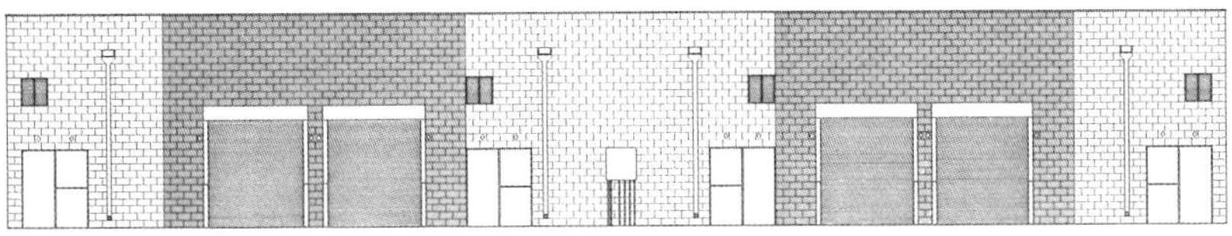

REAR ELEVATION

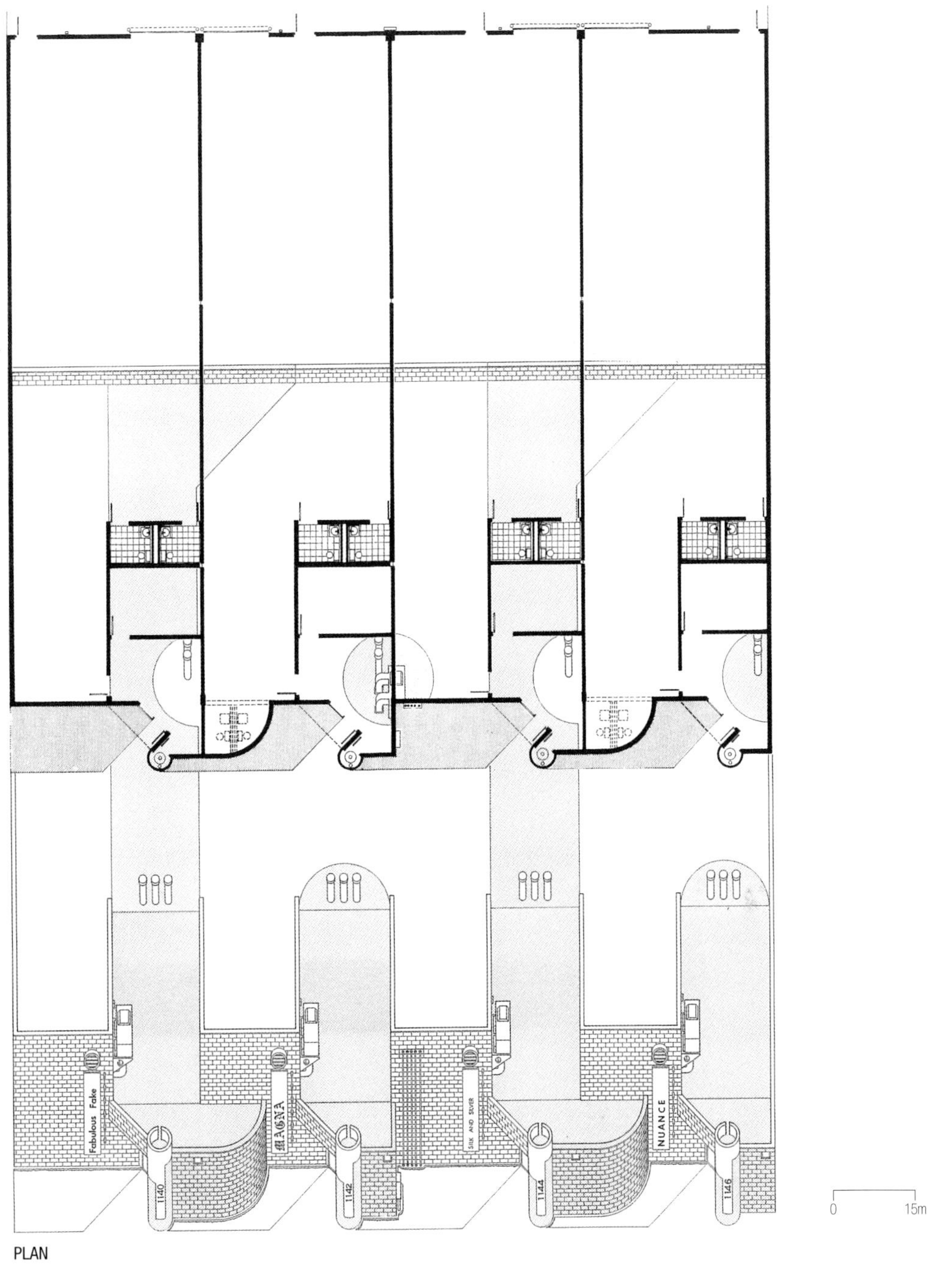

PLAN

1140
1142
1144

INTERIOR PRODUCTS, INC.
GLASS

FOX
INDUSTRIAL
REALTY
1142

1144

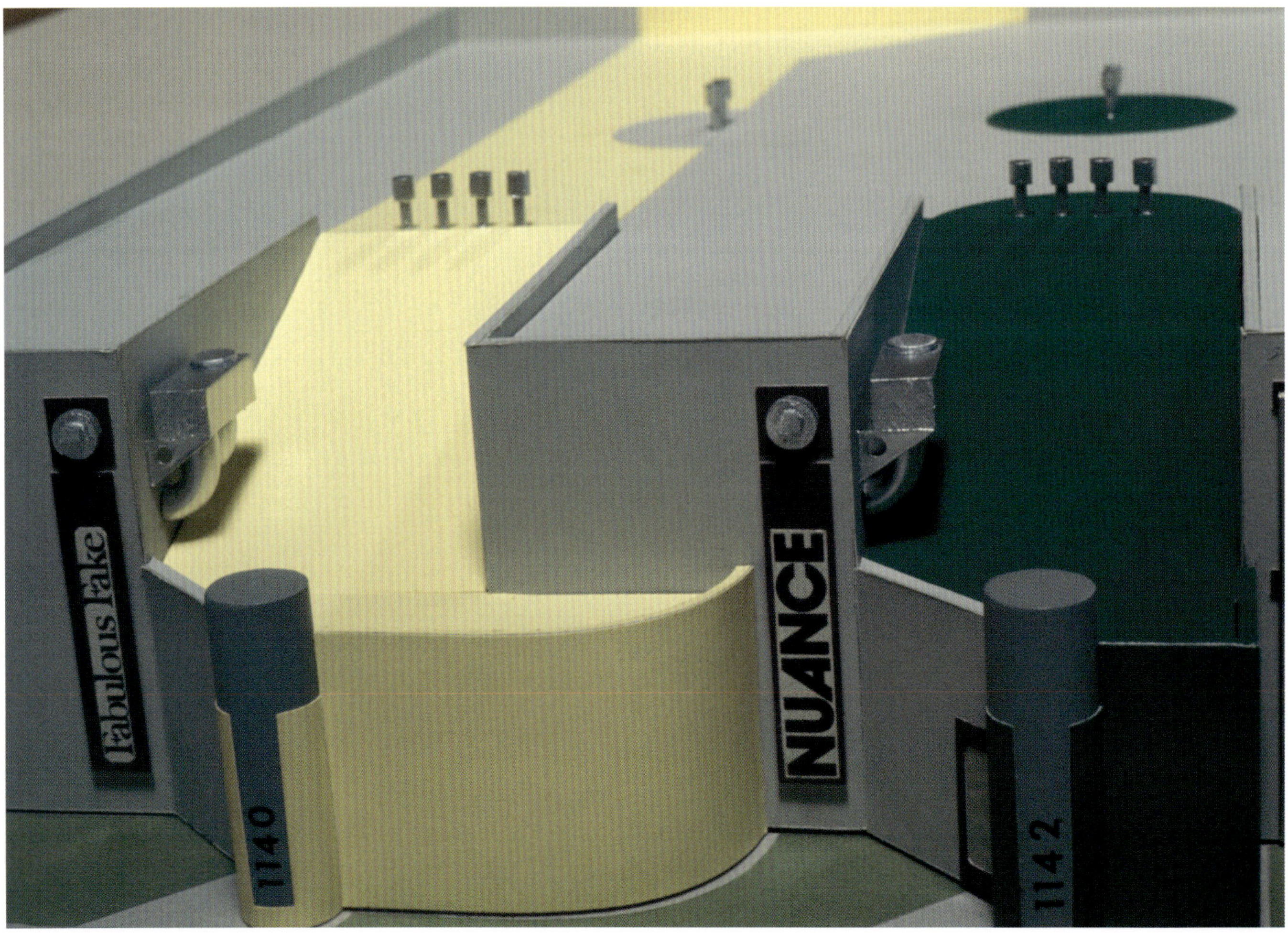
Fabulous Fake
NUANCE
1140
1142

1140
1142
1144

NUANCE
SILK AND SILVER

PETAL HOUSE

Petal House was originally built in the 1950s, one story with a detached garage, just north of the Santa Monica freeway in west Los Angeles. The project was a unique opportunity for the architect to share with the owners in the asking of a number of fundamental questions about the conception of the building and its meaning in their lives.

Together we considered whether we could acknowledge both the original bungalow design and simultaneously suggest a very different prospect for the building's future. Together we asked—because we really were not certain—what is a roof, what is a door, a wall, a window? Together we wondered whether we could exploit the freeway adjacency, and ultimately constructed a roof deck and spa from which the owners could alternatively view or avoid that jam-packed thoroughfare. Together we wondered about the possibility of working at home—not an obvious professional decision at that time—and constructed an in-house office/studio over the garage.

Each room, each wall, each space, each surface in the project became an opportunity for the exploration of shape, light, material, and fabrication techniques, so that finally, we came to understand the house less as a resolute design conclusion, and more as a series of conceptual propositions we considered and explored.

The investigation extended to construction details: the plywood and wood stud zone that connected the old roof to the new floor above, was exposed; hand rails were constructed of rope; a crucial column that combined rotation and vertical loading became a steel and wood expression of the resolution of those structural forces.

Petal House expresses the joy of discovery in design, use, and fabrication, and imagines that process as open and on-going—a sharing between owner and architect. If the house upholds that legacy it will be an enduring success.

Location West Los Angeles, California, United States
Client Private client
Size 2100 ft² (195 m²)
Date 1982

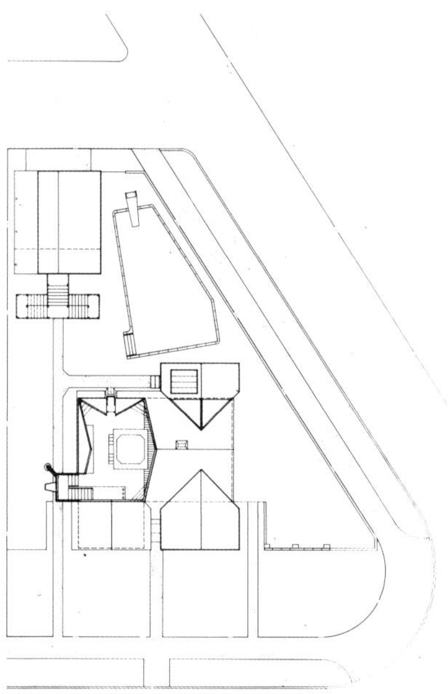

SITE PLAN

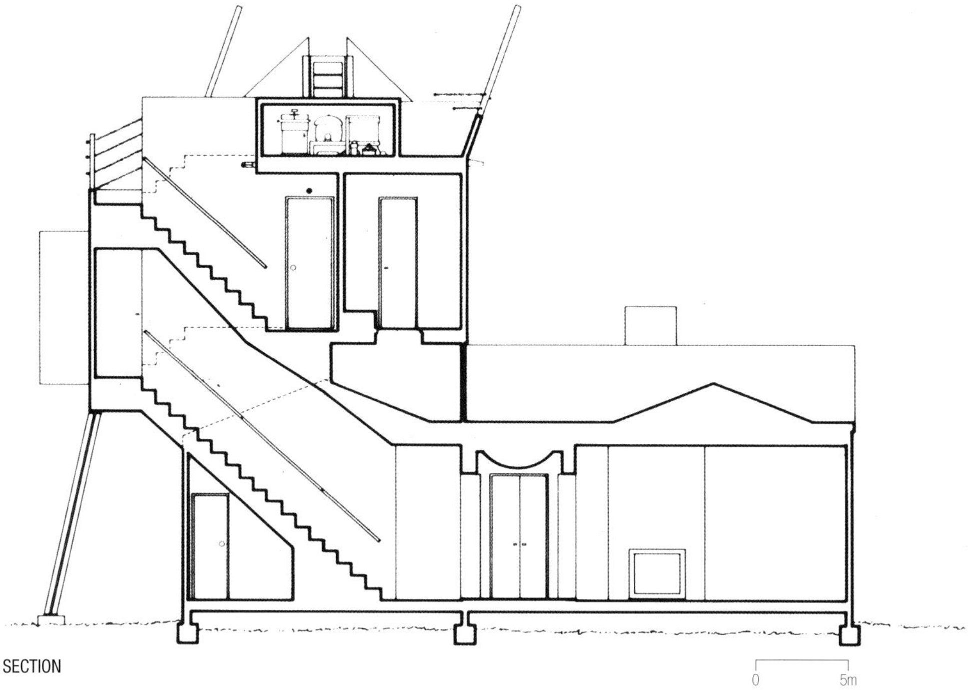

SECTION

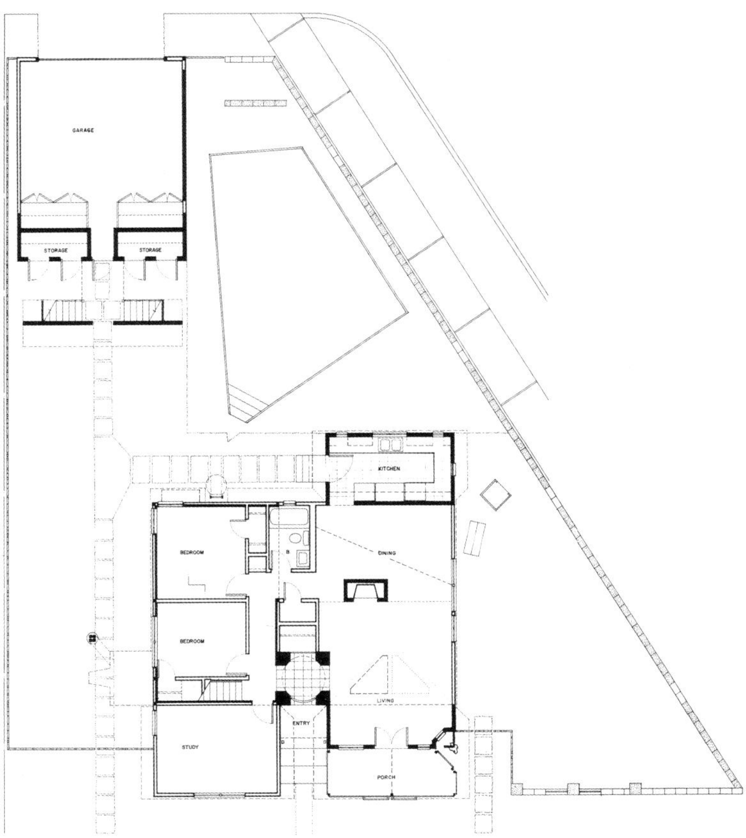

FIRST-FLOOR PLAN

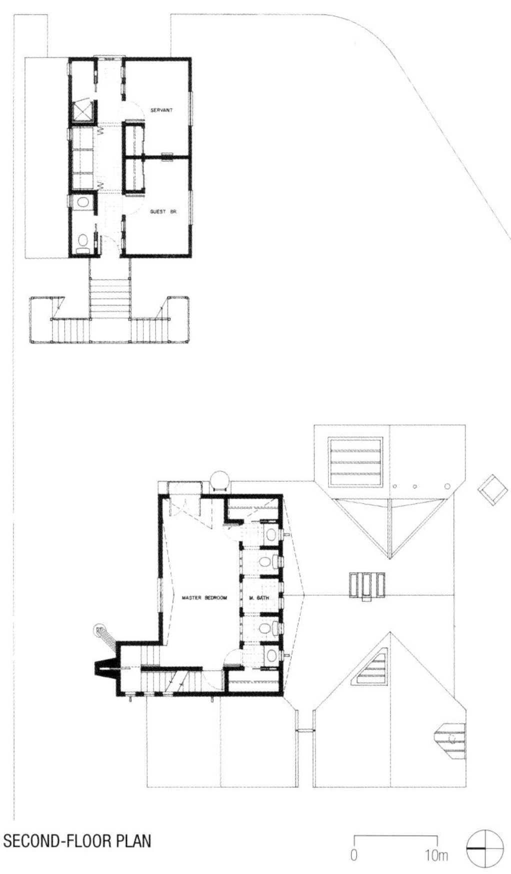

SECOND-FLOOR PLAN

UC IRVINE CENTRAL HOUSING OFFICE BUILDING

The Central Housing Office Building is constructed on a gently sloping site facing a major campus entry point at the University of California, Irvine. The building fronts onto a student walk that connects the east residential end of the campus with the administrative buildings to the west. This walk rises about 15 feet (4.6 meters) so the administrative and academic center of the campus to the west of the site views the building from above.

The Central Housing Office is in charge of on-campus dormitories and apartments. The building comprises four departments. Lobby, cashiers, conference room, and parking for 25 cars complete the program.

The building is positioned north–south on the site with the northwest corner facing the major auto entry. Users are typically pedestrians who enter along the ramp connecting the east–west campus walk to a centrally located building lobby.

The Central Housing Office Building accommodates a staff of 25 who assist faculty, students, and administrators with housing problems. Two types of work spaces are provided: open workstations where the housing staff meet the public, and executive office space.

The internal organization of the project reflects the two office types. The building is a composite of two gable roof volumes existing simultaneously within a single-plan rectangle. Each volume contains one of the two programmatic/spatial components in the building: public and/or open work area, and enclosed and/or private office space. Every working space is identifiable as part of one volumetric type or the other. The building lobby, accessed from two directions, is included as one of the five open office components, each of which has a large clerestory/roof skylight. The most important of the open work areas, Housing Support Services, is also identified with a major clerestory window in the east wall.

In longitudinal section from north to south, the building floor approximates the sloping site profile, while the transverse section varies as interior functions alternate from public to private and back again. Levels are connected with ramps. All spaces are rectilinear in plan. This creates an interior simply organized in plan, yet diverse, personal, and anti-institutional in section.

Location Irvine, California, United States
Client University of California
Size 10,000 ft^2 (930 m^2)
Date 1989

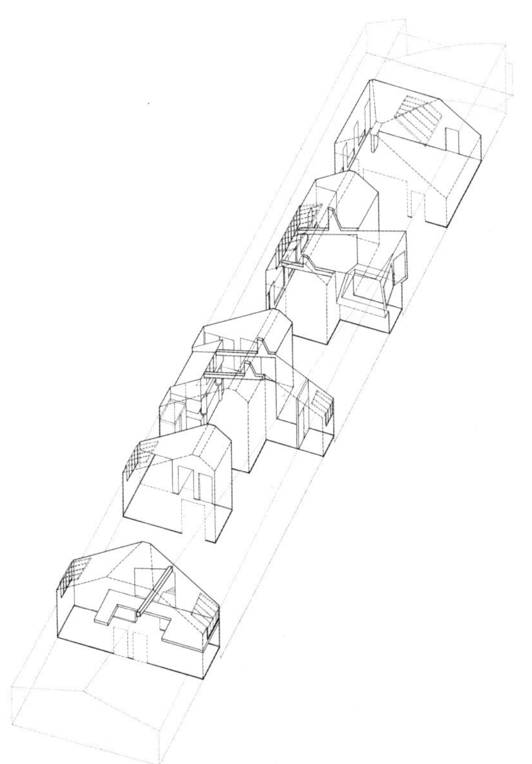

AXONOMETRIC

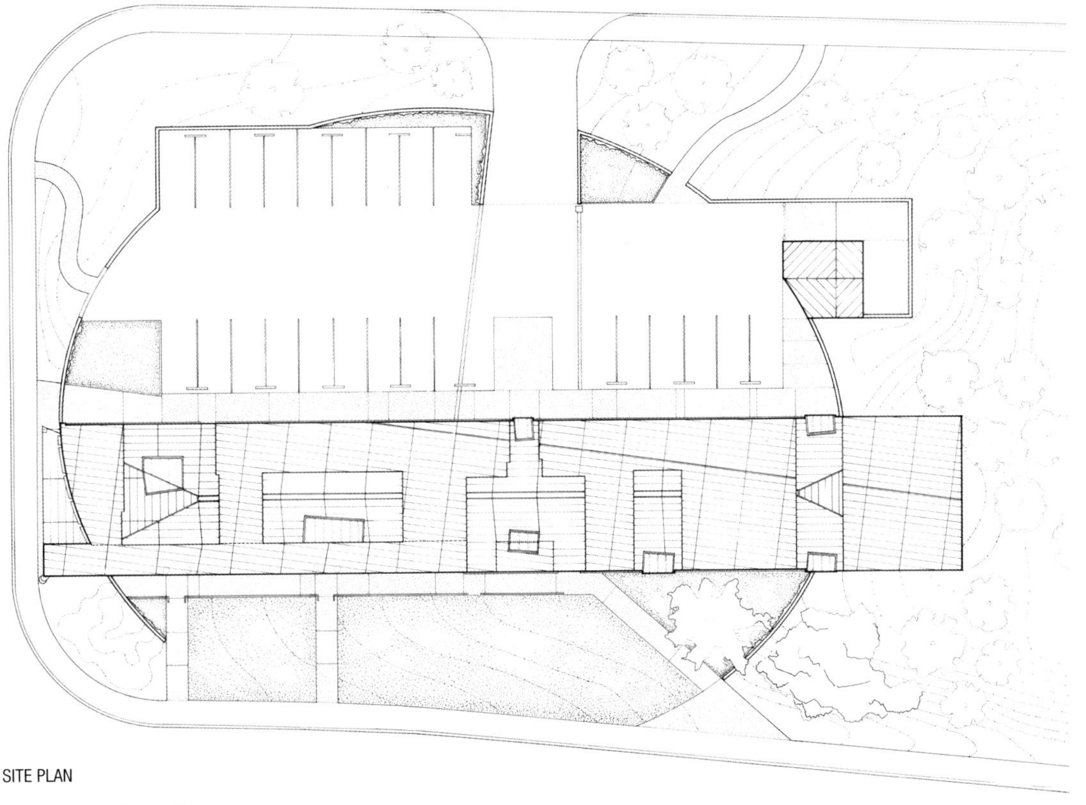

SITE PLAN

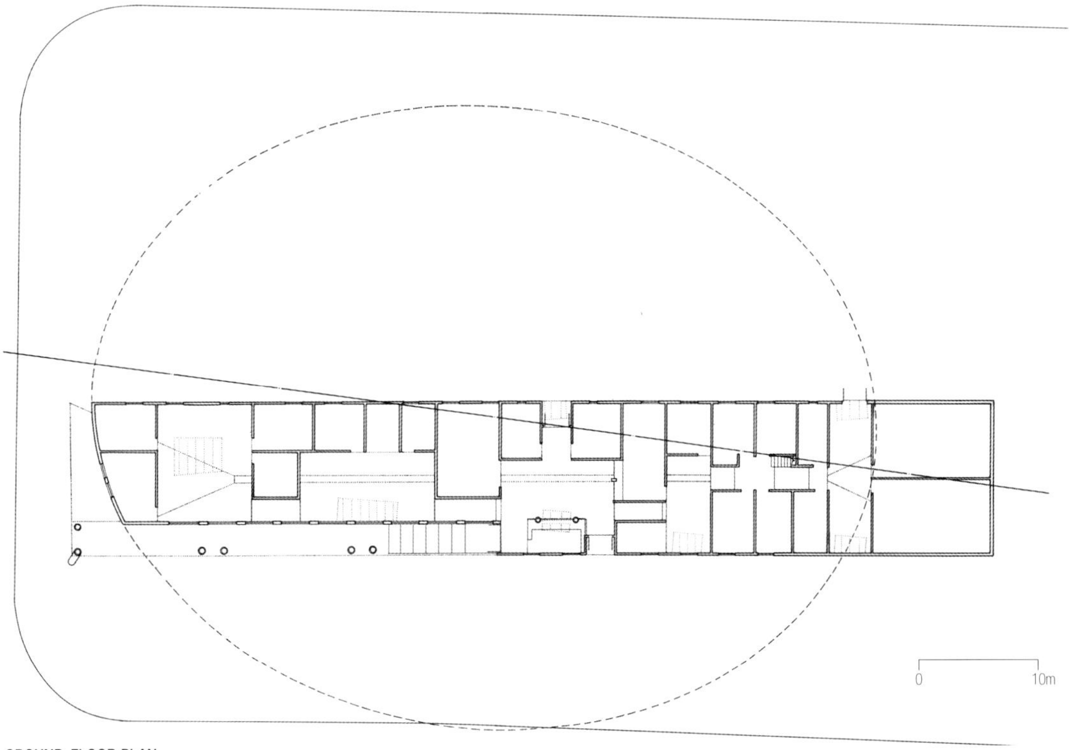

GROUND-FLOOR PLAN

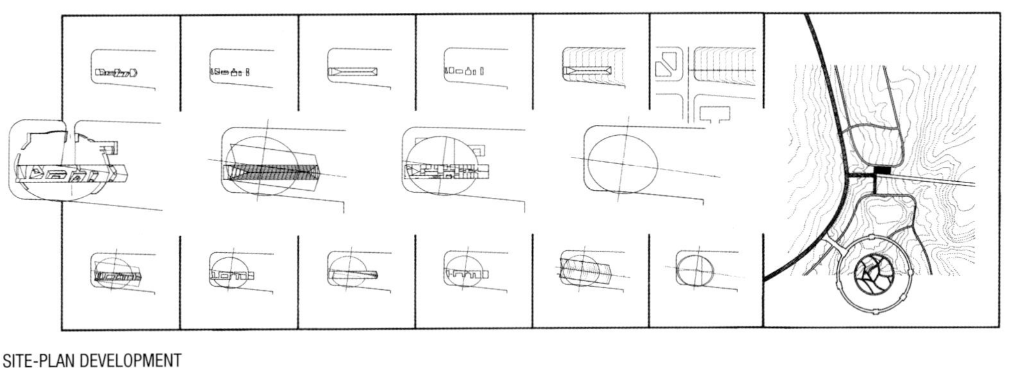

SITE-PLAN DEVELOPMENT

STOP

STOP

LAWSON-WESTEN HOUSE

Location Los Angeles, California, United States
Client Private client
Size 5100 ft^2 (473.8 m^2)
Date 1993

The Lawson-Westen house is located on a 14,400-square-foot (1340-square-meter) suburban site on the west side of Los Angeles. The house is positioned on the north side of the plot, leaving the south side and west end as an L-shaped garden. The clients had a very particular building program, a thoughtful reflection of how they live day to day, and how the housing of their substantial art collection would interrelate with the resolution of their practical concerns.

The kitchen, an entertainment and gathering space, is the center of the home's social agenda; a three-level cylindrical volume that contains the first-floor dining and cooking areas, with various living spaces attached to the open volume on floors one, two, and three.

A second-floor walkway and bridge connects the adults' sleeping area, adjacent to the cylinder on the west, with the children's sleeping area on the east. The bridge passes above/through the triple-height living room, then on through the second level of the cylinder to the adults' bedroom and bath. Within the cylinder, the bridge meets a stair that follows the profile of the cylinder wall, hanging out over kitchen and living-room areas, rising to a third-floor study at the top of the cylinder. Up another stair that follows the curve is a small outdoor deck.

The front wall of the building is poured-in-place concrete. The remainder of the exterior walls are cement plaster, applied with a wet trowel, rendering them extremely smooth.

The building investigates window types, and represents those types as an assembly of windows—a single large window comprising a number of pieces—on the south elevation, next to the garden. That window represents all the window types that are found singly elsewhere on the exterior walls.

Geometrically the center of the cylinder's conical roof is not synonymous with the center of the cylinder. That explains why the intersection between cone roof and cylinder is a line that rises and falls, rather than the horizontal line that would separate the two if their centers were the same. The cone's apex is flattened, creating the small ocean-view deck on the fourth floor. The roof of the cylinder is then theoretically inscribed with a vertical slice drawn across the cone from north to south, which describes a parabolic curve or arc. Using the

MODEL

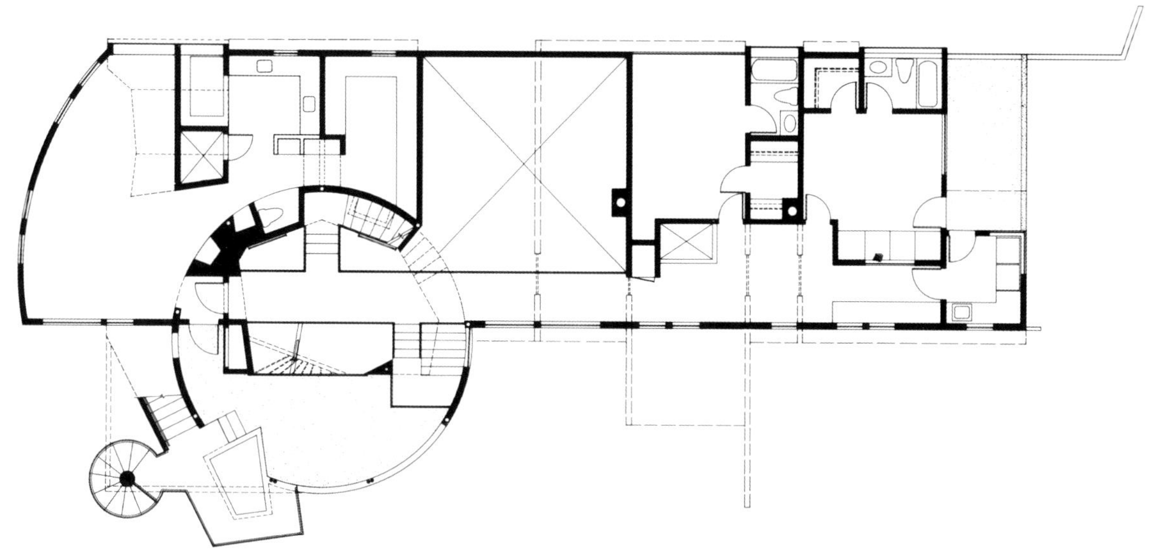

THIRD-FLOOR PLAN

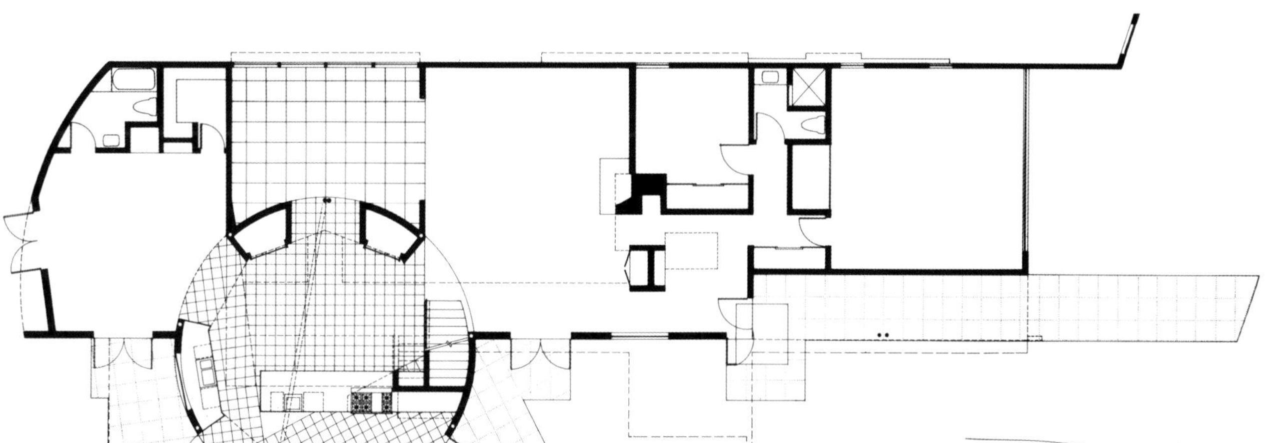

FIRST-FLOOR PLAN

SITE PLAN

theoretical curve as a template, the arc is extended east from the slice in the cone to the street end of the building, describing the vaulted roof that encloses the remainder of the house. The single roof-supporting glue-laminated and steel rib, fully extended over the entry door—one of a sequence that support the vault—marks the full extension of the inscribed east–west parabolic line in the cone roof.

PTERODACTYL

Location Culver City, California, United States
Client Samitaur Constructs
Size 16,000 ft^2 (1486.4 m^2)
Date 2015

The Pterodactyl comprises an office building and parking garage occupying a vacant site opposite the Stealth Building in a complex of new and remodeled buildings in Culver City. In terms of square footage, the garage is large—800 cars—and the offices small—16,000 square feet (1486.4 square meters). But, by intention, the view from the west—the primary elevation facing the parking lot—emphasizes the office building presence, and minimizes the parking lot visibility.

The parking structure is four stories, an open steel frame with blown-on fireproofing covering the structural steel. The entry elevation expresses the automobile movement system by stacking both entry and exit ramps on the west garage face. Automobile entry is at the visual center of that elevation, between the two ramps.

The two-story office space begins on the fourth floor of the garage. The first office floor shares the fourth-floor parking deck. The center portion of the office building is a three-level space that steps down across the second and third parking floors, attached to the front façade of the parking structure, and suspended over the auto entry/exit area above the first floor.

The office building is formed by the intersection of nine elevated rectangular boxes, lifted one level above the garage roof, stacked either on top of or adjacent to each other. The boxes are supported on the steel column grid extended from the parking structure two levels above the fourth-floor deck. An interior second-floor bridge, running north–south, connects the boxes. Each box is glazed on the north façade, with glazing running perpendicular to the entry elevation.

The four-level parking structure is of straightforward and inexpensive construction—steel frame, metal decks, regular bays, and ingress/egress ramps at opposite ends of the public, west face of the project. The required fireproofing of the structural steel was introduced as a finish material, and precisely applied to the steel frame but not to the metal deck spanning between the beams.

The 800-car structure is the conceptual podium for the rooftop office building. Buildings in the area are three stories or less, so the office building on the roof affords spectacular vistas of the entire city from

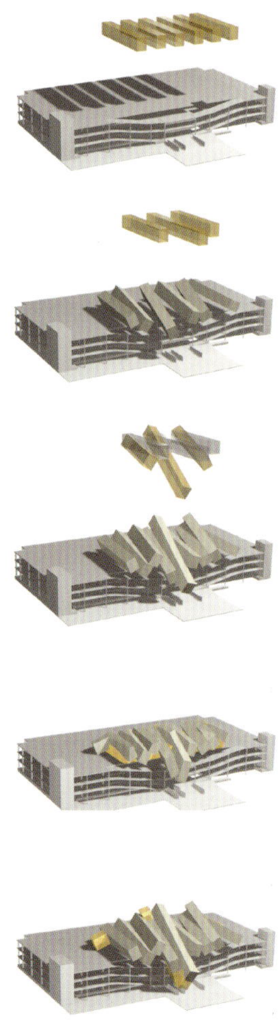

MASSING DIAGRAM

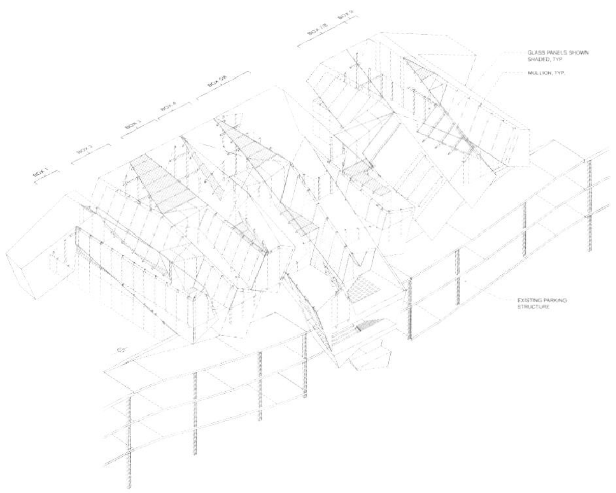

GLAZING

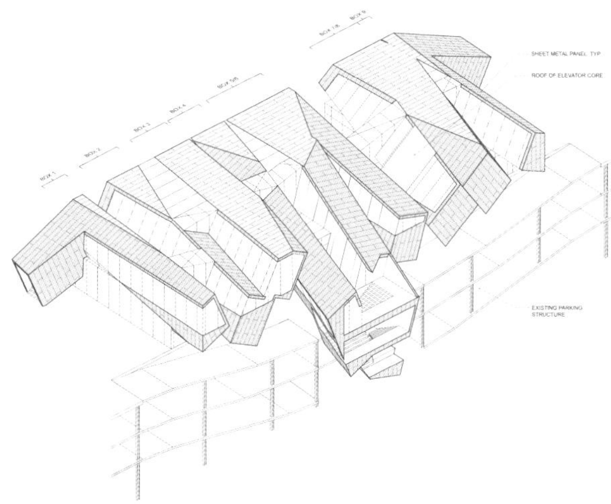

METAL PANELS

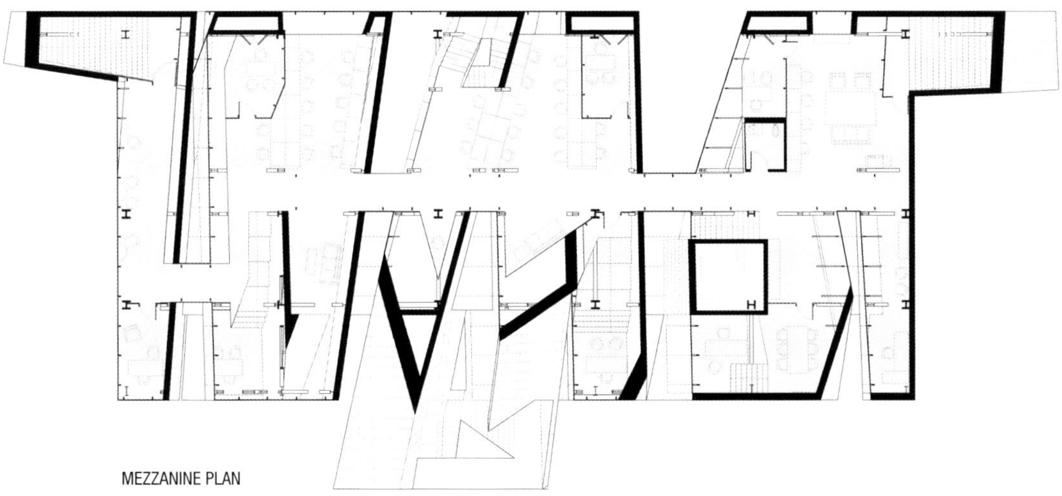

MEZZANINE PLAN

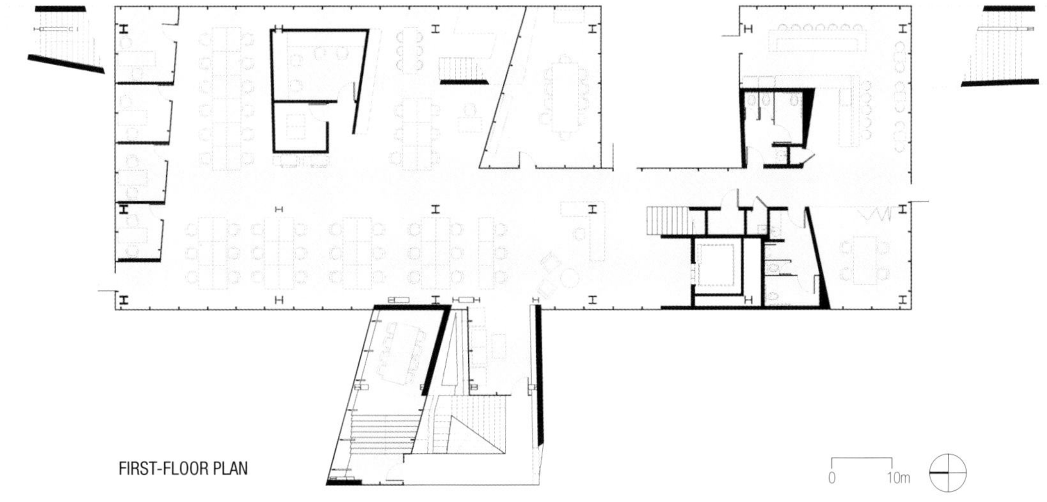

FIRST-FLOOR PLAN

downtown to the Santa Monica Mountains to the Westside of Los Angeles and the Pacific Ocean.

The main office floor is rectangular in plan and enclosed by a glass wall that extends vertically to meet the elevated boxes supported one level above the main floor, with the box second floor designed as a sometimes-open-to-the-floor-below mezzanine. The main floor is entirely open plan, while the mezzanine is compartmentalized as the closed area portion of the program requires.

UMBRELLA

The Umbrella, located directly behind Stealth, was the first of a number of projects that have explored complex compound curving arrangements and pushed the limits of material technology.

Two adjoining warehouses in Culver City, constructed in the 1940s, were redesigned as a performance and recording venue for an experimental performance series called the Green Umbrella, the Los Angeles Philharmonic's long-running new-music program. The Philharmonic ultimately decided to remain in downtown Los Angeles, and the orchestra program was changed to accommodate office, production, and post-production facilities for a graphics and online-media design firm. The outdoor performance venue, the rooftop 'umbrella,' originally designed to accommodate 30 performing musicians, was retained in the second scheme.

The block-like volumes of the existing buildings, one with a sawtooth sky-lit roof, the other with a bowstring-supported roof, remain essentially as they were. The interiors include a lobby, four avid bays, two conference centers, large open work spaces, and 20 private offices, most of which are located on a newly constructed second floor.

The defining conceptual object is an outdoor amphitheater—the originally intended Philharmonic venue—inserted into the northwest corner of the existing bowstring building, and cantilevering over the entry ramp and walkway to the lobby. The 'umbrella' is a performance arena, the slope of which is determined by the curving top chords of two original trusses, once supporting the bowstring roof, now salvaged from the corner demolition, and reused upside down to define the bowl seating profile.

With steel amendments, these trusses extend over the entry walk to support the cantilevered seating. A curving steel pipe marks the existing roof edge of the bowstring structure, and the perimeter cut for the new 'umbrella.' The free ends of that pipe project, one from the north elevation, one from the west, and are supported by a new steel truss with a curved bottom, configured with the inverted reused wood bowstrings as precedents for the shape. The terraced seating steps down the bowl from the edge of the roof to the edge of the cantilever, where a small conductor's podium is situated.

Location Culver City, California, United States
Client Samitaur Constructs
Size 17,000 ft² (1580 m²)
Date 1999

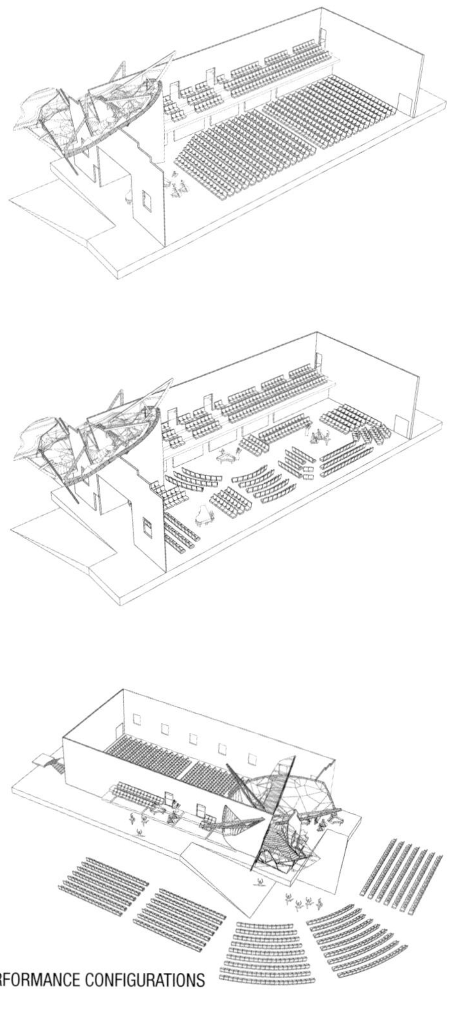

PERFORMANCE CONFIGURATIONS

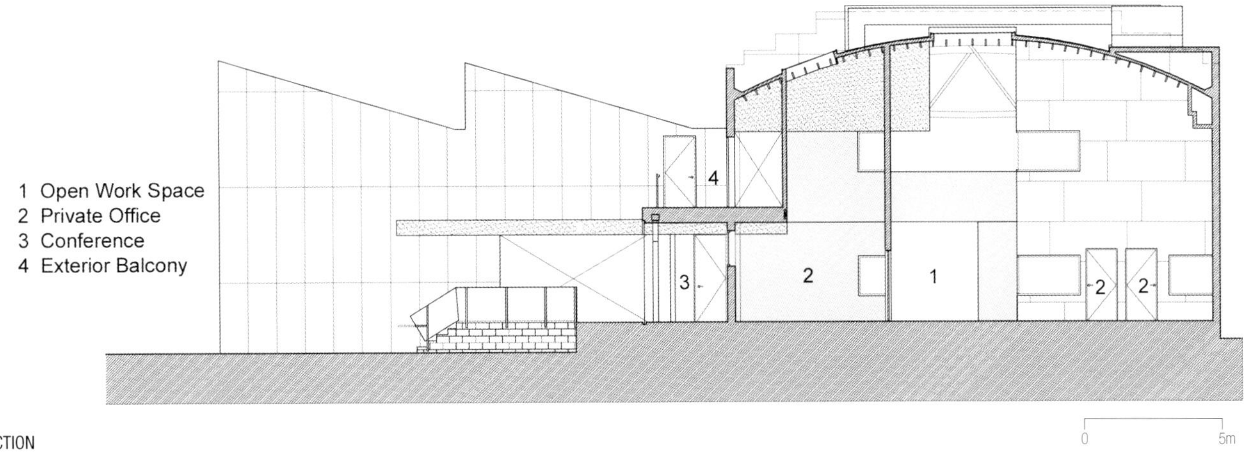

SECTION

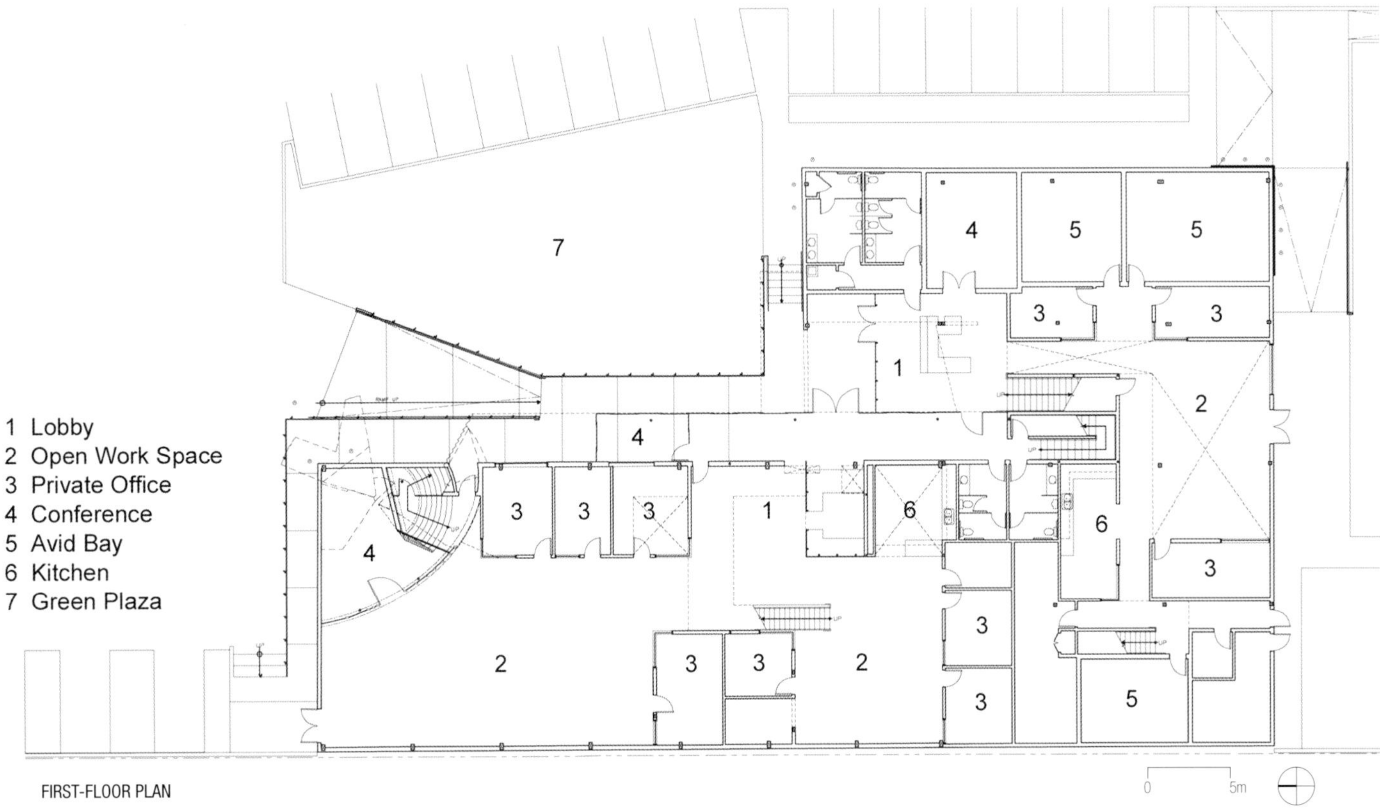

FIRST-FLOOR PLAN

Adjacent to the performers' seating area, within the ring, is an irregularly shaped, sprayed-on concrete roof that both encloses a new conference space below the bowl and provides the requisite undulating acoustic surface for music performance on the rooftop theater.

Seventeen slumped, laminated, overlapping glass panels, supported on a frame of steel pipes, provide a double-curving, transparent canopy over the musicians' seating. Each of the 17 panels is unique, with matching adjacent edges facilitating the panel overlap. The construction of the bent glass umbrella roof is the first time curving, laminated glass has been successfully engineered, fabricated, and installed.

STEALTH

At the point where the contiguous Wedgewood Holly warehouses of Slash and Backslash met Hayden Avenue, a gateway was needed to serve as the entrance to a new office campus.

The design concept for Stealth originated with a requirement for the excavation and removal of contaminated soil on the west side of the former industrial site. One of three contiguous warehouse structures was demolished to provide ground access to the area where the polluted soil was to be removed. A concrete block wall was constructed to enclose the two remaining warehouses to the east, and Stealth was constructed to the west, against the new wall. A portion of the excavated area underneath the overhanging new structure was regraded and landscaped, forming a sunken garden and meeting space.

The north end of the remaining warehouse was designed as a performance and meeting area. The stage is enclosed by a movable wall of steel doors that open onto the new garden. The stage can seat 150, with a further 600 in the garden, for a theater-in-the-round performance. The new block wall that separates the old warehouses from the new building has two openings: the north aperture forms the theater proscenium, which holds the sliding steel doors; the south opening admits vehicular traffic, which passes through the wall on the way to a parking area at the rear of the site.

The new structure has a three-sided north elevation, and a four-sided south elevation. Over its 300-foot (90-meter) length, the building section transforms, changing its interior and exterior shape continuously from triangle to square or from square to triangle.

The steel-frame structure approximates a plan grid on the south end, facilitating a simple organization of tenant space on the two floors. The center of the building houses a glazed elevator lobby on the ground floor, and open decks and bathrooms on floors one and two. The painted steel bathrooms and related mechanical equipment structures on the decks were prefabricated off site and craned into place. Visitors enter the lobby at ground level, and proceed via the elevator up to open pedestrian walks and then into the tenant spaces.

Location Culver City, California, United States
Client Samitaur Constructs
Size 48,000 ft^2 (4460 m^2)
Date 2001

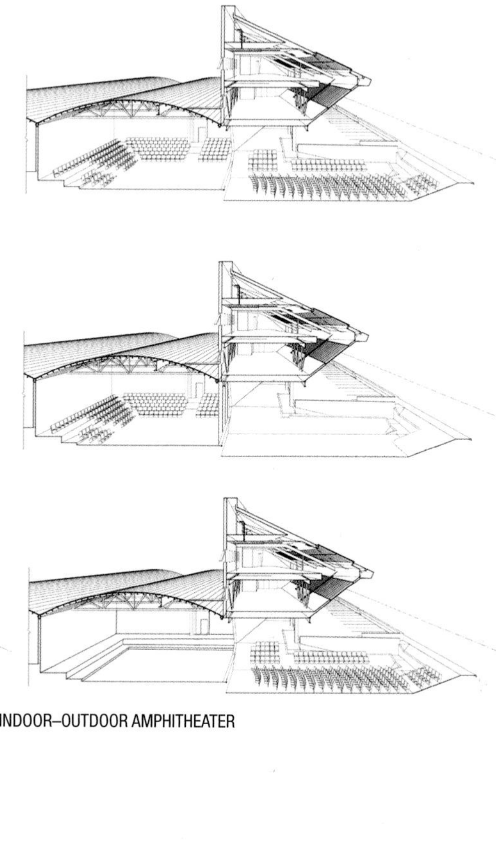

INDOOR–OUTDOOR AMPHITHEATER

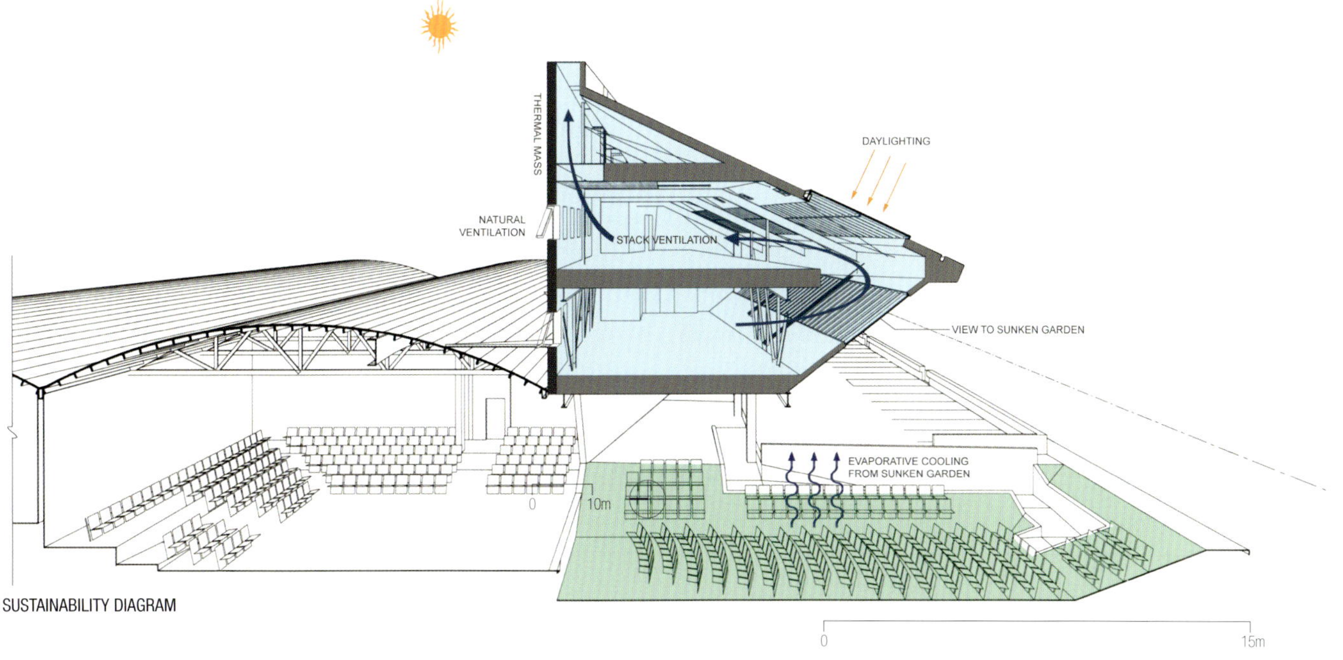

SUSTAINABILITY DIAGRAM

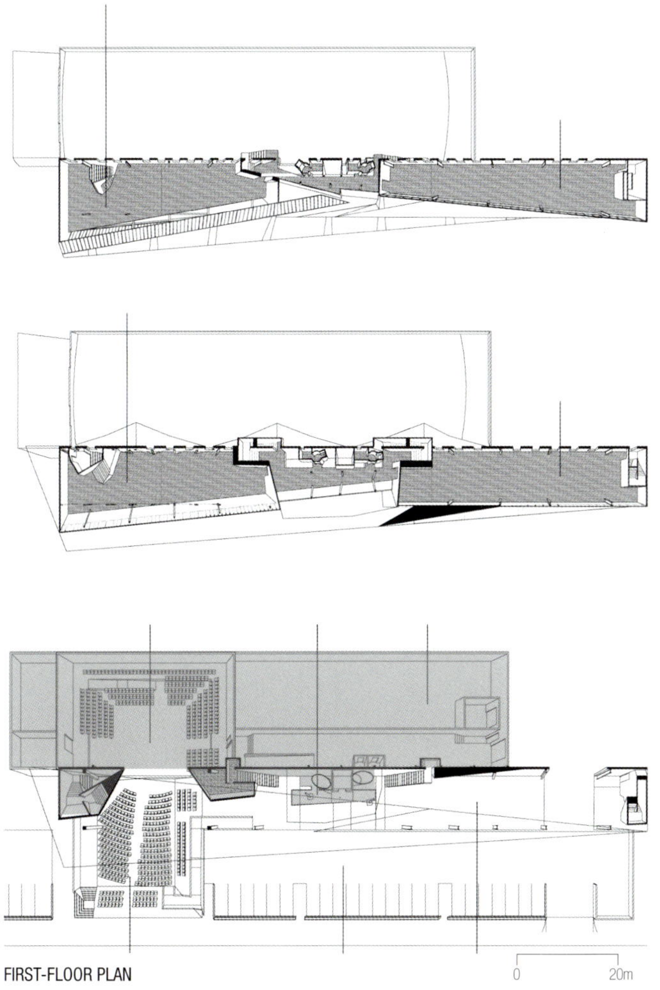

FIRST-FLOOR PLAN

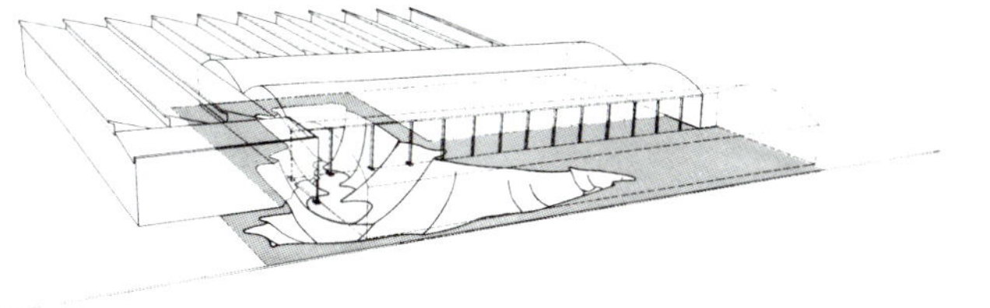

EXCAVATION

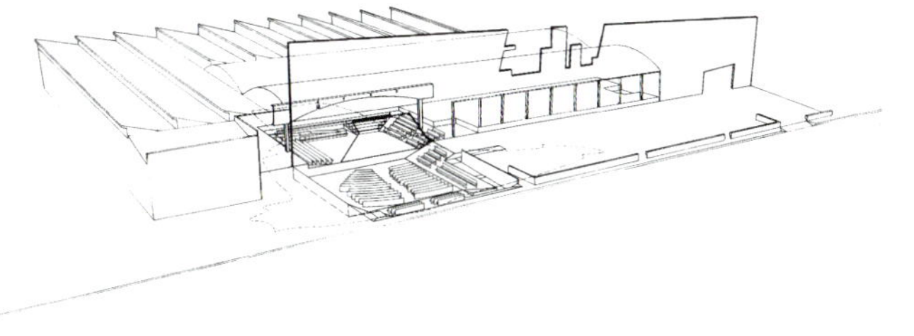

GARDEN

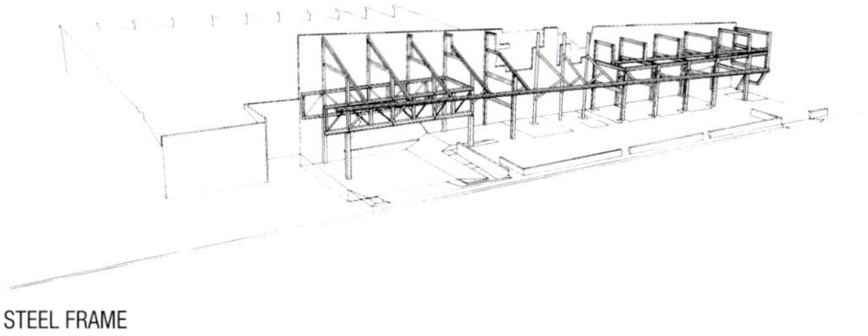

STEEL FRAME

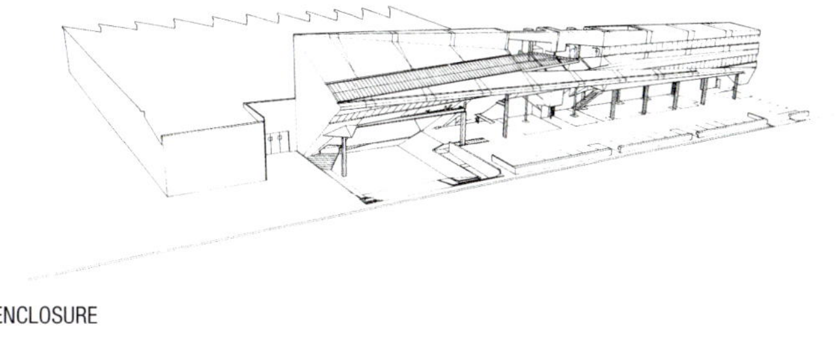

ENCLOSURE

SAMITAUR TOWER

Location Culver City, California, United States
Client Samitaur Constructs
Size 5000 ft^2 (465 m^2)
Date 2010

Conceptually, the tower has both introverted and extroverted planning objectives. Within the burgeoning area of new media companies, graphic designers, and general office tenants, the tower symbolizes the advent of this important new urban development, providing a changing art display for local viewing, and offering a variety of graphic content and data on its five screens, promoting upcoming events and the achievements of local tenants.

Externally, the tower displays culturally significant content and local event information, along with art and graphic presentations of all sorts, available to in-car audiences who pass the site area, traveling on a number of local thoroughfares in the Culver City/West Los Angeles area. In addition to the large number of cars passing the site, the Expo Line has an estimated ridership of 30,000 passengers per day with two local stops several blocks east and west of the site. The presence of the train riders guarantees an enormous daily audience of tower art viewers, as well as an increase in pedestrians in the area, who will walk past the tower from the train stops to local businesses.

The tower consists of five circular steel rings, approximately 30 feet (9 meters) in diameter. The rings are stacked vertically at 12-foot (4-meter) floor-to-floor intervals and staggered in plan, back and forth—to the north, east, south, and west—in order to establish proximity and viewing angles for various levels at various heights. Projection screens at each floor can be seen from cars on surrounding surface streets, from freeways, by passengers at train stops, from onboard the moving trains, and from pedestrians at a variety of key walking and viewing points. Between each pair of staggered horizontal circular steel planes, the curving, conical projection screens are installed. Behind the screens are a number of digital projectors, 10 in all, that will rear-project onto the translucent acrylic screens. Inside the screens, steel decks are provided for viewers to look out at the city, and for a maintenance staff who will service the projectors and screens.

The tower has a glazed elevator in an enclosed glass shaft, and an open stairway to the top, so the tower will be used as a viewing platform to overlook the city. However, its primary objective is to distribute art and other relevant content to the local and in-transit audiences passing by.

SCREEN AUDIENCES

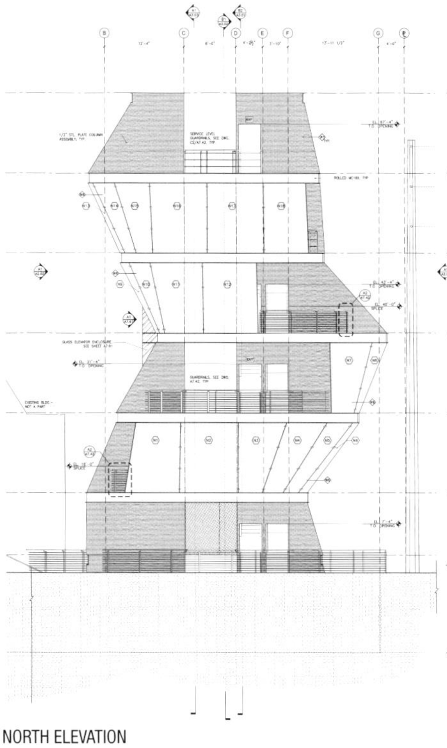

NORTH ELEVATION

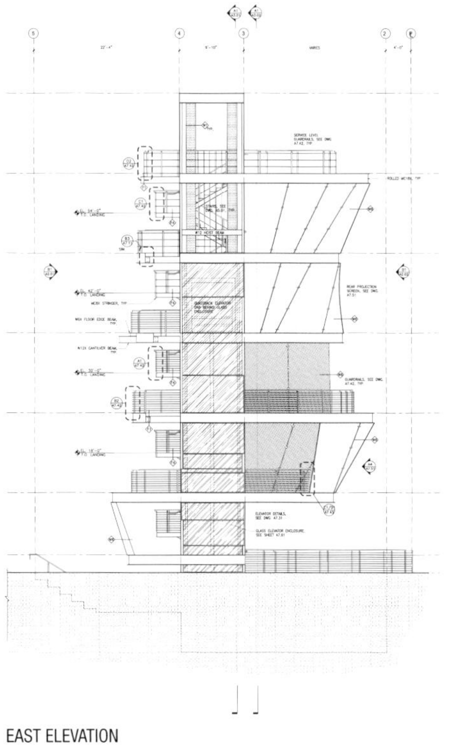

EAST ELEVATION

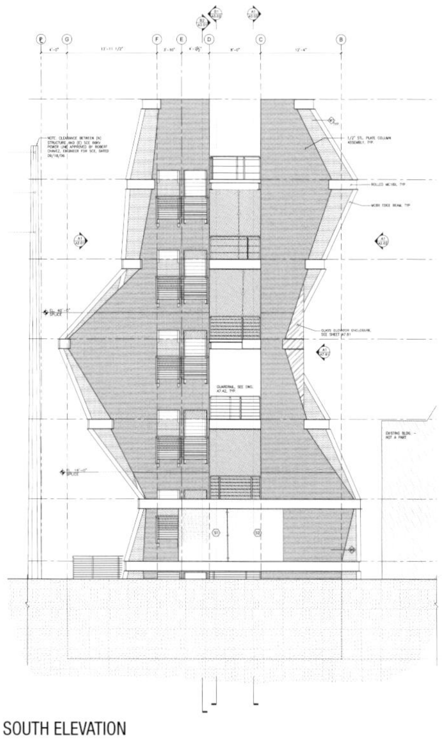

SOUTH ELEVATION

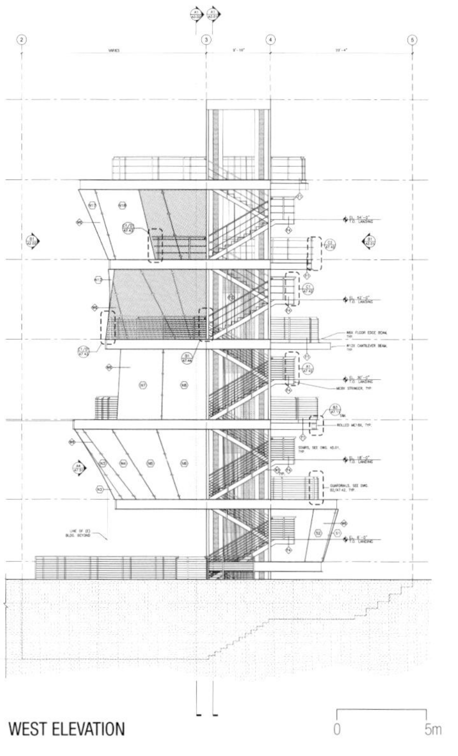

WEST ELEVATION

The tower is fabricated from standard structural steel sections—wide flange beams and columns, and channels—with panelized walls made of half-inch-thick (10-millimeter-thick) steel plate. All the shapes and components were shop fabricated, and delivered to the site for erection. Because of earthquake-design constraints, the tower is supported on a deep foundation of concrete piles with a continuous grade beam tying the piles together.

3520
3522

SAMITAUR

The Samitaur Office Building in South Los Angeles once again extended the boundary of the new city and began a series of investigations into combining and manipulating Euclidean geometry to form complex spatial sequences.

The new site had a troubled past, and was located near the Fedco Building which served as a backdrop to one of the most infamous scenes from the 1992 Los Angeles riots.

Samitaur utilizes a building site above a private road. The road continues to operate as a conventional road, and the new building is an air-rights structure, one of the few such projects to be constructed over an automobile right-of-way in the United States. The new building is supported on a steel column-and-beam system 15 feet (4.5 meters) above the road, to allow sufficient vertical clearance for trucks and automobiles to pass underneath. The air-rights building is a simple, rectangular block, 110 feet (34 meters) long, 30 feet (9 meters) wide, and 45 feet (14 meters) high, the height limit in that area of Los Angeles, supported by steel pipe columns, and girders that span the original road width. The new columns land either on the road outside existing structures, or within the adjacent buildings that adjoin the road. Existing buildings on either side of the road are remodeled to provide additional ground-floor office space for Kodak Cineon, the original building tenant.

There are two geometric anomalies in the otherwise rectangular building block. First, the double cone entry-and-exit stair, outdoor lounge and roof deck spaces on the southeast corner of the project, identifying the building from the access road by which cars enter the site. The second spatial exception to the block is the west-facing, pentagonal courtyard, with open-air bridge, pool, fountain, and outdoor seating for employees, that cantilevers over the automobile egress road directly below.

The interior plan for the building in the air includes open and closed office space and conference rooms. On the ground are the multimedia classrooms, lounges, open offices, and production space. In the center of the rectangular block building is the bathroom and utility core, one of two double-height volumes within the otherwise regular floor-to-floor height structure.

Location Los Angeles, California, United States
Client Samitaur Constructs
Size 57,000 ft^2 (5300 m^2)
Date 1996

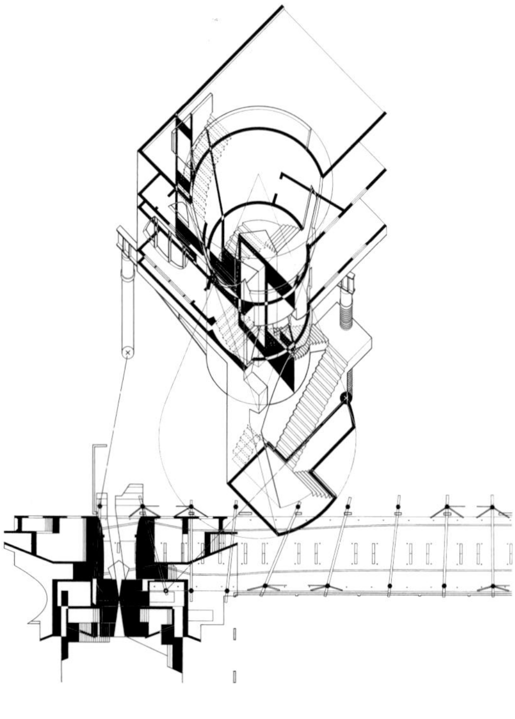

SECTION—AXONOMETRIC

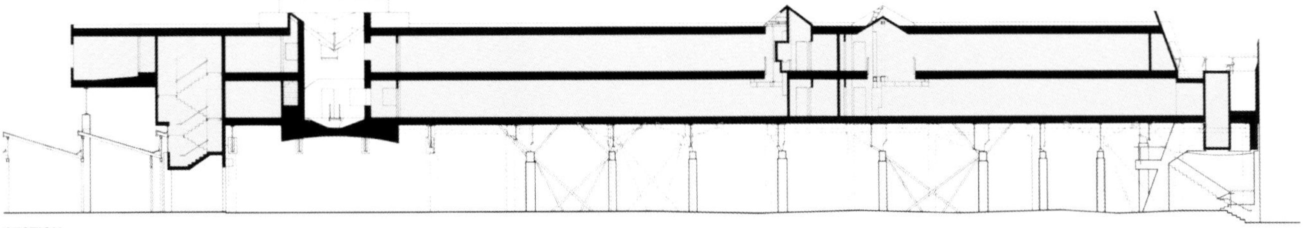

SECTION

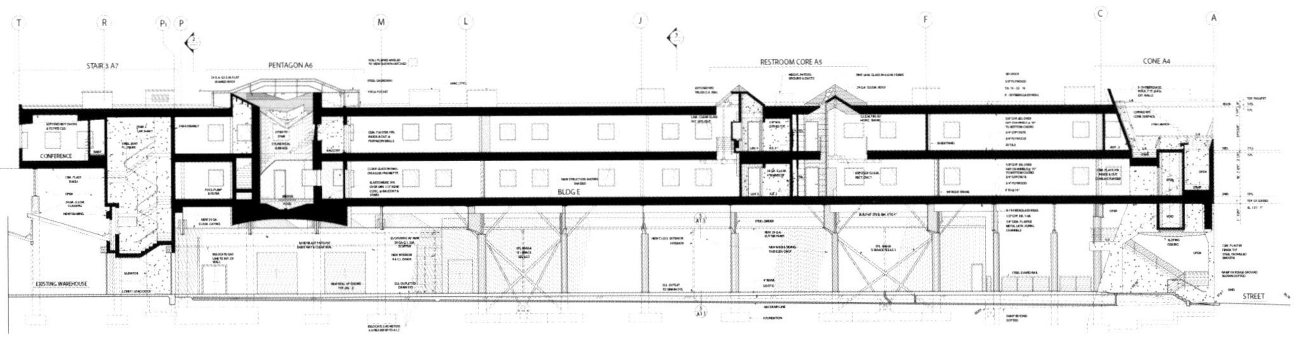

SECTION

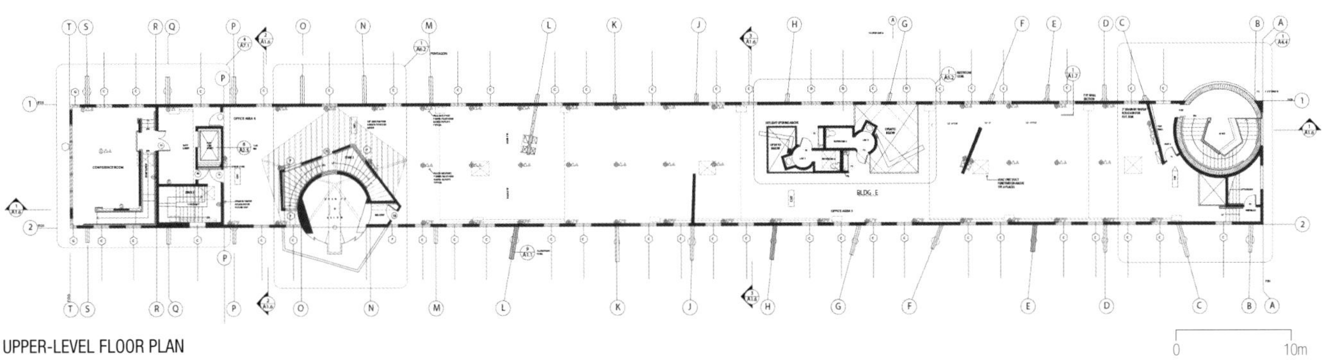

UPPER-LEVEL FLOOR PLAN

The remodeled sawtooth-roofed building at the end of the access road holds Kodak's commissary and classroom spaces, and the elevator lobby that leads to the second and third floors of the new office structure. Off the elevator lobby on the second floor is a double-height conference space that looks west to the Santa Monica Freeway, Wilshire Boulevard, and the Santa Monica Mountains, providing a sense of orientation to what is so often a more complex, less intelligible vision of Los Angeles.

BOX

The Box is an intervention that modifies the organization and structure of an existing warehouse on National Boulevard in Culver City.

The Box has three conceptual parts: the first is a cylindrical reception area located on the ground floor of the existing warehouse building, and extending vertically to intersect the single-story, truss-supported roof. The existing roof was removed and replaced with glass at the intersection of the roof and the cylinder.

A new exterior stair leads to a second-level roof deck, supported on the original truss system of the roof above the reception area. The space between the new deck and the cylindrical incision in the roof is glazed to bring natural light into the reception area.

The conference space above is a private third-floor volume with three-sided corner windows raised to eye level—preventing views of the local neighborhood streets, and allowing views only of the sky and the tops of the trees across the street in the park.

The conference space is lifted on steel legs which lean to form the floor-support beams. The beams are positioned as two planes that cross as an 'X' in plan, with a spherical cut-out in the webs of the two beams providing clearance for occupants on the second-floor open deck, between the conference space and reception. The Box appears to roll on a steel sphere.

The Box is a hybridized version of the conventional, orthogonal box shape. The traditional geometric precept becomes an amended object, which transforms the box to a still recognizable but not quite regular box shape.

The three-sided corner windows in the northwest and southeast corners are themselves box analogues, positioned on opposite corners of the conference space, opening the corners to views. The three-sided corner windows, when added together, form a theoretical glass box.

The various Box elements are one material and one color, an almost black cement plaster both inside and out. Roof, interior and exterior walls, and ceilings are a consistent, smooth, troweled surface. No material distinctions are made between roof and wall, and none are made between the inside and outside surfaces of the building.

Location Culver City, California, United States
Client Samitaur Constructs
Size 12,000 ft^2 (1115 m^2)
Date 1994

MODEL

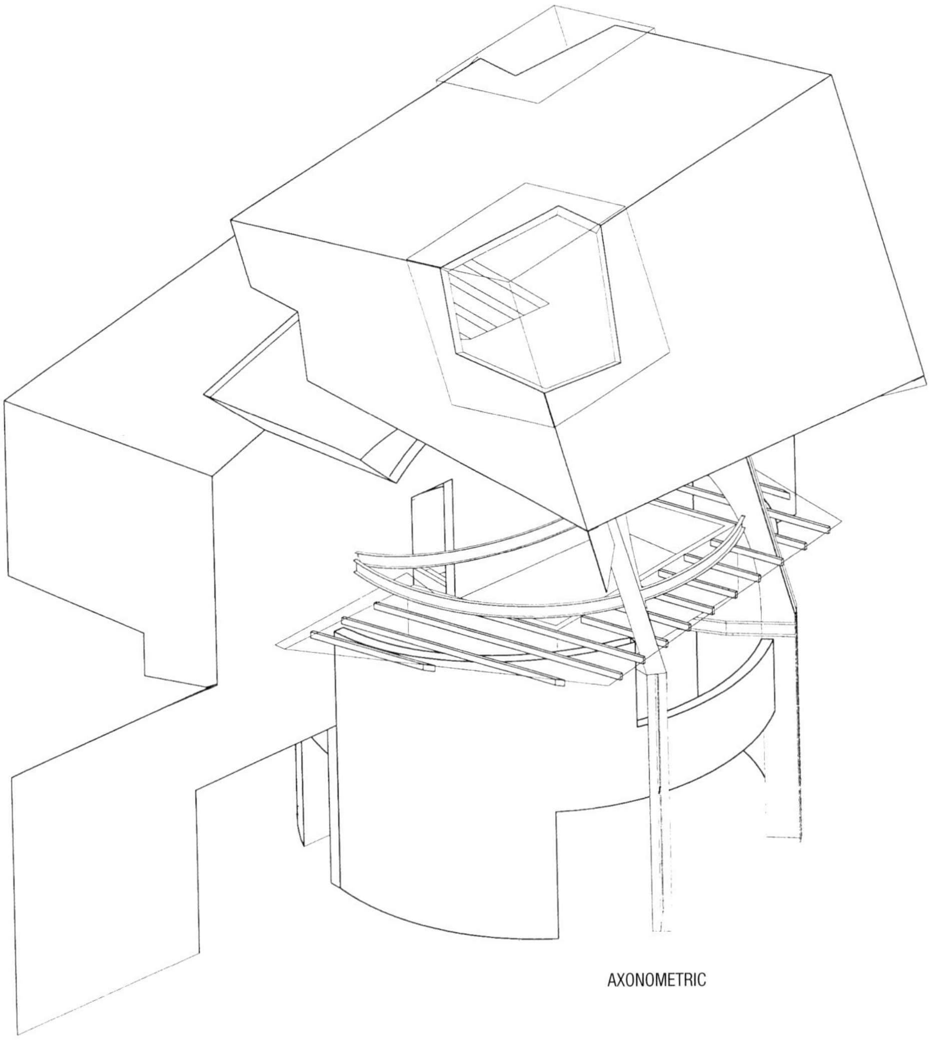

AXONOMETRIC

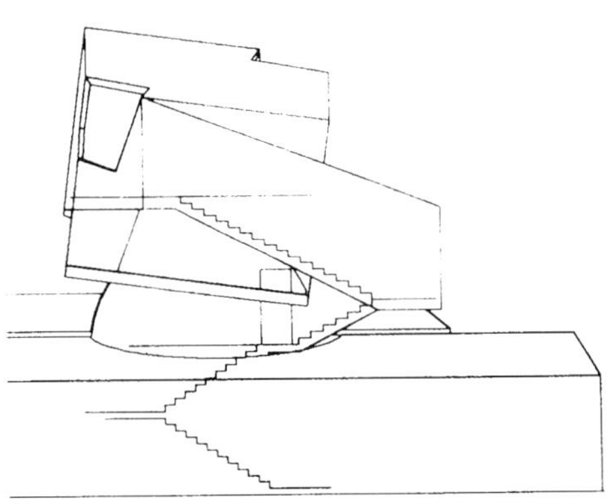

EAST ELEVATION

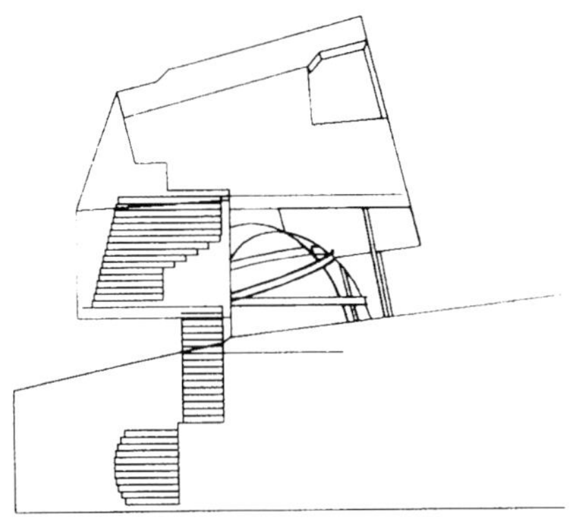

NORTH ELEVATION

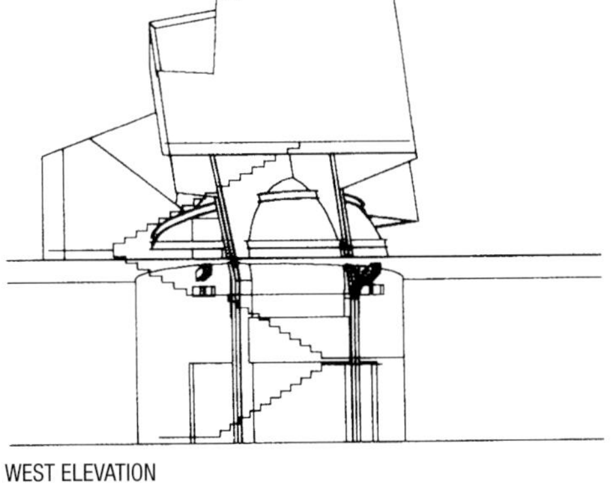

WEST ELEVATION

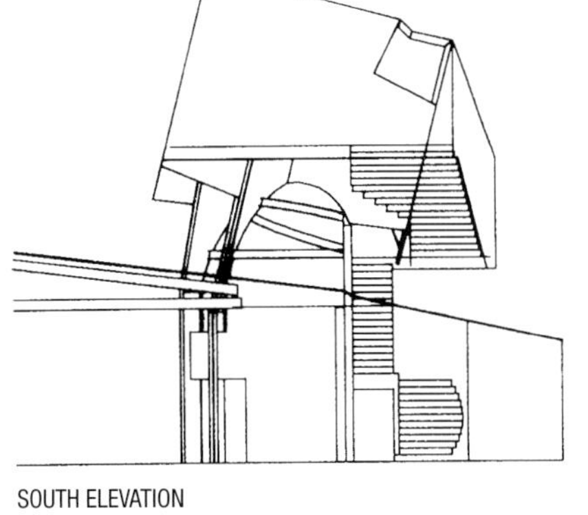

SOUTH ELEVATION

0 5m

BEEHIVE

Location Culver City, California, United States
Client Samitaur Constructs
Size 11,000 ft^2 (1020 m^2)
Date 2001

The Beehive includes a conference facility and a reception area for a web-hosting company. The project also includes a two-story rectangular volume that holds office space. The project is inserted in the midst of an existing grouping of contiguous warehouse buildings.

The main entrance and reception area are on the first floor. A stair encircles the street face of the lobby and leads to the second-level conference room. An exterior stair on the east elevation leads from the conference floor to a terraced roof-deck. The deck steps up toward the southwest, providing informal seating for staff and clients, overlooking the local park just across the boulevard, and with a view of the city in all directions. The stepped seating surrounds a pyramidal skylight that brings light to the conference, reception, and open stairway areas.

The shape of the exterior Beehive wall is determined by the positioning of four steel-tube columns that support both the walls and the roof. Each column inclines outward, and then inward as the volume of the interior space increases on the second floor, then decreases as the volume rises to the roof-deck. Each column inclines at a different angle, and each column varies in length.

At the point where each column changes inclination, the steel tube is severed and stitched back together with two steel plates to reveal the joint.

Curved horizontal ring-beams span between the columns, and define the shape dictated by the plan of the columns. The exterior surface of the building is a shingled system of glass and Rheinzink® panels that slip over and under one another at each horizontal ring. The shingling is visible on the interior and exterior of the structure.

Panel widths vary as a function of the curvature of the pipe beams. The more pronounced the curve, the smaller the panel module.

The Beehive and adjacent buildings are set back from the street to create a garden to the north and west. The new grass mounds serve as informal seating, and also sequester the area immediately in front of the buildings creating some separation from the highly trafficked adjacent street.

MODEL

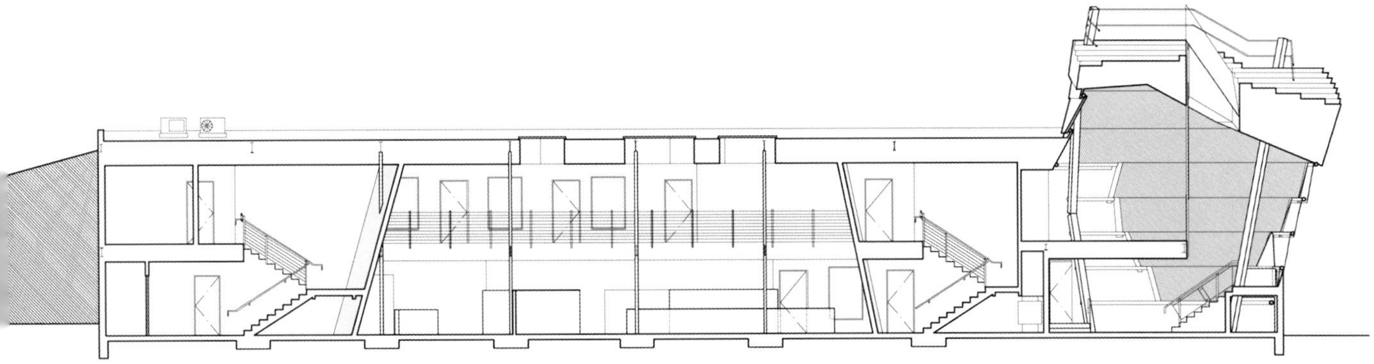

SECTION

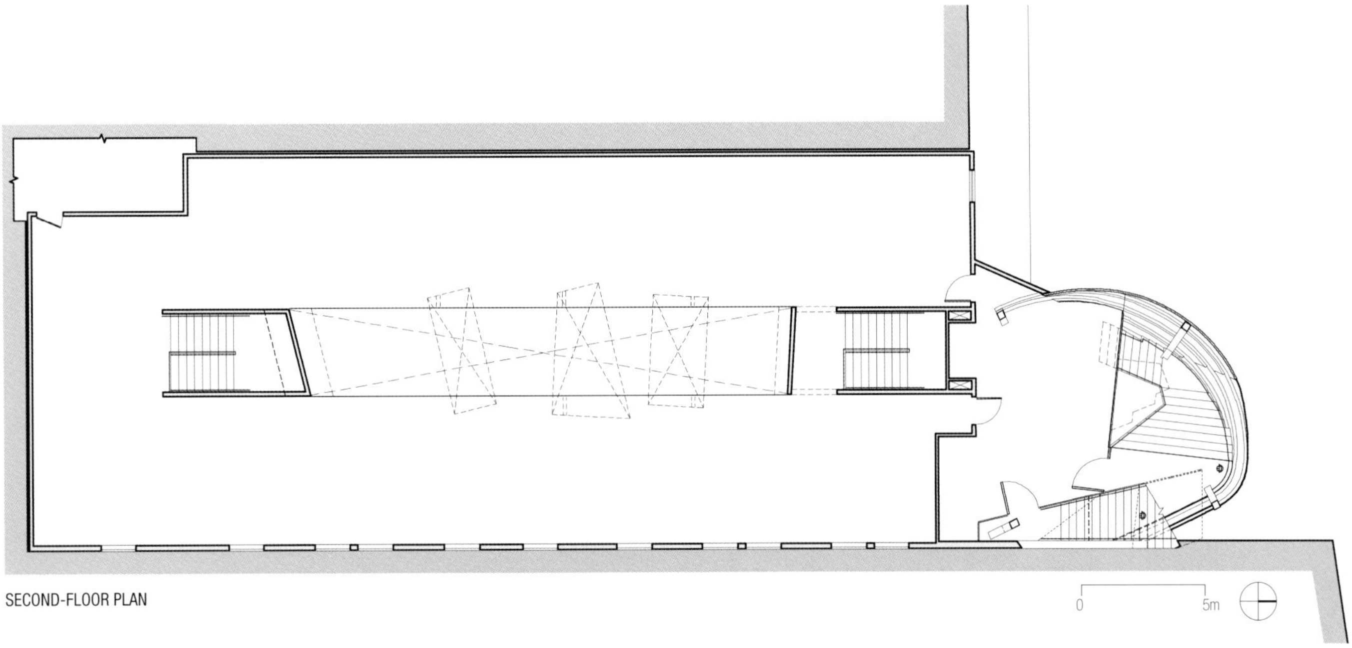

SECOND-FLOOR PLAN

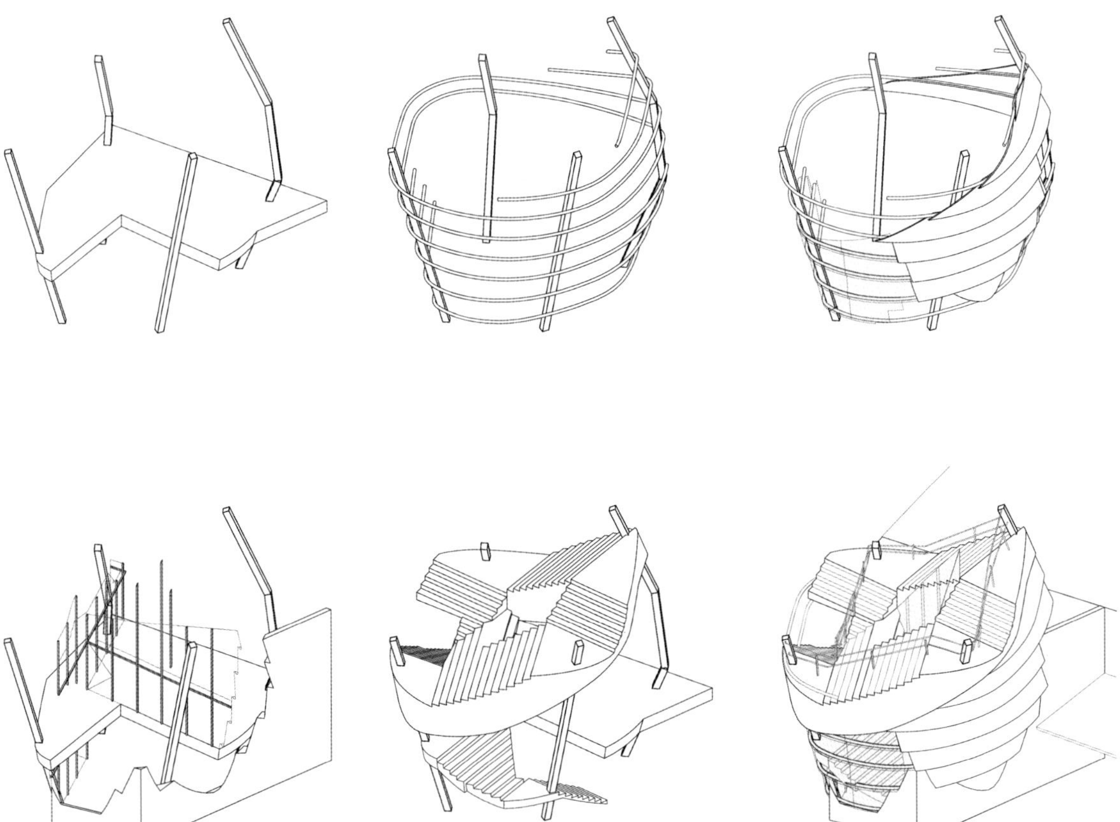

STRUCTURAL DIAGRAMS

3555 HAYDEN

Location Culver City, California, United States
Client Samitaur Constructs
Size 25,000 ft^2 (2325 m^2)
Date 2007

The existing building was a one-story brick warehouse, built in the early 1950s. A two-story masonry box at the west end of the building was added in the late 1990s, replacing a portion of the original brick structure, which is used as office space. The double-floor height addition to the original building is a new sound stage and studio for use by film production companies in the area. The 2007 third-floor addition is placed on top of the sound studio, providing space for additional offices.

In order to support the third-floor addition, a new perimeter of steel beams, supported on the steel and concrete block structure of the sound studio, was built on the existing studio roof. Steel columns are added to the new perimeter steel frame on the existing roof of the sound studio to support the new, undulating roof of the third floor. The roof shape is determined by averaging the city-mandated height limit, so that the portion of the roof that extends over that limit is offset by an equal area of roof below the limit.

The roof geometry is constructed with 42-foot-long (13-meter-long) glue-laminated wooden beams spanning in a north–south orientation, and two-foot-by-eight-foot (0.6-meter-by-2.4-meter) wooden rafters spanning from beam to beam. Each glue-laminated wooden beam was milled to a unique curvature, and has a continuously changing, beveled edge on the top surface to accommodate the varying slope of the roof over the span of the beam.

Because the entire wooden structure is exposed to the third-floor interior, the roof construction needed to insulate the plywood diaphragm roof. The finished surface, applied over the cement board, is a translucent spray-applied fiberglass material, developed specifically for this project. It waterproofs the entire external surface of the building, and conforms seamlessly to its unique curvature. Half-round ridge-bumps (analogue topographic lines) were placed horizontally along the sloping roof, to slow and redirect the flow of water off the roof.

The third-floor addition is subdivided into three interior working spaces by two intervening, 42-foot-long (12.8-meter-long), mullion-less, structural, glass skylights, which span the glazed six-foot (1.8-meter) zone between the three separate office modules. On the north side of the sound studio roof, an exterior courtyard in the middle module is cut into the façade and roof, and enclosed by slanted glass. The aluminum

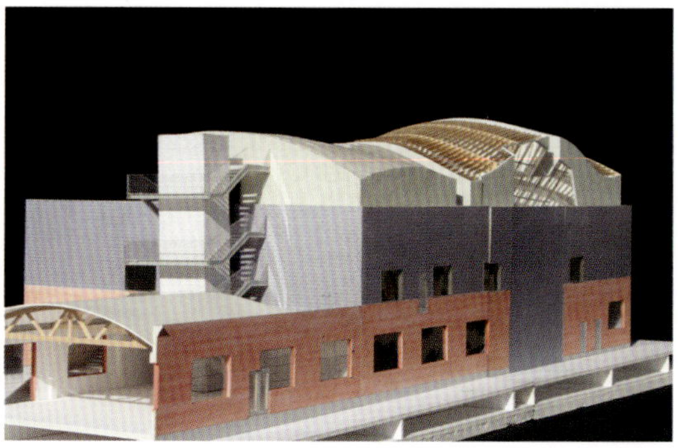

MODEL

SECTION PERSPECTIVE

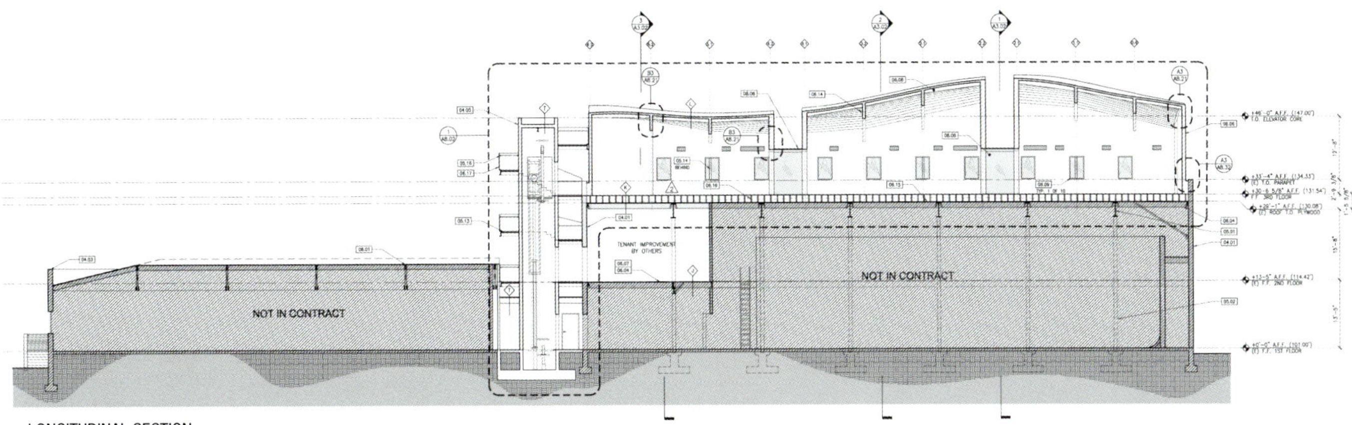

LONGITUDINAL SECTION

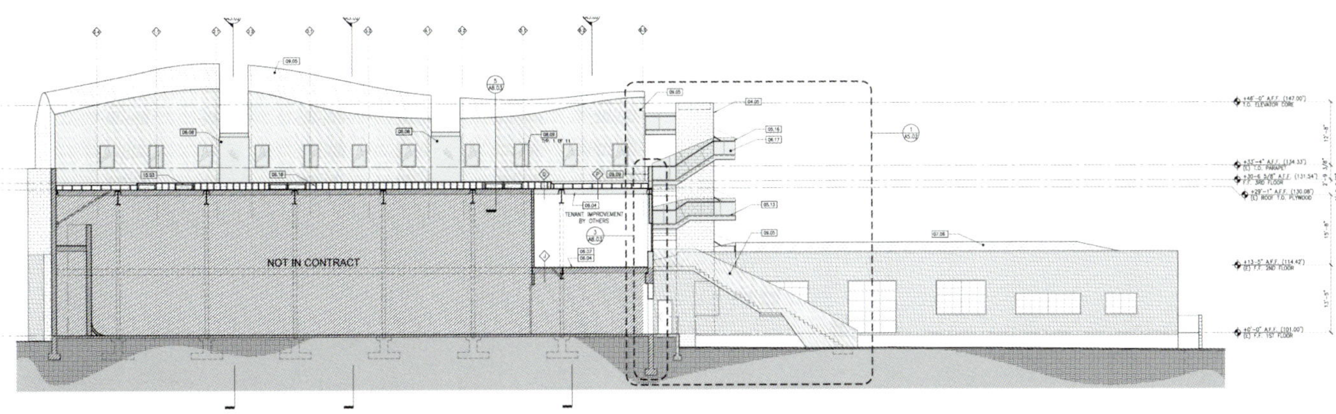

LONGITUDINAL SECTION

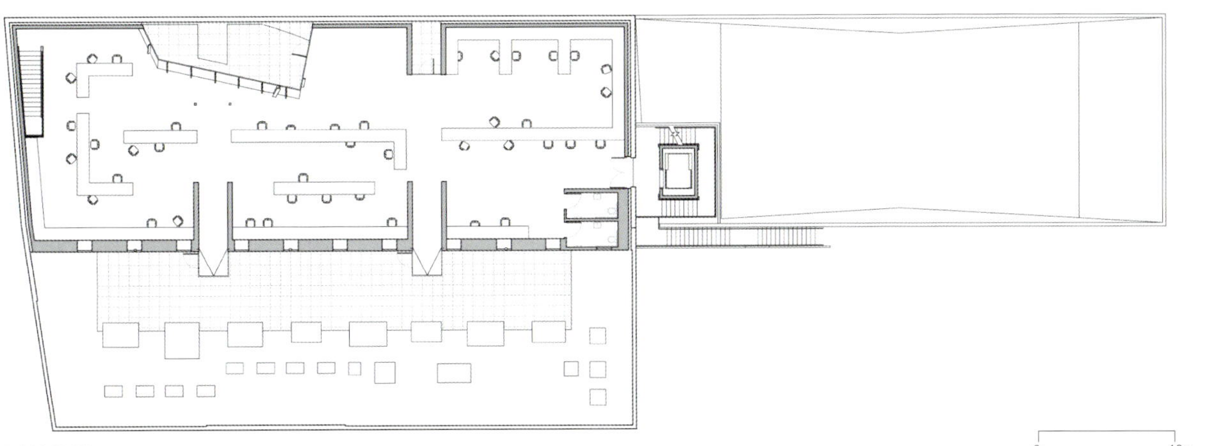

FLOOR PLAN

storefront system was reinforced with steel tubes to support the acute angle of the inclined glazing.

On the south elevation, two glazed, six-foot-wide (1.8-meter-wide) boxes with glass doors extend onto a roof platform to provide an exterior deck area for use by the third-floor tenants.

3535 HAYDEN

Located roughly midway between the IRS and Hayden Tower sites, the 3535 Hayden project is a new four-story, steel-frame structure constructed over the wooden posts and trusses of an old warehouse on the site. The original building was demolished except for the posts and long-span bowstring truss structure, which was preserved. New steel-tube columns and wide flange beams are positioned over, under, around, and through the original trusses and posts, so that the built conclusion is a spatial amalgamation of two distinct construction types rarely found together in a single building.

The wooden structure is no longer functional—it supports only itself—with the exception of the last structural bay along the north elevation, where half the vaulted, truss-supported roof of the original warehouse is preserved above the new design studio. The wooden post supports at the center of the original bowstring truss spanning the warehouse bays now define the center line of the primary public circulation hallway, running the length of the building, extending east and west from the central lobby.

The incomplete top chords of the modified original trusses project through the south wall facing the parking, and are used to support a new steel angle, sun-control system to protect the south wall windows. Over the entrance on the south side is the only remaining complete truss, projecting into the parking lot to mark the entry doors. Above the doors is an inclined, cantilevering orthogonal block that contains a third-floor conference room.

The lobby to the building is a three-story, conical volume with circulation corridors extending east and west. An open stair encircles the lobby on the west side. Bridges on levels two and three span the lobby, connecting the elevator core with the floor areas. Behind the reception desk is the primary conference space, enclosed at ground level, and glazed on the second-floor wall adjoining the second-level bridge over the lobby. Events in the conference room are visible from the second- and third-floor lobby bridges. The fourth floor is an executive floor, enclosed by the third-floor ceiling from the lobby below, accessible by elevator.

Location Culver City, California, United States
Client Samitaur Constructs
Size 53,000 ft^2 (4924 m^2)
Date 1997

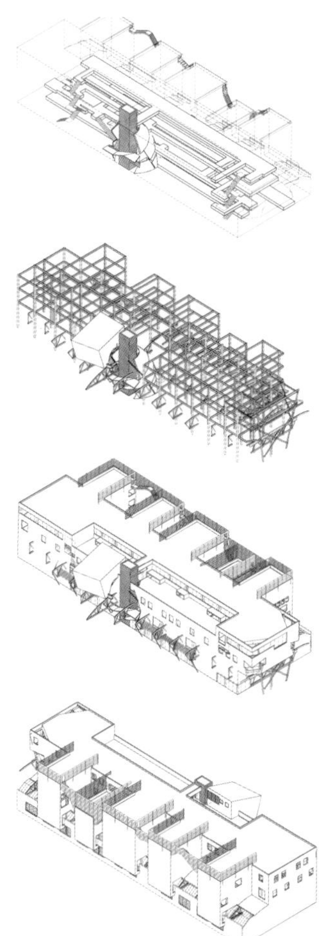

CIRCULATION AND STRUCTURE

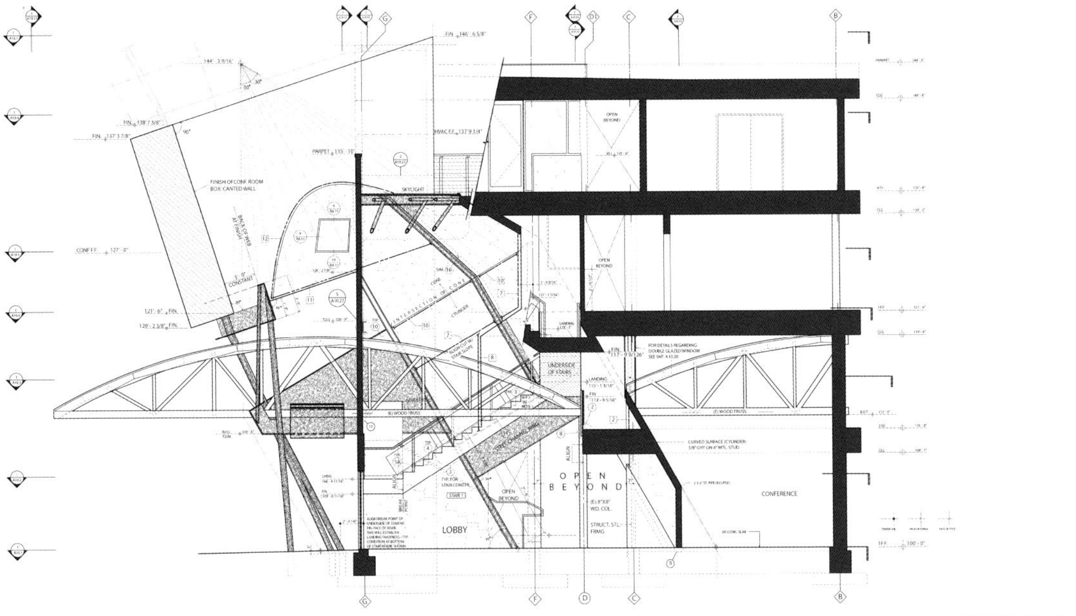

SECTION

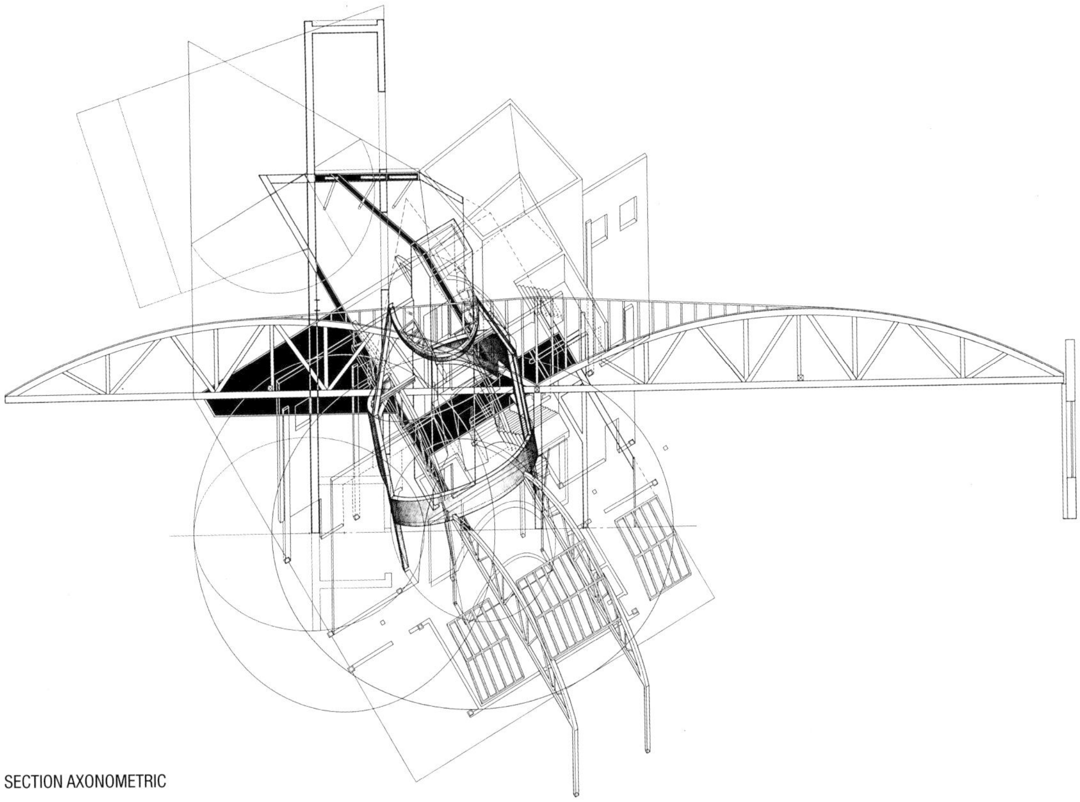

SECTION AXONOMETRIC

The curving steel beams that form the interior lobby cone extend out through the south elevation of the building to support a steel canopy over the entrance. The canopy, end-supported by the two curving beams, passes through two of the wooden trusses that also extend over the entry area.

Floors one, two, and three contain a mixture of office, production, library, and computer spaces. On the ground floor is a kitchen, and an indoor and outdoor dining area that includes a walled, landscaped garden at the east end of the building.

UCLA
UCLA

8522 NATIONAL

Location Culver City, California, United States
Client Samitaur Constructs
Size 43,000 ft^2 (3994.8 m^2)
Date 1988

Located along busy National Boulevard, five warehouses adjoin one another, forming a single building. The first building was constructed in the 1920s and the others followed during the 1930s and 1940s. All are long-span spaces with clerestory windows along truss lines. There was never any design attempt to coordinate an earlier building with a later one. Buildings were simply added as additional square footage when required.

The strategy was to convert the industrial building to office space for creative industries supporting the local film industry. The building required a unifying organizational system to coalesce the disparate parts while maintaining the character of the original buildings.

A steel canopy was constructed across the street elevation, propped on wooden struts, extending from the existing cement-plaster wall. An elliptical entry court was cut into the original building and supported by new concrete block, exposing a piece of interior truss structure to the street.

A pedestrian entry ramp leads from the sidewalk into the open court, through the entry door to an interior path arranged either side of an existing column system running along the center of the path, and supporting the existing trussed roof. The interior façades along the path consist of three superimposed components: an orthogonal frame, an arch wall, and a glass wall. These elements run at different modules based on their individual needs and intersect irregularly along the length of the path.

The path leads to a lobby midway along the route. The newly skylit volume is a partial ellipse in plan. The path then turns left and leads to a large meeting room. A third ellipse, inclined in section, has been built into an existing room, now used for conferences, with original walls of concrete block.

The walls of the new meeting room are wood-framed and clad with birch plywood. Wooden beams are bolted to the existing perimeter walls and serve as ledgers spanning the existing corners on the diagonal. Wooden studs are placed above and below the wooden beams, cantilevering past the beams to form the elliptical cone shape.

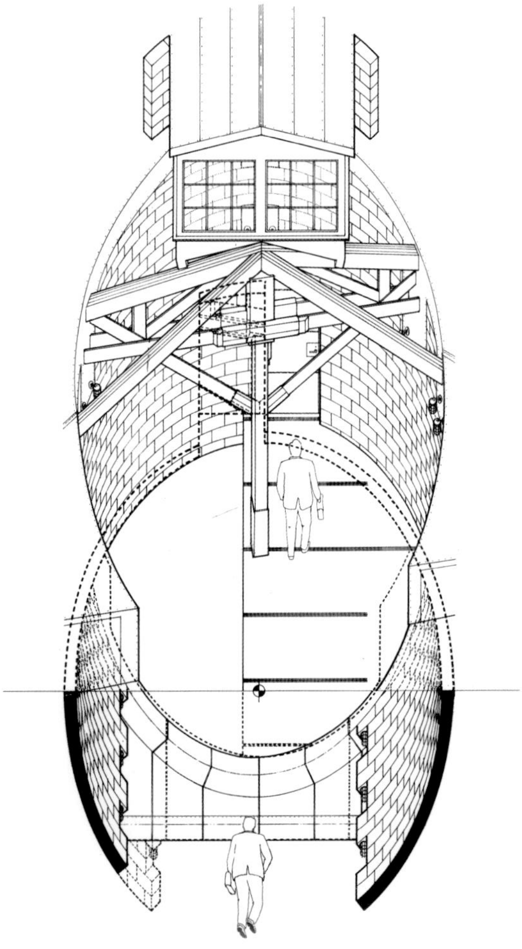

ENTRY AXONOMETRIC

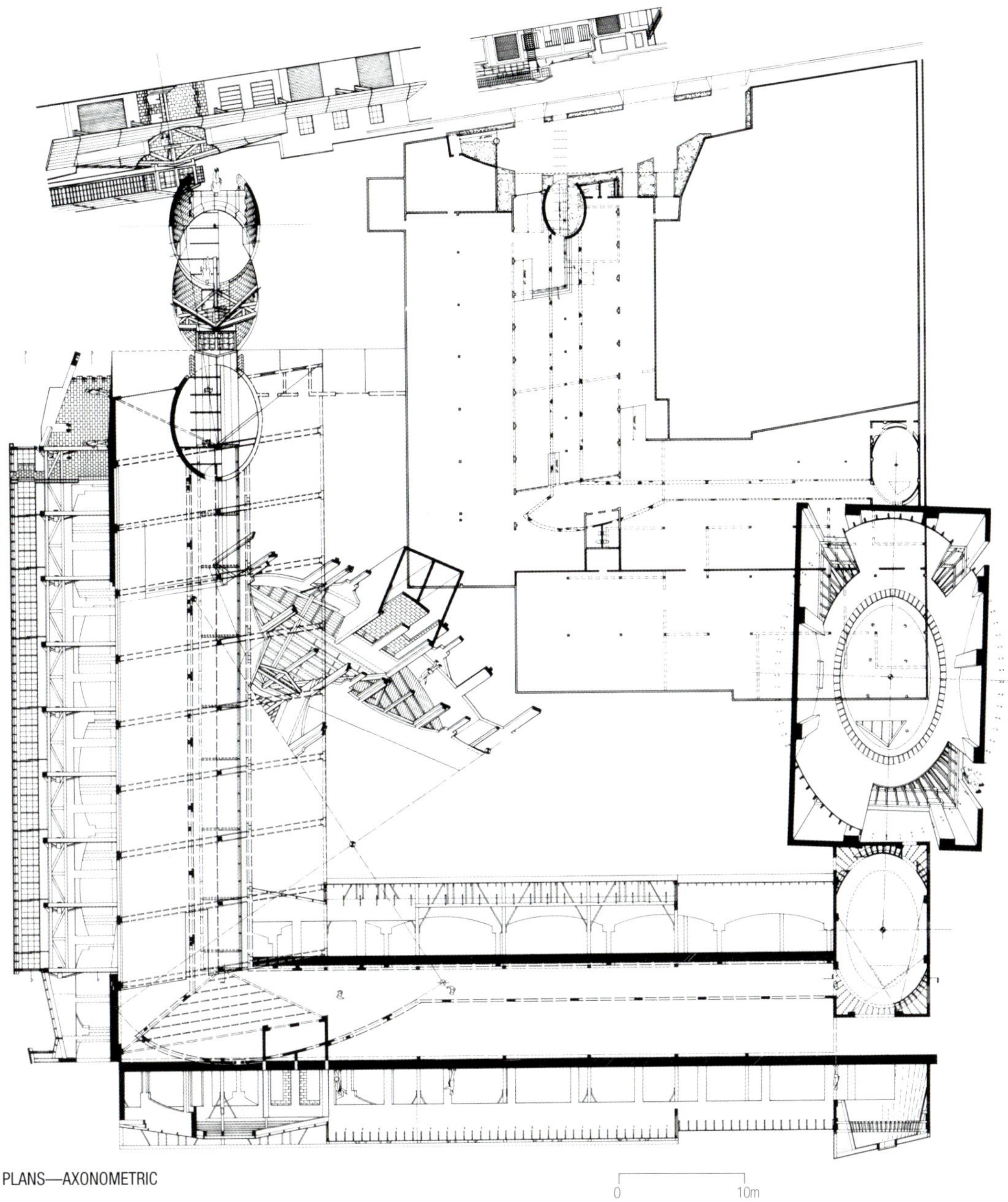

PLANS—AXONOMETRIC

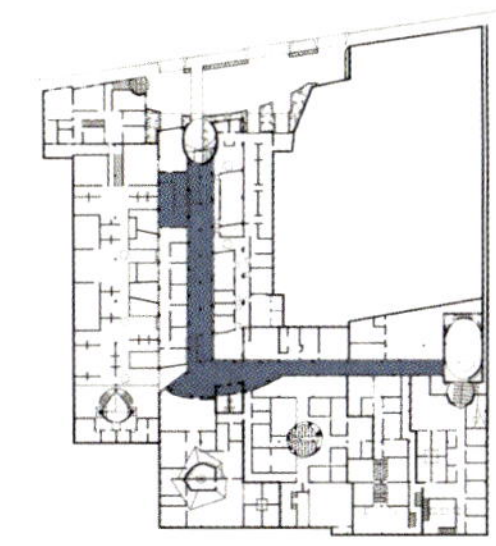

SHARED SPACE

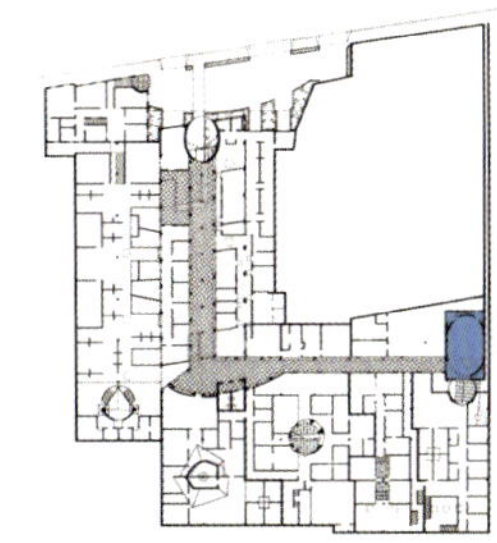

CONFERENCE

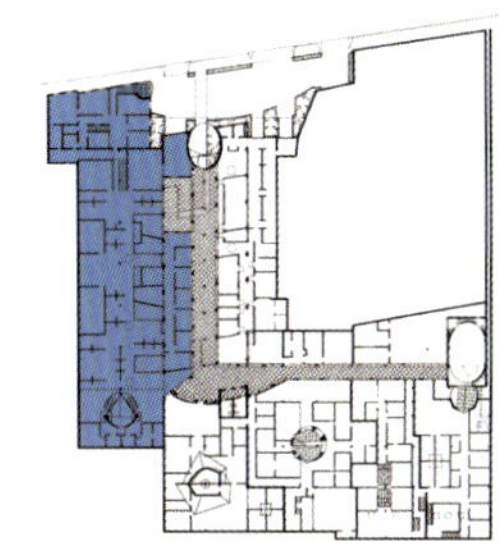

SMA

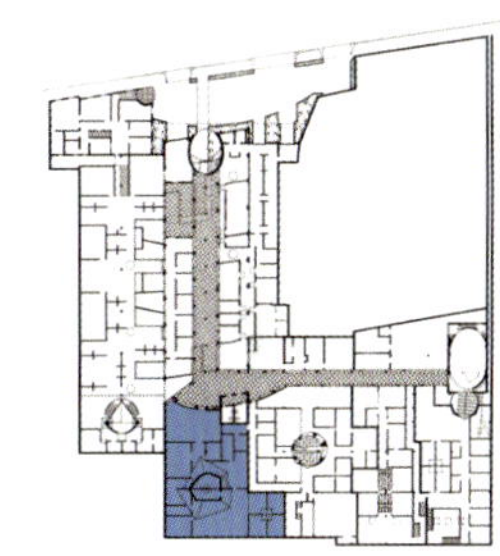

QRC

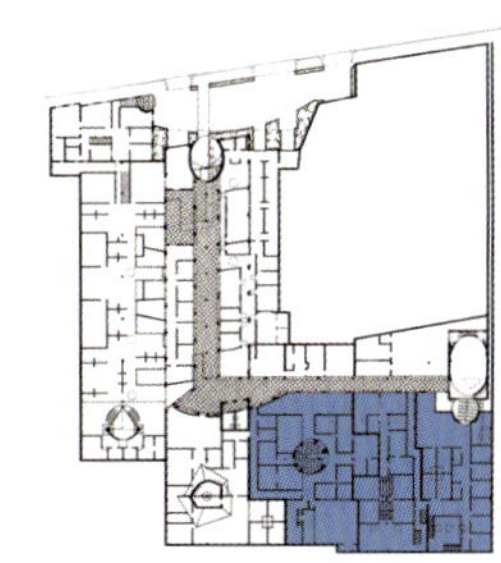

GOALEN GRUUB

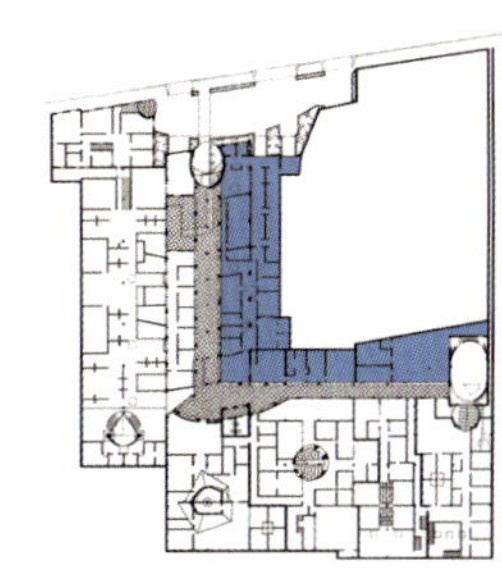

HYBRID ARTS

The interior path and lobby organization allows the owner to subdivide and lease the spaces on either side of the path in a variety of ways, or simply to lease to a single tenant. Over the years, this flexible arrangement has accommodated a wide variety of tenant configurations.

Five significant design-industry tenants moved into the building, which quickly caught the attention of the international architecture and design community. The building garnered numerous design awards including AIA National awards for both architecture and interior design. The success of 8522 confirmed the strategy for the neighborhood and prompted a provisional master plan for the area and a number of more ambitious projects nearby.

WAFFLE

Location Culver City, California, United States
Client Samitaur Constructs
Size 5500 ft^2 (511 m^2)
Date Under construction — 2017

The Ten Towers project indicated that the existing tower frame was too far removed from the street to be fully effective. It was decided that the existing frame would become the site of the Cactus Tower, and a second tower would be located along Hayden Avenue.

The conceptual focus of the project will be the new tower located at the eastern edge of the site, adjacent to Hayden Avenue. The new tower has the same plan size and height as the existing tower.

A preliminary study model made from a square pile of note paper describes a tower that is not quite a regular box, nor a clear, spatial departure from the regular box. Rather, the model suggests a conceptually soft geometry—a twisted tower. The proposed horizontal and vertical 'fins' and the glazing enclosure system were thoroughly evaluated. Glazing components are never curved, so the curving surfaces are conveyed as the aggregate of a sequence of straight lines that continually shift position across the four tower elevations.

The Waffle sustains the soft geometry analogue, but replaces the horizontal and vertical glass supports with half-inch steel plate—plasma-cut, brise soleil frames, with orthogonal, double-glazed window panels that enclose and waterproof the building.

The original tower block twists along its height and rotates slightly, both clockwise at the top and counterclockwise toward the bottom. The plan shape and size are maintained as the tower volume pivots. The curvature of the form is conveyed by the horizontal and vertical steel plate grid that frames the glass enclosure. As the curvature increases, the spacing between plates is decreased to maintain the planar glass-panel subdivision.

The internal structural frame closely follows the exterior shape. Four corner columns undergo a series of compound miters to reflect the curving form. The building comprises a ground floor, a mezzanine, a second floor, and a covered roof deck connected by an internal stair and elevator.

The Waffle will house an exclusive restaurant. A secondary support building will be built just to the west of the site. New garden seating will be constructed directly adjacent to the Waffle.

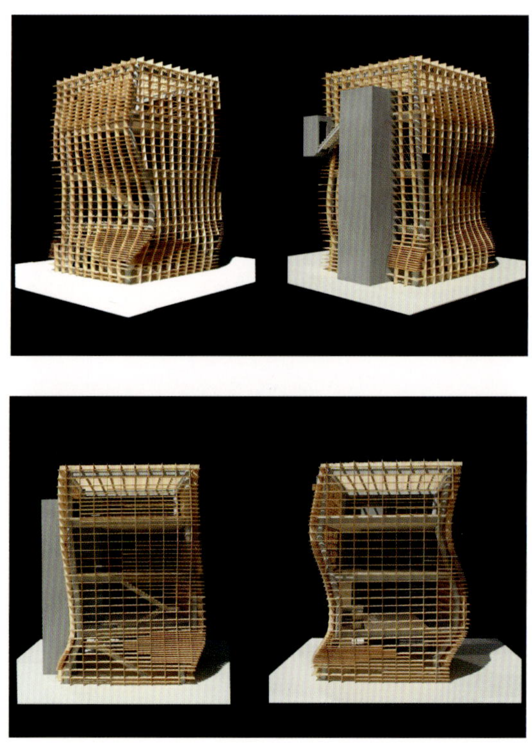

MODEL

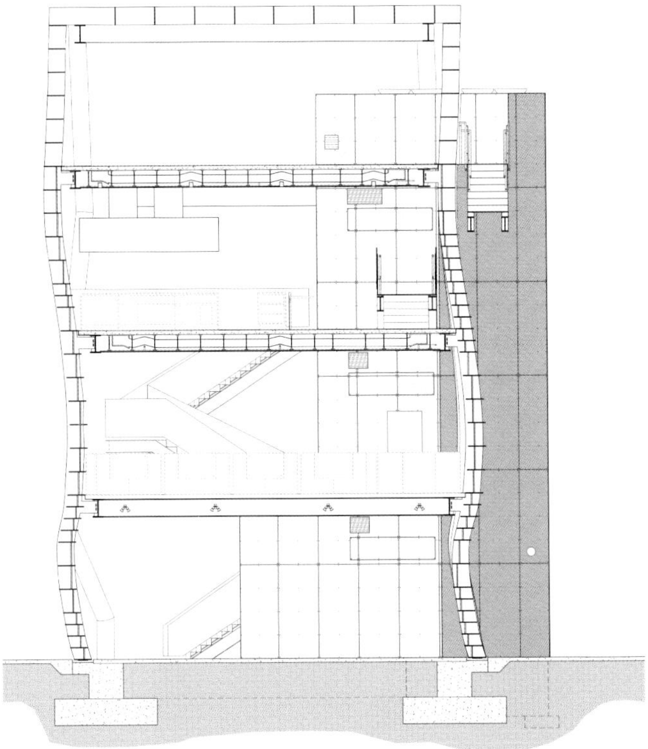

SECTION

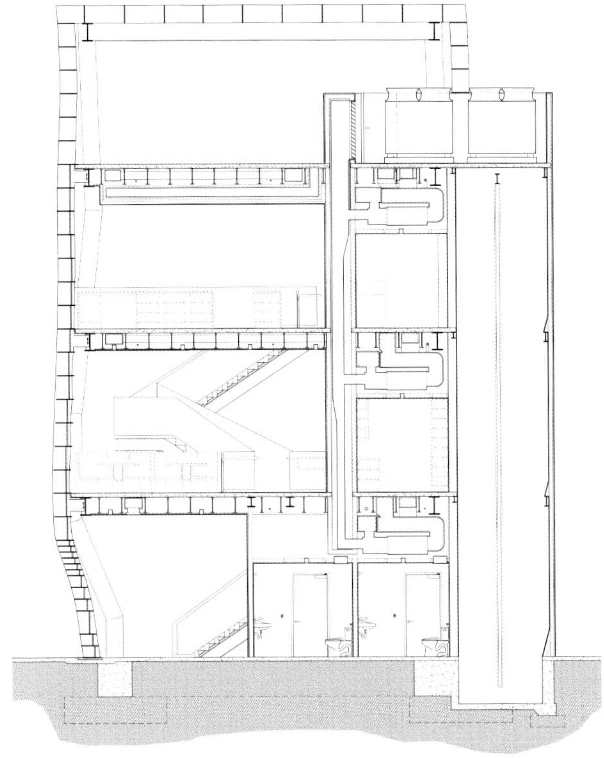

SECTION

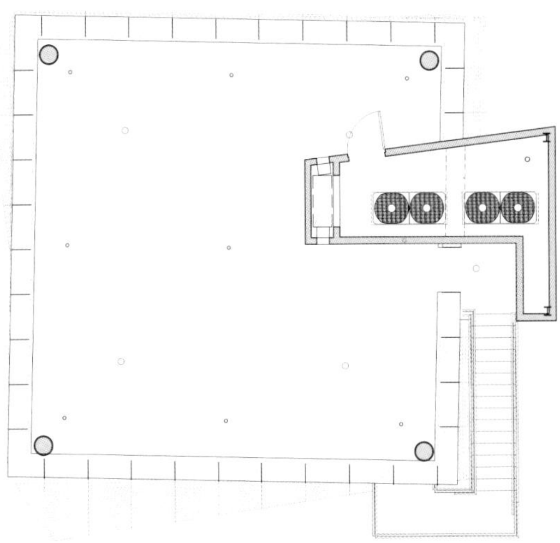

ROOF PLAN

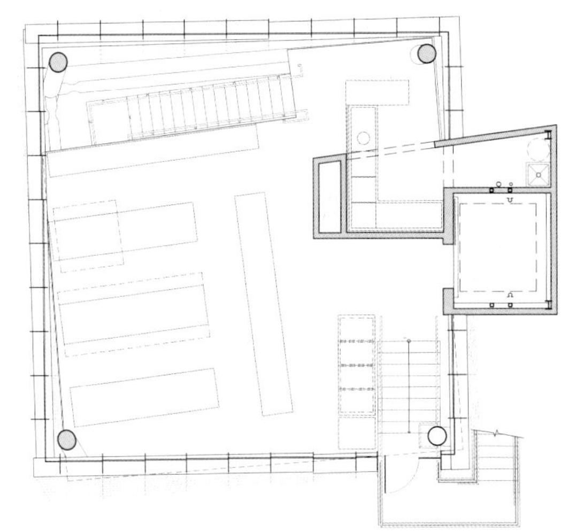

THIRD-FLOOR PLAN

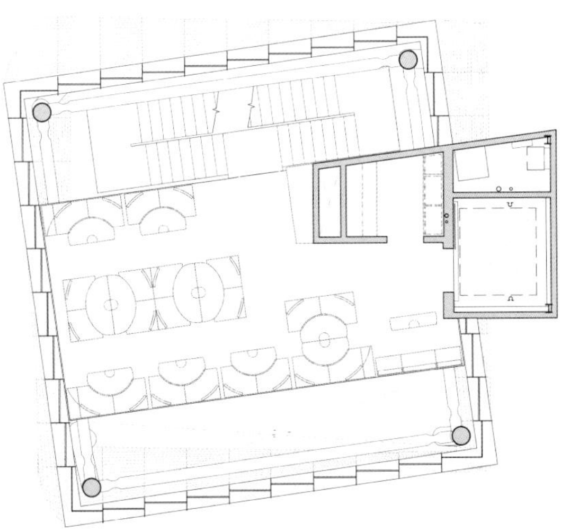

MEZZANINE PLAN

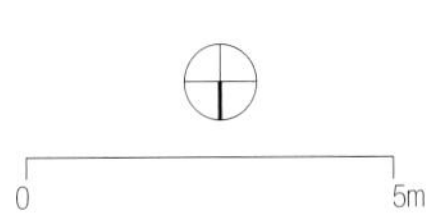

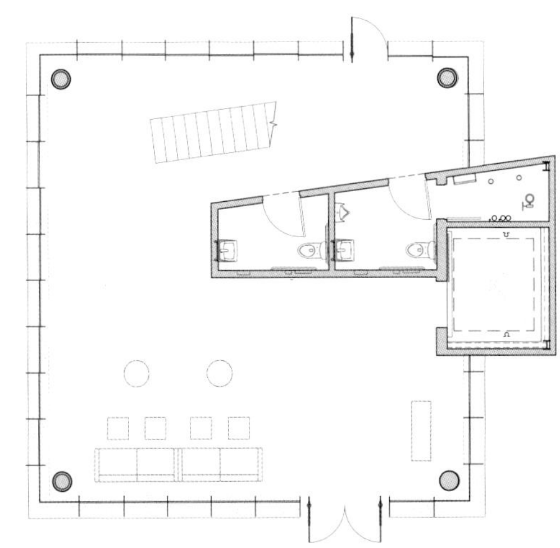

FIRST-FLOOR PLAN

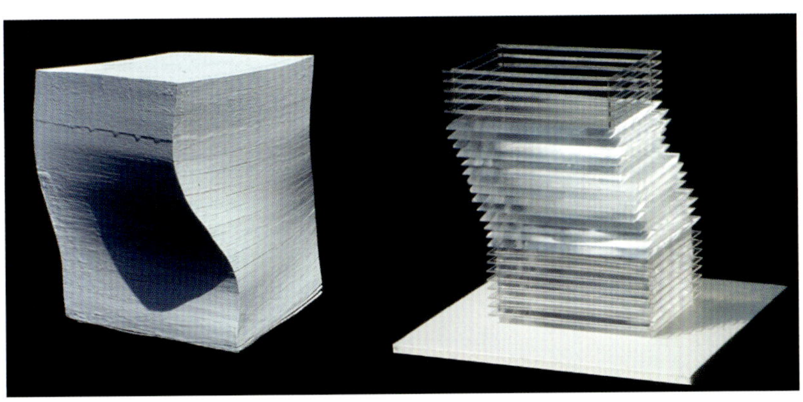

CACTUS TOWER

Location Culver City, California, United States
Client Samitaur Constructs
Size 20,000 ft² (1858.1 m²)
Date 2010

Existing walls are poured concrete, and the existing roof structure is a sequence of wooden bowstring trusses. The building was originally used for light manufacturing, and was constructed in the 1940s. A large steel frame, located just outside the warehouse, once housed an industrial press.

The old industrial press tower has been stripped, revealing a ramshackle steel support structure, and a supporting concrete block wall. The intention is to use the existing structure to accommodate an outdoor meeting and gathering area. The steel frame is re-engineered, and the block wall repaired.

A new 'green structure' is installed midway up the tower, providing a canopy/pavilion that defines a space for outdoor work and relaxation. This new structure comprises 28 steel pots, each holding sufficient earth for a single Mexican fence post cactus. The pots are positioned in six parallel lines, running east–west. Each pot line is a linear sequence of five cacti, and a new structural truss spanning from one edge of the original steel structure to the other. The pots are compression struts, five per truss, serving as the vertical chords of the new trusses that form the garden. The top chord of each new truss is an eight-inch (203-millimeter) steel 'T'; the bottom chord is a steel cable. Each pot is slotted from below, and the depth of each slotted pot varies as a function of the position of each pot in the truss sequence. The slots follow the line of the bottom chord from one end of the structure to the other. Perimeter pots have the deepest slots; centrally positioned pots, the least. Irrigation lines and lights, unseen from below, are located on the top chord 'T's. A ladder leading to the cacti is provided for maintenance. In the center of Cactus Tower, two pots are omitted from the sequence to allow for the penetration of the afternoon sun to the meeting-area floor.

As a consequence of its height, Cactus Tower is visible from long distances, a symbol of drought-tolerant greenery on the West Los Angeles skyline. Cactus Tower is the result of combining environmental advocacy, an outdoor space, and a new truss typology.

A new production studio, constructed of metal studs and drywall, and tightly wrapped with acoustic fabric, is designed and constructed within the 30,000-square-foot (2787.1-square-meter) shell. The

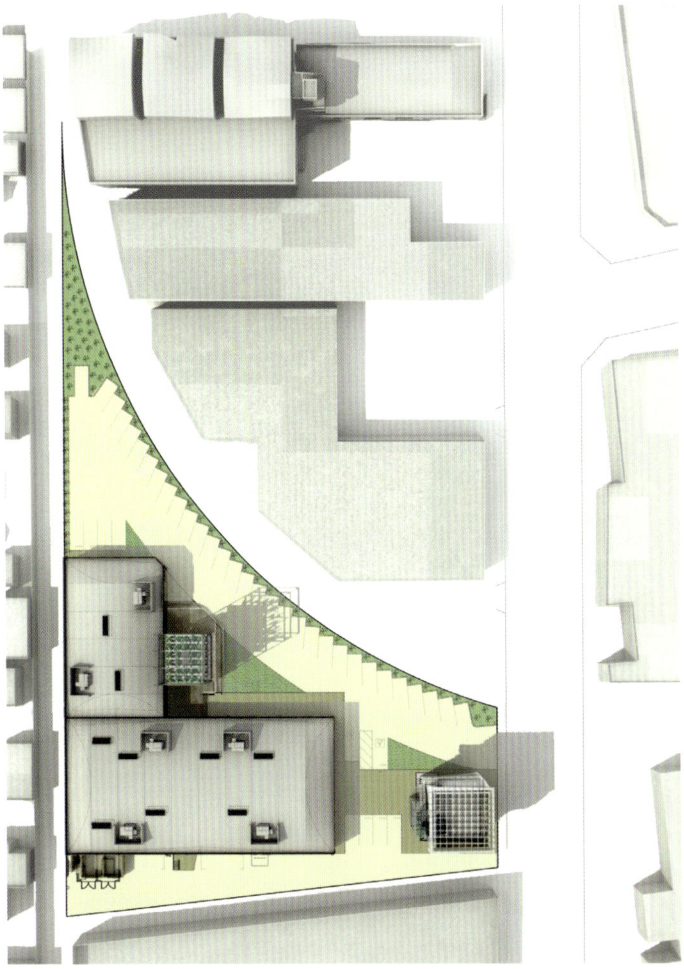

SITE PLAN 0 10m

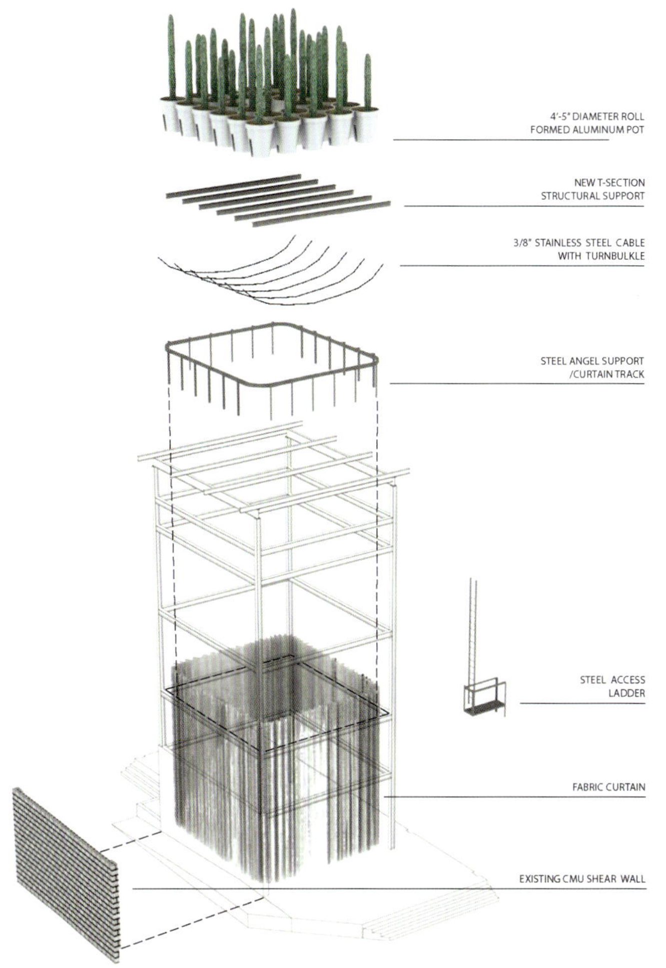

COMPONENT DIAGRAM

RENDERING

production facility is surrounded by a variety of open and closed conference facilities, private offices, post-production venues, and eating and relaxation accommodation. Three glass roll-up doors are installed on the perimeter walls of the existing concrete shell.

The two original warehouses will be spatially connected by demolishing an interior wall, then subdivided in accord with the tenant's interior requirements using metal-stud partitions to form closed office space and open work areas.

WHAT WALL?

Location Culver City, California, United States
Client Samitaur Constructs
Size 15,000 ft^2 (1393.5 m^2)
Date 1998

What Wall? is a small tenant improvement project located within the same block of warehouses as 8522 National, and positioned midway between IRS Records and Stealth along Hayden Avenue. The existing street elevation is a long, unadorned plaster wall with no openings.

The tenant for the new space is a software design company with conventional program requirements: private offices, open work and production areas, conference space, and the need for an iconic image to symbolize the company.

The technical and conceptual focus of the project is a 30-foot-by-30-foot (9.1-meter-by-9.1-meter) portion of a 165-foot-long (50.3-meter-long), 35-foot-high (10.7-meter-high), otherwise uninterrupted, cement plaster wall that faces the public entry and street. The original model studies of the wall were constructed with lemon rinds, a close facsimile to the irregular-curving surfaces that identify the built shape of the new wall.

Having arrived at the formal configuration, the lemon-rind model was reconstructed as a sequence of rectilinear blocks, positioned to approximate the predetermined shape of the curve. The original smooth curve was reconceptualized with off-the-shelf blocks as both wall shape and surface, to be visually identical from both inside and outside the new offices. The new 'replacement' wall that interrupts the original flat plaster surface was constructed of exactly 1000 concrete blocks, each eight inches by eight inches by eight inches (203 millimeters by 203 millimeters by 203 millimeters). Each block is specially cut to fit within the lemon-rind wall model. Each block is fabricated identically, but modified specifically in each case to fit the varying curvature of the new wall.

The blocks are supported on a framework of vertical and horizontal steel pipes that predetermine the essential curvature of the wall to which the blocks conform. A plywood grid, or analogue wall form, was used during construction as a supporting shape and scaffold in order to precisely position each block in the curving sequence.

Three steel windows are inserted within the block wall, providing light and views to the street from the new executive office and conference space directly behind it. The windows are first imagined as simple,

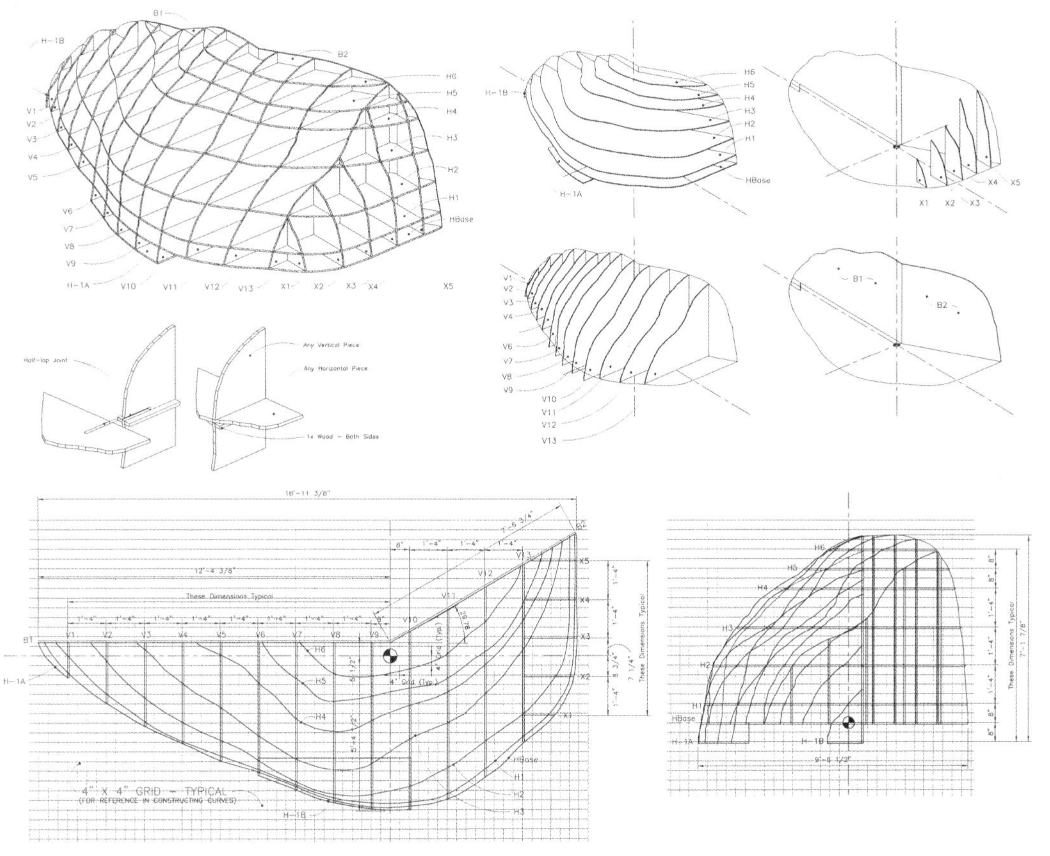

MASONRY FORMWORK

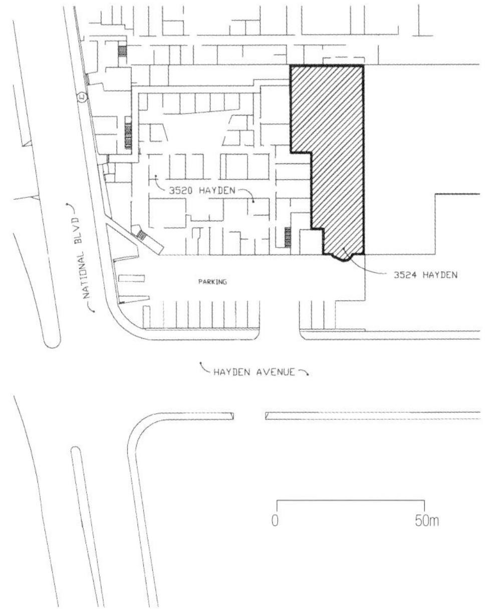

SITE PLAN

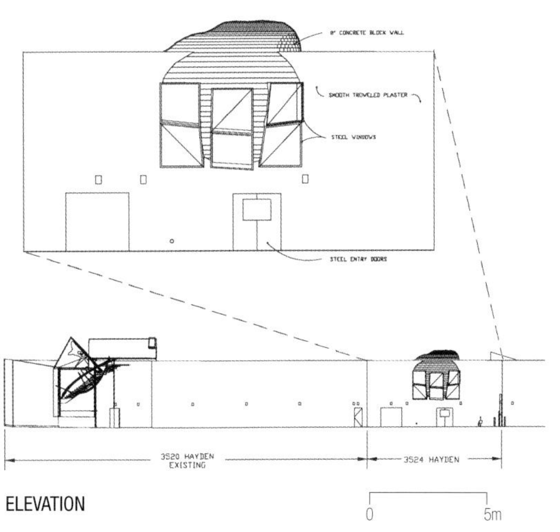

ELEVATION

orthogonal shapes in the curving wall elevation. The frames are then modified to accommodate the curving surface, so that the steel frames incline in and out, following the a priori curved section of the wall as straight line analogues. The glass is then triangulated to fit within the folded steel edges of the frames.

Where the block wall shape loops over the roof line, a clerestory window, invisible from the street, is positioned between the curving top of the new wall and the existing warehouse roof below, admitting natural light from the south on to the curving interior surface of the blocks.

RESERVED
PARKING ONLY

NO PARKING ANY TIME
NO PARKING ANY TIME
3524

PARAMOUNT LAUNDRY

Location Culver City, California, United States
Client Samitaur Constructs
Size 24,000 ft^2 (2229.7 m^2)
Date 1989

Based on the early success of 8522 National, the project site expanded within the Culver City neighborhood. A new site location was added—much closer to downtown Culver City, and directly adjacent to the backlot of Sony Pictures.

The new site, located along Ince Boulevard, was a smaller satellite campus of four buildings. Two of the buildings to be modified fronted Ince (Paramount Laundry and Lindblade Tower) and ultimately shared some common design elements.

The Paramount Laundry project is a remodeling of an existing concrete structure with a wooden truss roof, used by Paramount Studios in the 1940s. The building is a mix of open work areas, private offices, and conference space. A three-story entry lobby was inserted at the street entrance to provide direct stairway access to each of two new office floors above, and to organize circulation to ground-floor office and conference areas. Adjacent to the lobby is the primary work space, a three-story volume with a new third-level bridge spanning overhead, connecting two separate sections of the new third floor. The bridge was made possible by cutting and removing the bottom chords of the existing roof truss structure, providing the vertical clearance needed to circulate across the bridge. The severed trusses were resupported with a new steel structure made of angles and tubes.

The bridge has a lounge and seating area in the center, a unique vantage point from which the working staff can relax and view their co-workers on the floors below. The bridge structure is supported by vitrified-clay columns filled with reinforced concrete. The clay pipes, used here for the first time as permanent form-work for reinforced concrete, are typically used for plumbing installations underground. The new clay columns also support a new second-floor level with an enclosed media and conference center housed underneath.

Above the bridge is a new vault-like volume, positioned above the existing clerestory roof, aligned with the bridge directly below, and bringing added natural light and space to the bridge and the floor areas beneath.

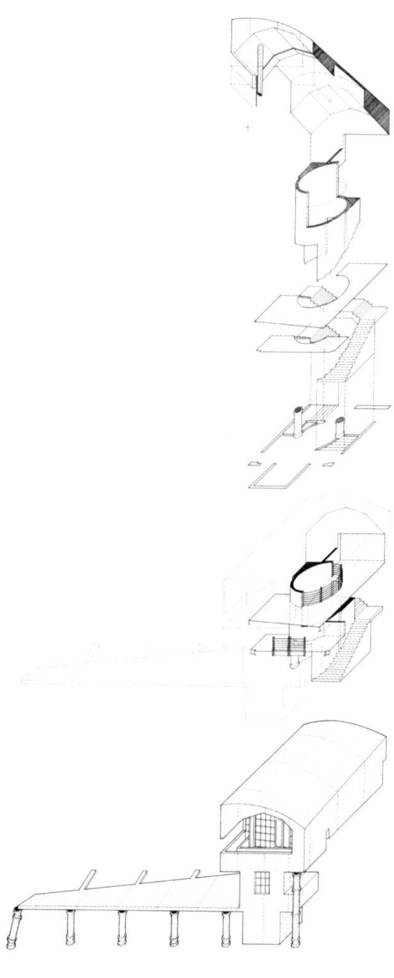

AXONOMETRIC

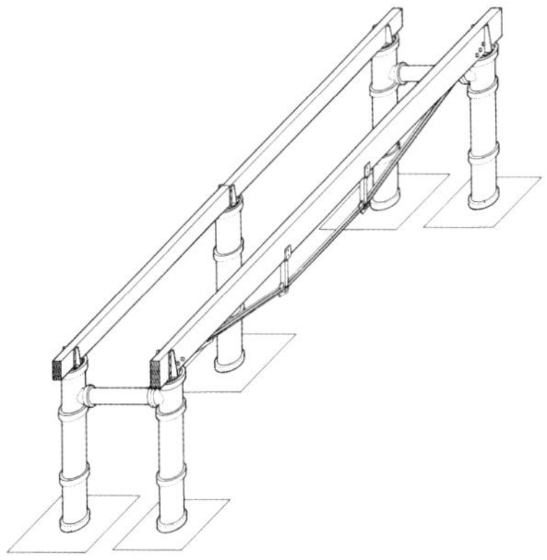

PRIMARY STRUCTURE

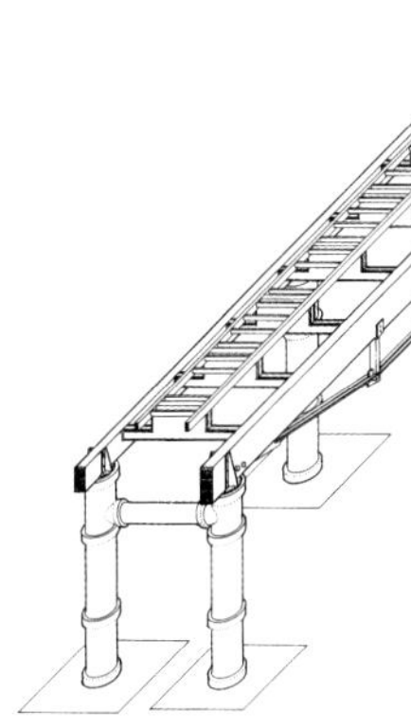

BRIDGE FRAMING

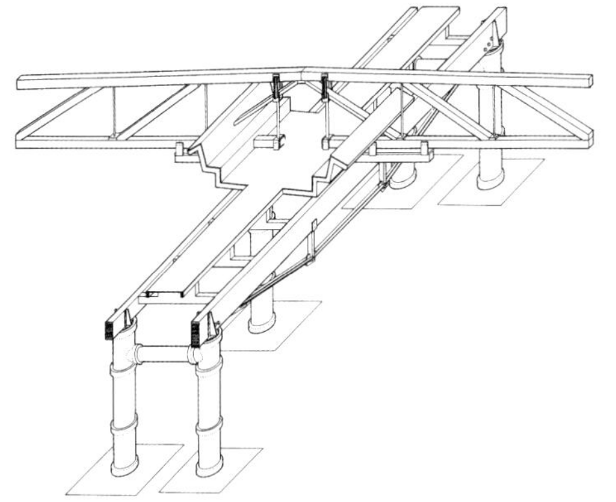

BRIDGE/TRUSS INTERSECTION

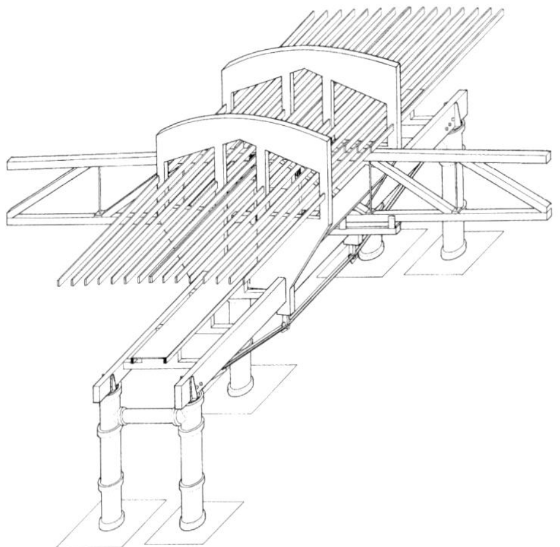

EXTEND HEIGHT

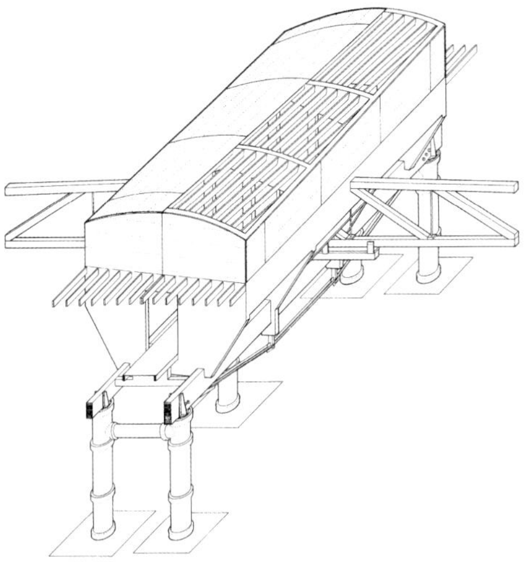

NEW ROOF

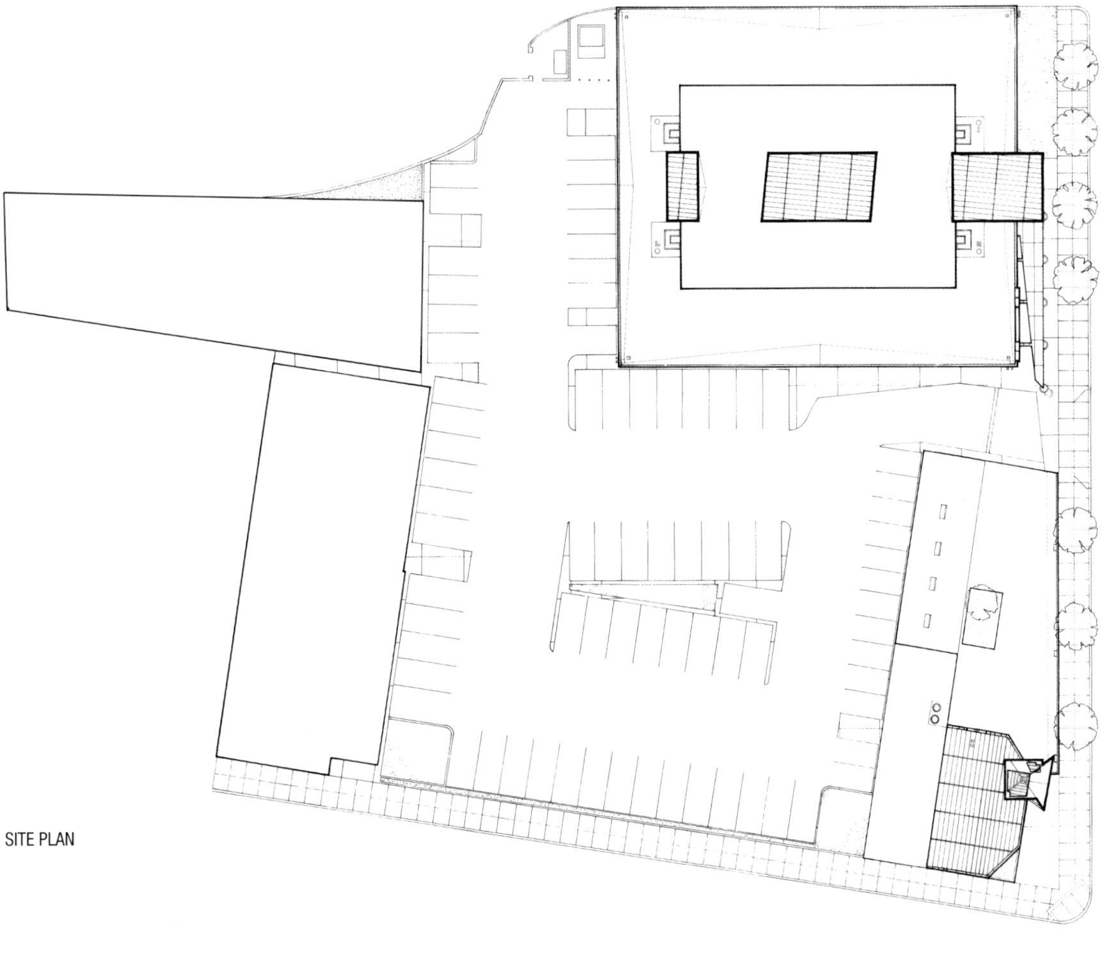

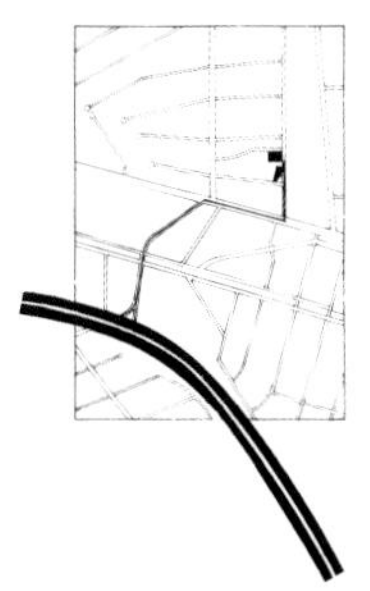

SITE PLAN

PARAMOUNT
LAUNDRY COMPANY

GARY GROUP

The project for Gary Group marked the beginning of a shift in methods of seeing, thinking, and building.

The new site was a small satellite campus of four buildings, which would eventually be expanded to include a fifth.

The remodeled warehouse provides management offices and production design space for an entertainment and marketing firm. The original building was a conjunction of two warehouses, one on the south end of the site, with a vaulted, truss-supported wooden roof, the other on the north, facing both a street entry to the north, and a parking lot entry to the west.

There are no permanently owned offices. There is no operational sequence or chronology for the building interior. Rather it can be entered at a number of points, and used in a variety of ways.

The building has two primary entrances. The first, facing Lindblade Street to the north, is a cut into a freestanding, street-facing concrete block wall built as a new street elevation, and placed in front of the original warehouse wall. The wall tilts back toward the original structure, and rests on steel ribs attached to the existing building.

The second entrance, through a wall newly embellished with chains, wires, rebar ladders, climbing vines, and windows, opens to pedestrian traffic from the parking lot.

Inside the first volume, five work spaces are grouped with five black bamboo-landscaped courtyards in a cruciform plan. At the center of the plan crossing is a pool, open to the sky. Steel showerheads drop water through a marble chute into the pool. Workers gather around the pool to talk and relax. A corridor connects the five work spaces and pool to a private conference room. A conical steel cap supported on glulam wood and steel legs encloses and defines the perimeter of the conference volume. South of the corridor is the second warehouse, which adds a new second floor that includes private offices and open work counters. Two large aluminum, glass, and sheet-metal funnels, cut from the existing bowstring truss-supported roof, bring natural light to the second-floor work areas below the vault.

Location Culver City, California, United States
Client Samitaur Constructs
Size 8000 ft^2 (743.2 m^2)
Date 1990

CONFERENCE ROOM MODEL

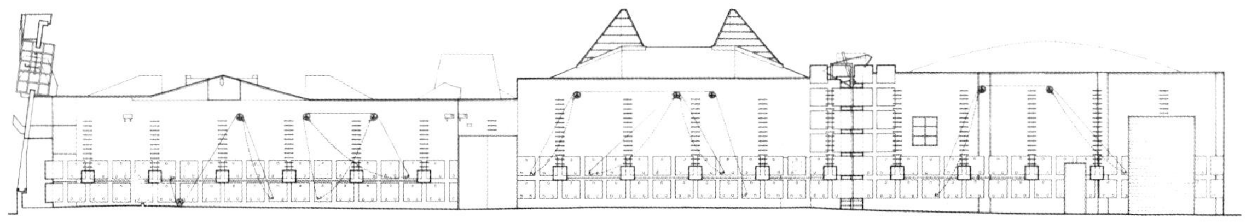

ELEVATION

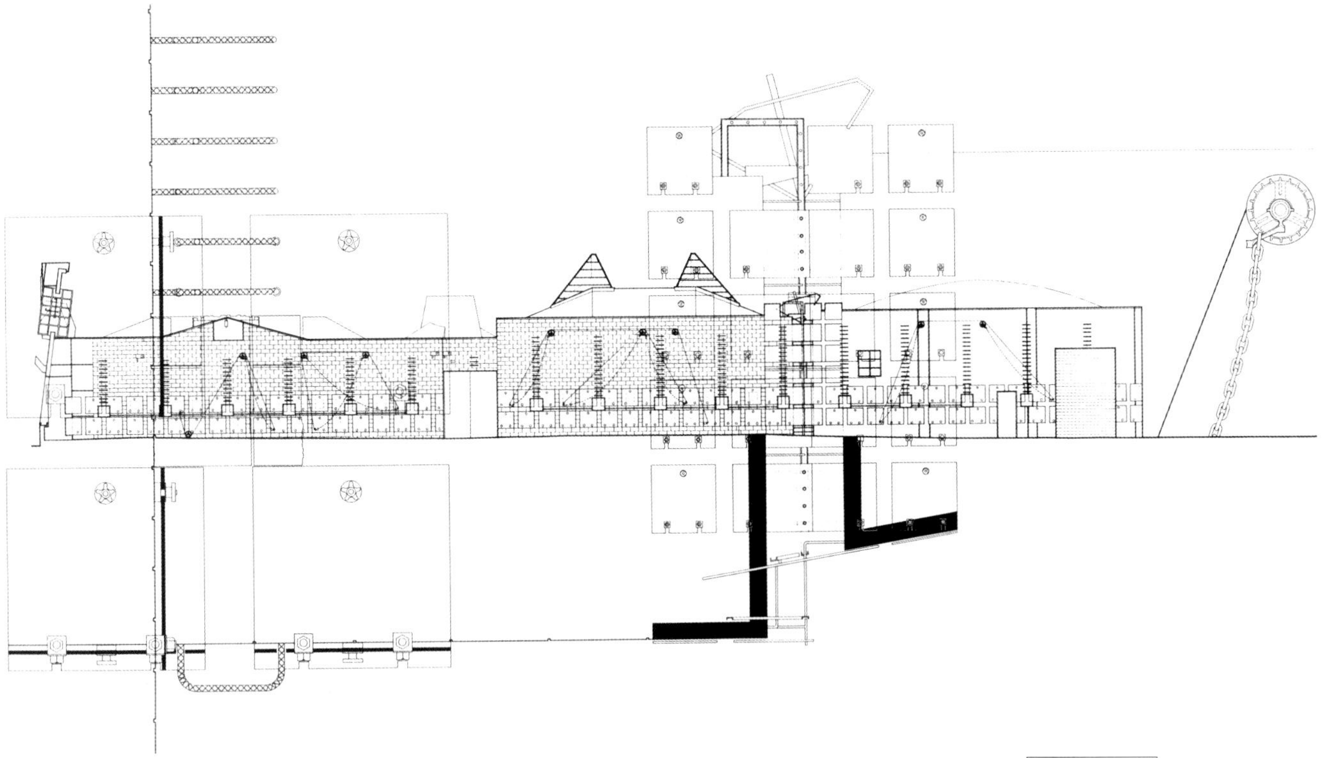

ELEVATION/DETAILS

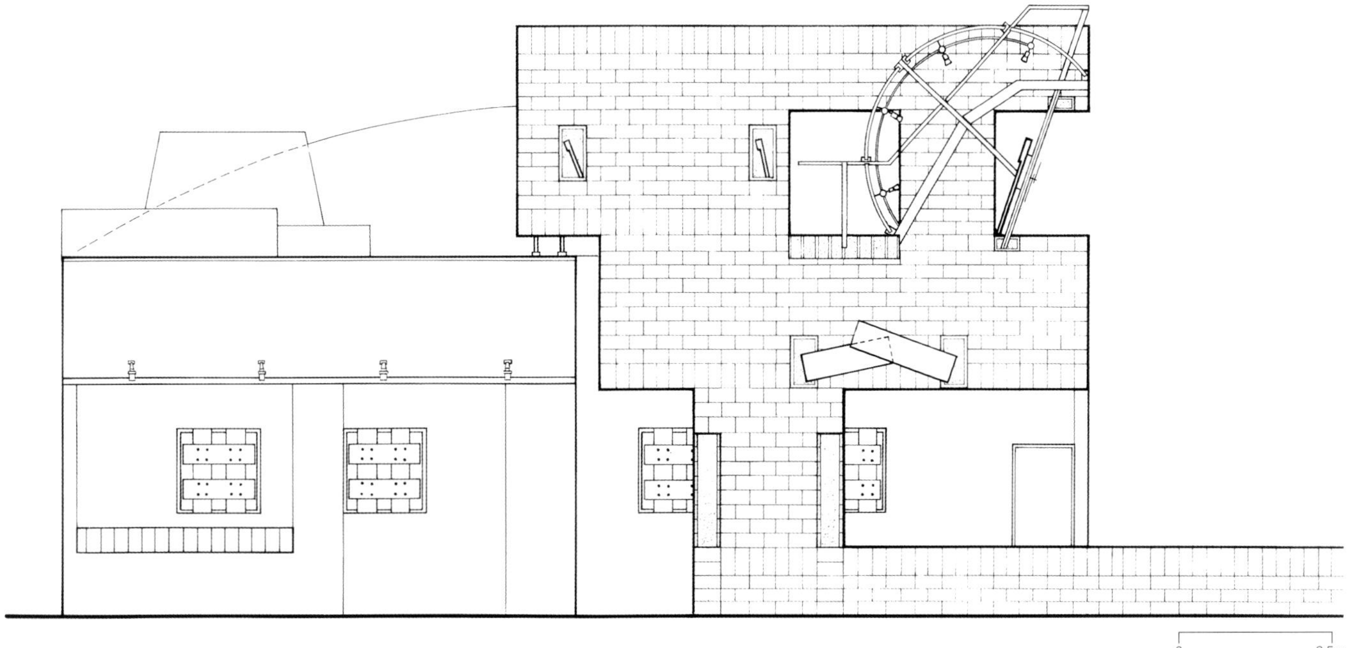

ELEVATION

GARY

GARY
GROUP

AUSTRIA UNDER CONSTRUCTION

Location Venice, Italy
Client Austrian Federal Ministry for Education, Arts and Culture
Size 10,000 ft² (929 m²)
Date 2010

Architecture at its best suggests that the world could be other than it is, that the world progresses, and that architecture can facilitate that progress. New prospects for the city. New visions for design and building. A new built world for the inhabitants of a new world. Hope and optimism. That is the promise.

Innovative conceptions from Austria's architects extend around the globe, from East Asia to Europe, the Middle East, Africa, Central and South America. Reciprocally, contributions from our colleagues abroad are constructed in Austria. Austria re-imagines the art of building and city-making in the world. Foreign architects re-imagine buildings and cities in Austria. Austria exports. Austria imports. New architecture 'under construction.'

That dual capacity to contribute inventively and to welcome new possibilities openly is the essential strength of the Austrian architectural mind, and was the subject of this exhibition proposal for the Austrian Pavilion in Venice, 2010.

Austrian culture at its best is culture 'under construction'—reconceiving, re-evaluating, re-imagining its meanings. That on-going exploration can never appear simply as a homogeneous body of built work. Rather there are several powerful, alternative prospects which reflect an enduring debate regarding priorities. Architecture as poetry? Architecture as sociology? Architecture as culture? Architecture as urbanism? Architecture as an amalgamation of possibilities?

Architecture and urbanism propel cultures, re-inform sociologies, and explore technologies. Austrian architects at work internationally, and international architects at work in Austria are producing investigatory work that challenges the conventional pro forma with respect to aesthetics, technical means, relationships of art/media/architecture, ordering and organizational strategies, and alternative energy systems. Architects are also at work on the re-conception of the systems and methods that have traditionally governed contemporary cities—transportation, housing, and the use of natural resources; the inter-relationship of social, economic, and political concerns with the form of the city; and the integration of imported conceptions with local customs, traditions, and aspirations.

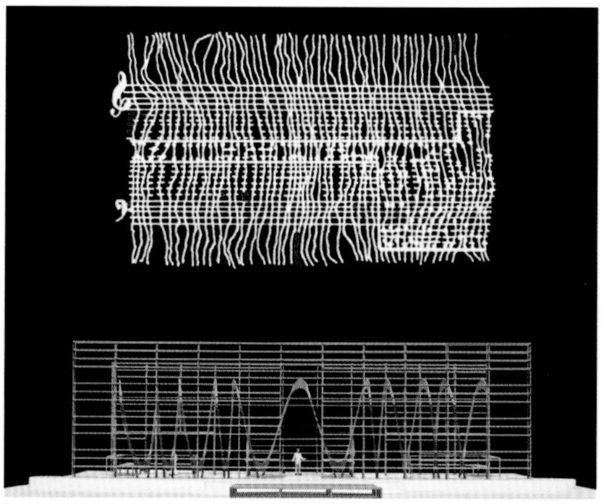

STRUCTURE

SECTION

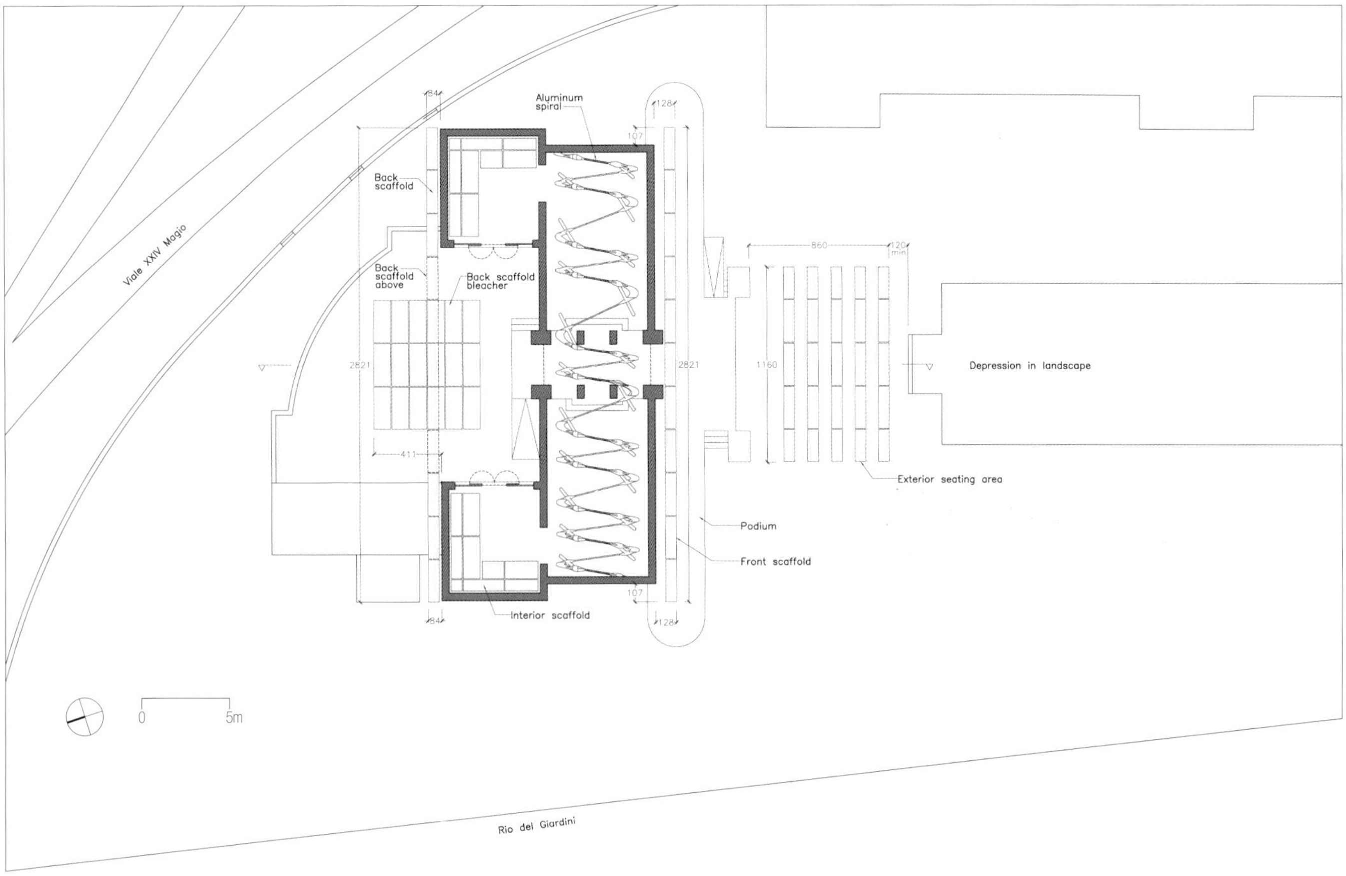

SITE PLAN

The proposal was to present the 2010 exhibition in the Austrian Pavilion at the Venice Biennale as a scaffolded building 'under construction', suggesting an international design and construction discourse in process.

We proposed to install modular, open scaffolding running the entire length of the entry elevation of the Pavilion, suggesting a building midway in the construction process. Similarly, in the interior of the Pavilion, we intended to mount additional open scaffolding through the entry space and the adjacent wings on either side.

The curatorial objective at the Austrian Pavilion was to use an imaginative design means to communicate the most imaginative prospects for contemporary Austrian architecture and urban design around the world as well as to contemporary Austria as both a unique repository of architectural talent, and an attentive welcomer of a new spirit of foreign architectural invention.

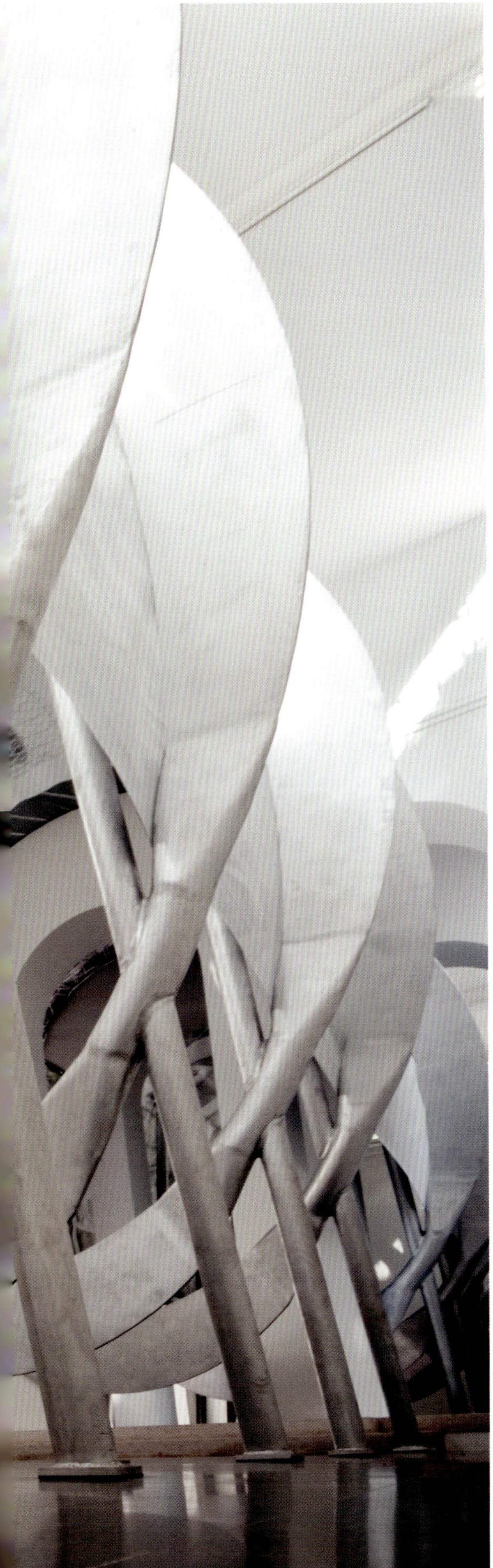

DANCING BLEACHERS

Location Wexner Center, Columbus, Ohio, United States
Client Wexner Center for the Arts
Date 1998

The art installation Dancing Bleachers was a part of the *Fabrications* exhibition that was organized and presented simultaneously by the Museum of Modern Art, New York, San Francisco Museum of Modern Art, and the Wexner Center for the Arts in Columbus, Ohio. Four projects were presented at each of the three venues. Dancing Bleachers was presented at the Wexner. In total, *Fabrications* presented full-scale architectural installations by each of 12 architects.

Dancing Bleachers contests the conception of building premised on the grid as a structural order, as a spatial order, as an organizational order. The new Wexner Center by Peter Eisenman is an exhaustive exploration of grid-derived space. The grid as a plan or section norm, or that same grid folded or bent variously accounts for the form and space, inside and out, of the Wexner gallery where Dancing Bleachers was installed. The grid, in an abstract conceptual sense, whether as a town plan or a curtain wall, is a system of equity, even neutrality, rather than hierarchy. In its essence, the grid has no center. The Dancing Bleachers project offered an alternative to the order of the grid. So the Dancing Bleachers exhibit challenged the design premise of the hall in which the exhibit was housed.

Dancing Bleachers originates as a sequence of curvilinear forms, and in that fundamental sense, it offers what the gallery space cannot—the concept of center. As an alternative to the order of the grid-based gallery space where it is housed, Dancing Bleachers consists of a concentric ring of seats, organized around a center or focal point where performance takes place. The connection of the ring structure to the gallery structure amends, temporarily, the single-mindedness of the grid.

The organization of curved-steel structural supports for the seats makes reference to a single center in plan. Because the design had to fit within the allotted space of the gallery, the conventional representation of seating was not plausible, nor was it necessary to the conception. The suggestion of a seated audience—the stepping steel rods—with imaginary performers at the conceptual center, was sufficient.

MODEL

Although substantially different, both in scale and as building typology, an essential connection exists between Dancing Bleachers and

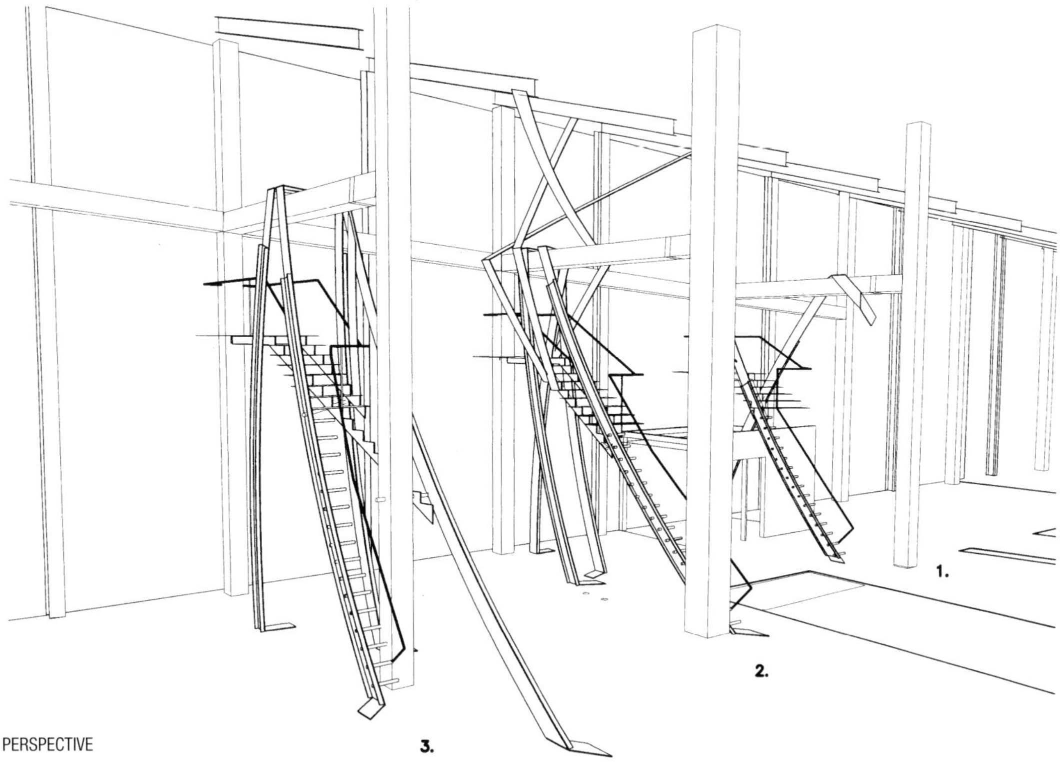

PERSPECTIVE

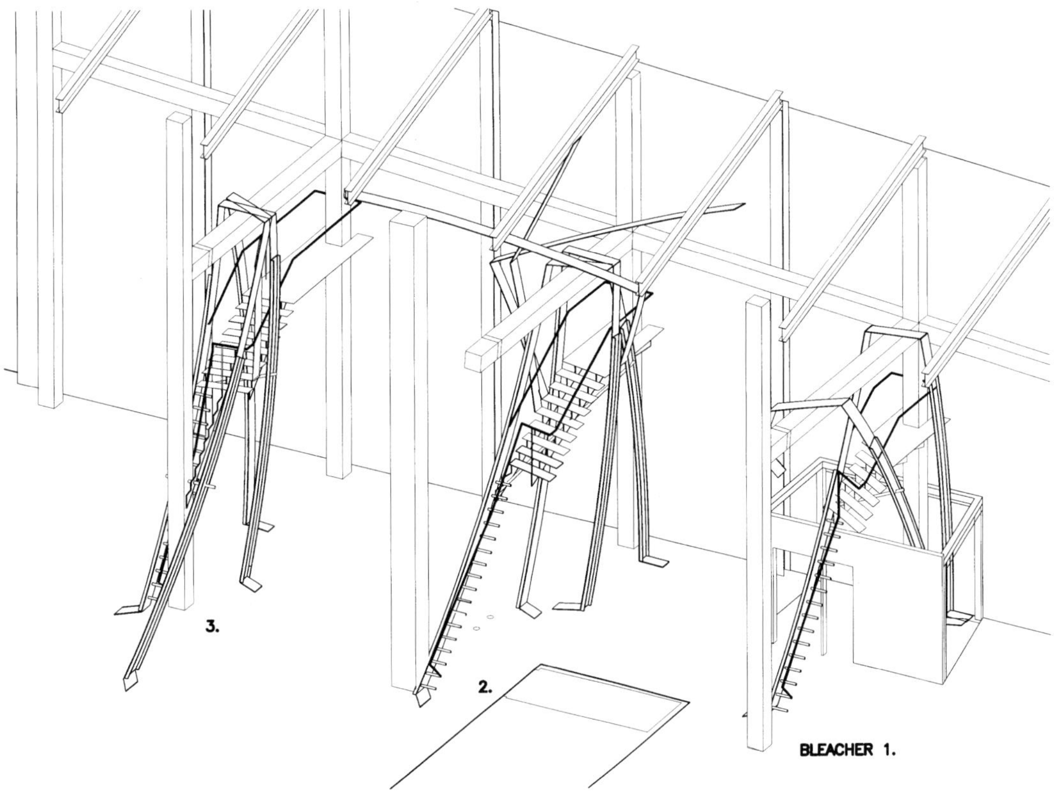

AXONOMETRIC

the Jefferson Tower [see (W)rapper]. Located in Los Angeles, the tower pursues a structural typology that challenges the traditional gridded structure and curtain wall, suggesting, as in the Wexner Center, that the concentric structural ribbons, being analogue to neither conventional columns nor beams, but to column-beams simultaneously, originate at a single center as the origin of the geometries that surround it. The two projects—exhibit and tower—were designed at roughly the same time in 1998.

Fabrications
Fabrications Full Scale

CATERPILLAR

Seeing is the second project in the Boone Children's Gallery produced by LACMA Lab, the experimental research and development unit within the Los Angeles County Museum of Art.

This exhibition explores the concept of 'seeing' by raising questions and challenging notions of expectation, perception, and viewpoint. Nine LA-based artists were commissioned to create participatory installations that investigate ways of seeing, drawing upon the permanent collection as a resource, springboard, or provocation for visitor engagement. The charge to the artist had two specific conditions: that the installation incorporate an object from the collection, and that it appeal equally to both child and adult.

This project explores the relationship between image and word through the physical form of language. A 36-foot-long (11-meter-long) walk-through 'caterpillar,' made from a see-through cardboard honeycomb stretched between four solid cardboard ribs, twists and snakes around structural elements in the gallery. The ribs are set at different heights, reaching a maximum height of 16 feet (4.9 meters), with a plywood platform sloping up and down through the architectural structure. Underneath each rib, set into the raised plywood floor, is one of the small cylinder seals from LACMA's permanent collection housed in lighted mirror bowls. The images produced by the seals are enlarged and printed on the first and last ribs, extending onto the gallery floor. Seen from the outside, the legs of the visitors inside become the legs of the caterpillar, animating the structure.

Location Los Angeles County Museum of Art, Los Angeles, California, United States
Client Los Angeles County Museum of Art
Date 2001

MODEL

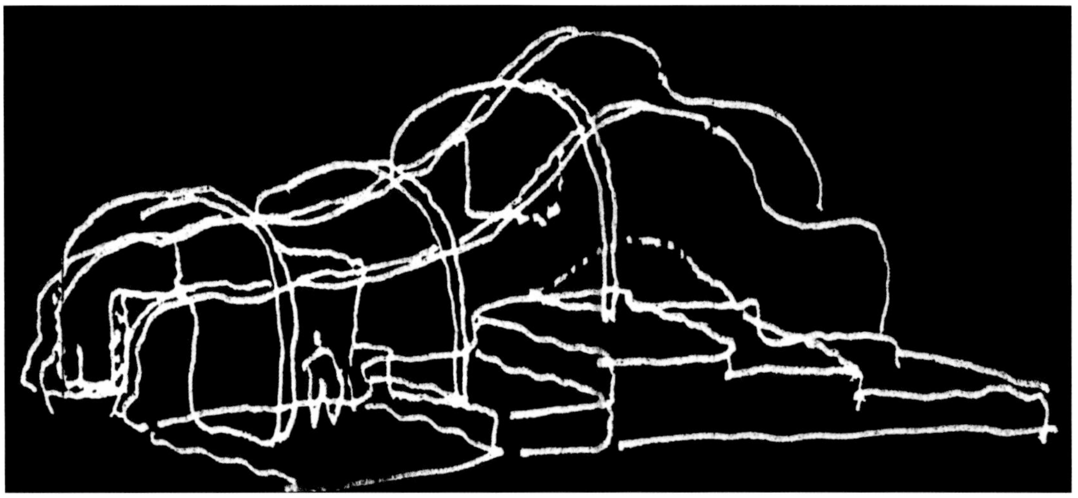

SKETCH

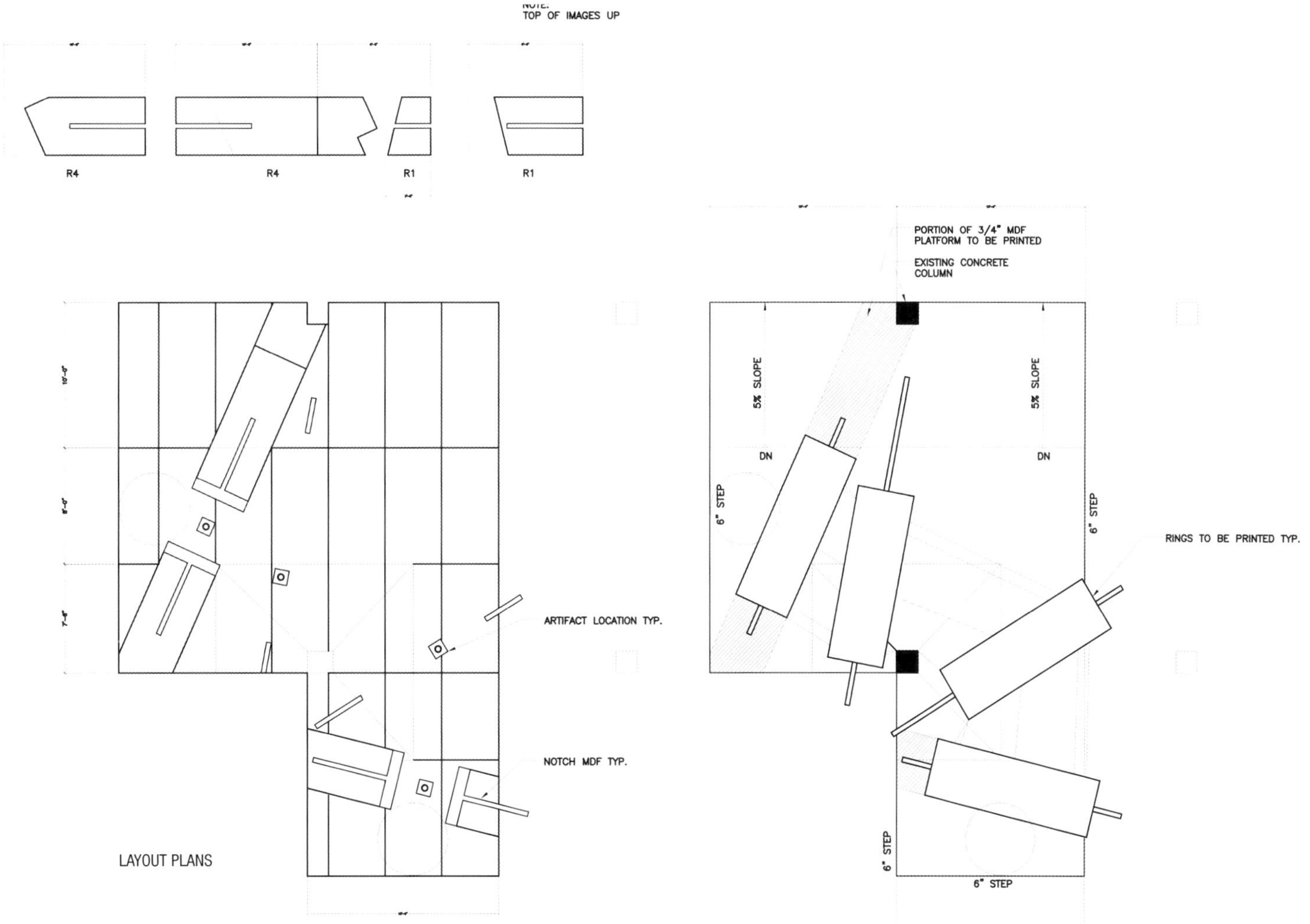

LAYOUT PLANS

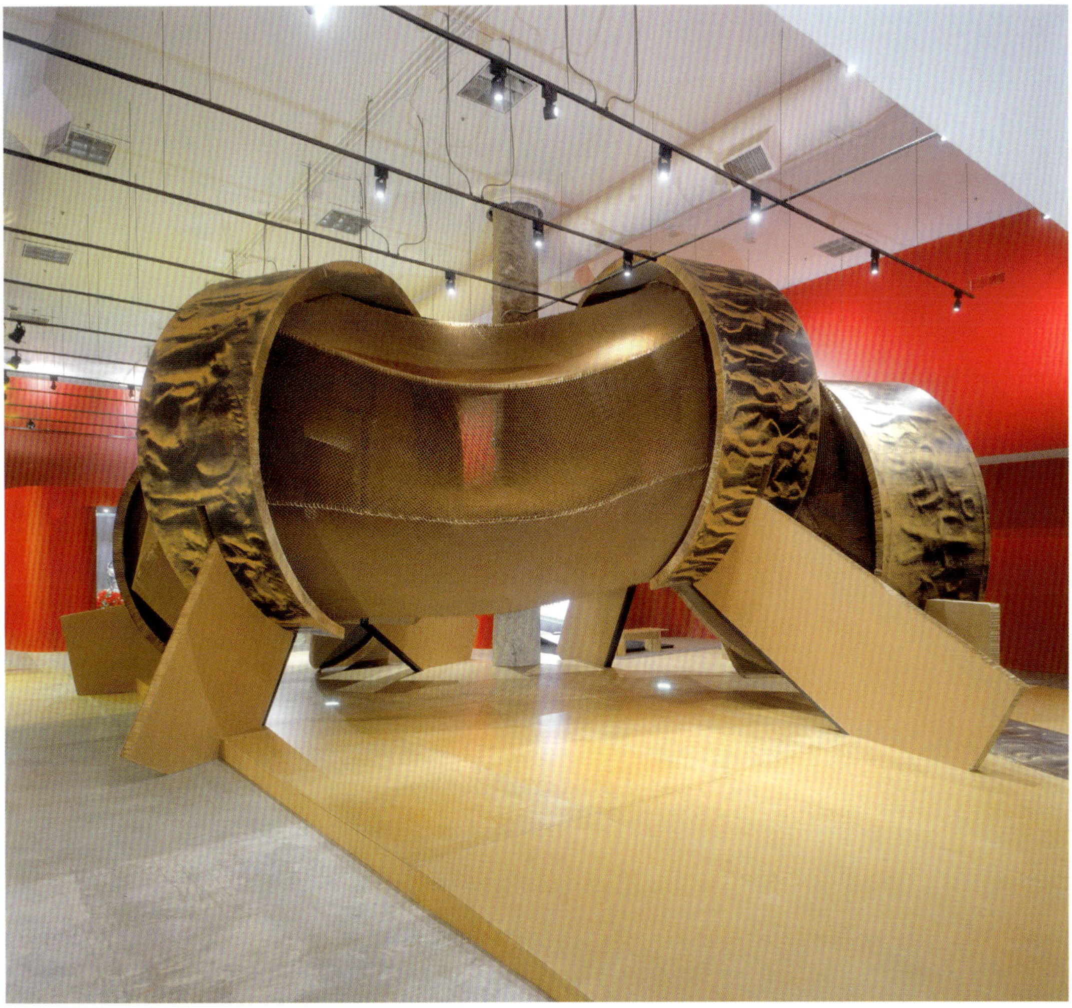

IF NOT NOW, WHEN?

The band language was developed on (W)rapper in parallel with the Wexner Center exhibit, Dancing Bleachers in 1998. The installation contested the conception of building premised on the grid as a structural order, as a spatial order, as an organizational order. The Wexner Center by Peter Eisenman is an exhaustive exploration of grid-derived space. The grid, in an abstract conceptual sense, whether as a town plan or a curtain wall, is a system of equity, even neutrality, rather than hierarchy. In its essence, the grid has no center.

Dancing Bleachers originates as a sequence of curvilinear forms, and in that fundamental sense, offers what the gallery space cannot—the concept of center. The connection of the ring structure to the gallery structure amends, temporarily, the single-mindedness of the grid.

The tower also pursues a structural typology that challenges the traditional gridded structure and curtain wall, suggesting that the concentric structural bands, analogue to neither conventional columns nor beams, but to column-beams simultaneously, originate at a single center as the origin of the geometries that surround it.

If Not Now, When? in 2009, re-examined both the content of the Wexner exhibition and the premises of (W)rapper. The ubiquitous grid is presented as a metal box, hung as a conceptual foil from the gallery roof. The bands and box intertwine, and remake the grid. The form language of the bands suggests the prospect of a center or of multiple centers, whether or not those centers are discoverable in the installation. The exhibit elevates the aluminum box, attached to the gallery roof, bound by plasma-cut aluminum bands that belong to the geometric and space-making order of curves.

The attached box confirms a speaker's area directly below. The speaker's space is surrounded by orthogonal rows of old chairs, likely to be empty, that provide permanent seats for an assembly that, as with Dancing Bleachers, may or may not take place.

Location Los Angeles, California, United States, Vienna, Austria
Client Southern California Institute of Architecture (SCI-Arc)
Date 2009

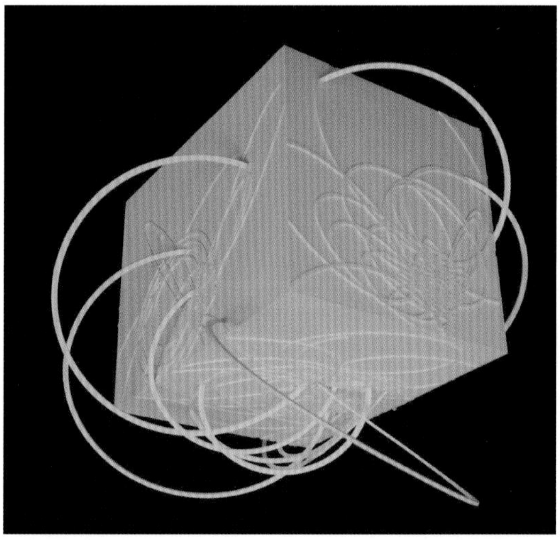

MODEL

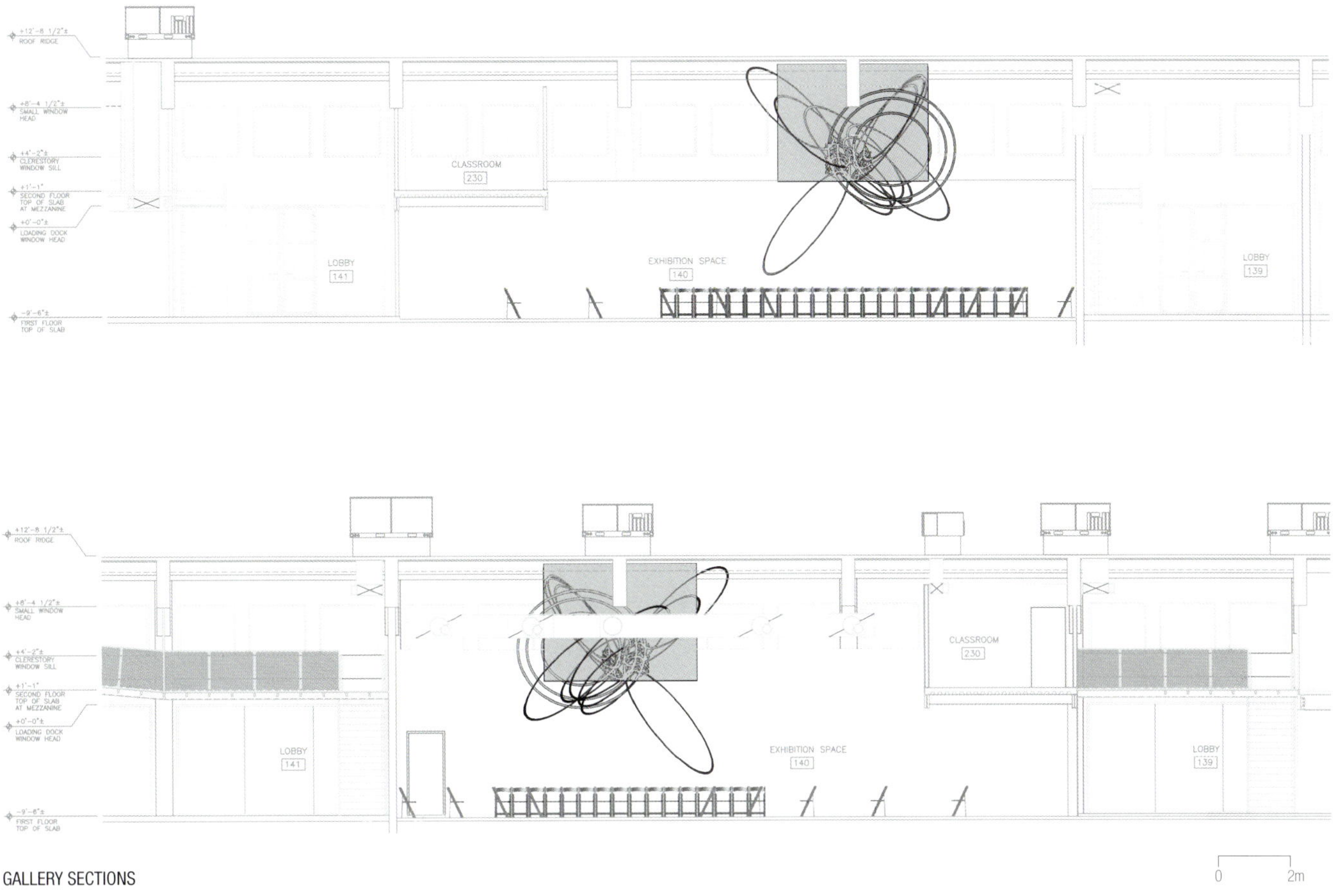

GALLERY SECTIONS

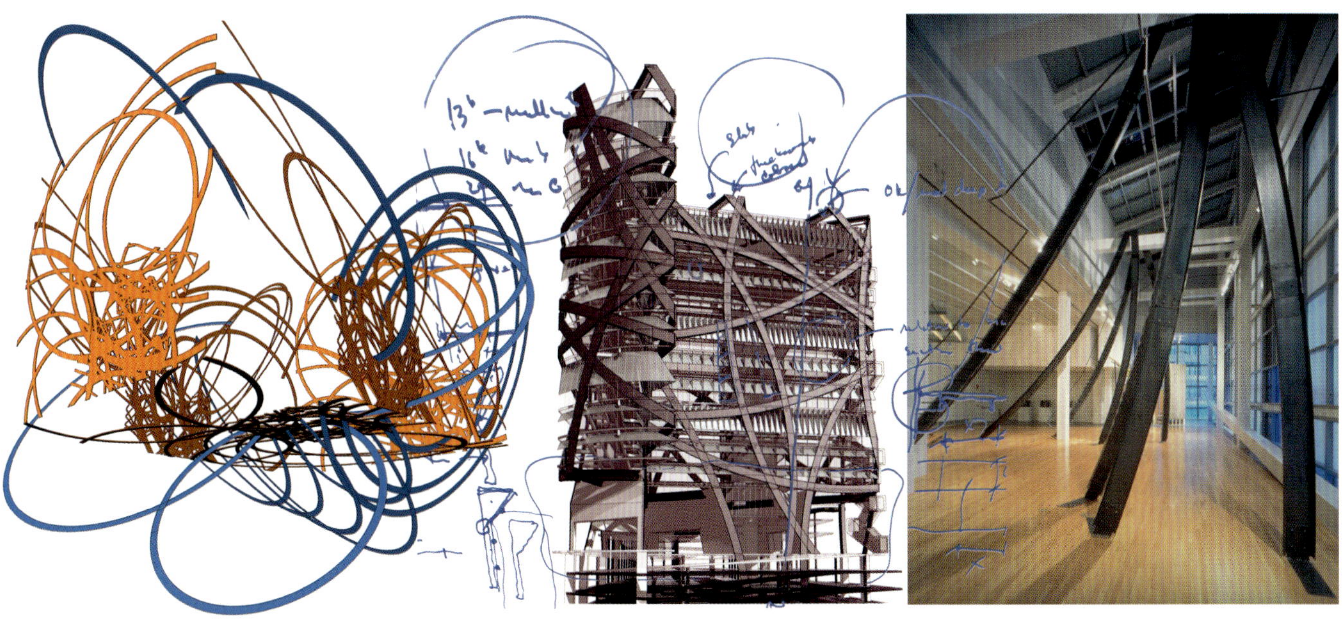

BAND EVOLUTION

(W)RAPPER

The original Jefferson Towers project—two 235-foot (71.6-meter) high-rise towers plus parking—was approved by the Los Angeles City Planning Commission and the Los Angeles City Council in 1999. At that time, it was the only high-rise proposal in the South Los Angeles area. The project carries with it the aspiration for the renewal of an area that has had more than its share of poverty, and the accompanying social pathologies. The conceptual strategy for the project was structural, and that strategy remains in the most recent version. A continuous system of curvilinear ribbons, neither beams nor columns, wraps the two contiguous boxes—T-shaped in plan—allowing a completely open, column-free interior.

The towers project was resurrected in 2006 as a single tower. A primary impetus for the return of the project was the advent of a surface commuter train system, running from downtown to the University of Southern California, south of downtown, then west along Jefferson Boulevard to a stop at Jefferson and La Cienega before continuing west to Santa Monica. That intersection is a primary crossing of major north–south and east–west traffic axes in Los Angeles. The project site is a block northwest of the train stop, and sits adjacent to the train route as the train turns north to a second stop, several blocks west of the site.

Due to its height and the relatively low buildings that surround the site, the project will have enormous prominence both as an object on an otherwise 45-foot-high (13.7-meter-high) skyline, and as an opportunity to provide long-distance views for the office building's tenants. Both these opportunities were persuasive arguments for the revival and redesign of the building.

The new tower and the new passenger railway and train stop are likely to become prominent symbols of the rebirth of South Los Angeles.

The new tower, with floor plates of 20,000 square feet (1858.1 square meters) per floor, is supported on curvilinear steel-tube ribbons, 2 feet by 5 feet (0.6 meters by 1.5 meters), filled with concrete. The ribbon system is located external to the floors, so the floor interiors are entirely open and flexible. The ribbons are resolved at the base of the tower as a series of intersecting hyperbolic concrete support walls that geometrically join ribbons on one elevation of the box with ribbons on the opposite side.

Location Los Angeles, California, United States
Client Samitaur Constructs
Size 183,000 ft^2 (17,001.3 m^2)
Date Under development

MODEL

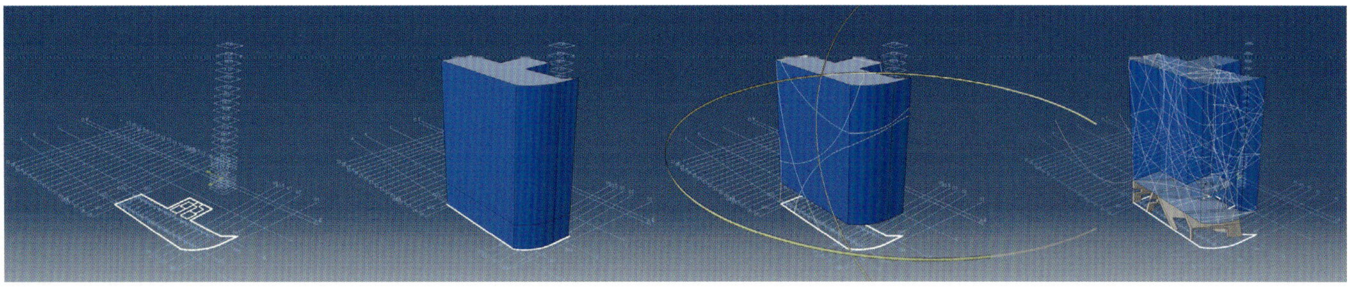

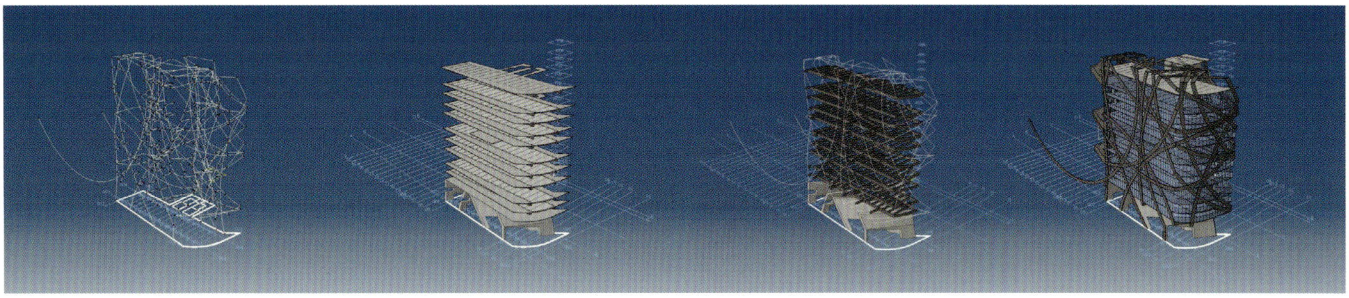

STRUCTURAL SOLIDS

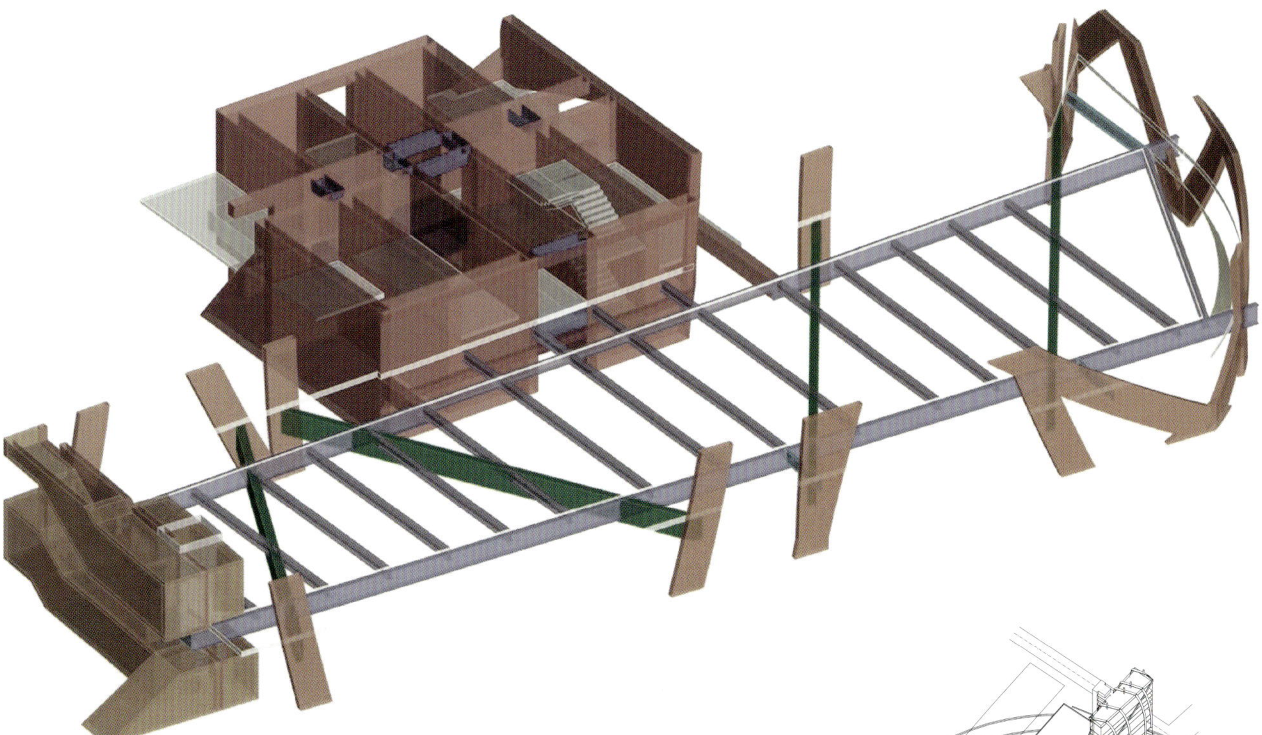

FLOOR FRAMING

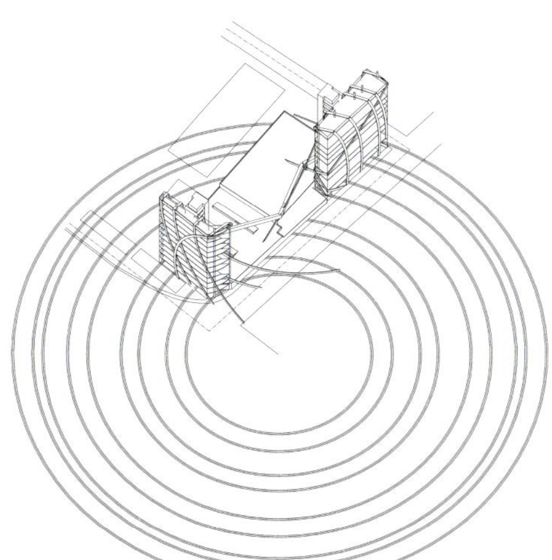

Rather than the conventional single floor-to-floor height, typical of most tower structures, this project offers three alternative floor-to-floor heights to its tenants, one at 13 feet 6 inches (4.1 meters), one at 16 feet (4.9 meters), and one at 24 feet (7.3 meters). The 24-foot (7.3-meter) volume occurs three times, and allows the construction of a glass-enclosed, acoustically segregated mezzanine floor.

SAMITAUR

WARNER PARKING AND RETAIL

Location Culver City, California, United States
Client Samitaur Constructs
Size 50,000 ft² (4645.2 m²)
Date Under development

The existing paved lot at 8511 Warner Drive has served as the primary parking lot for the Conjunctive Points complex for years. The site features large frontage to Warner Drive, with two vehicle entry/exit points. The site sits directly to the east of UCLA's satellite campus, and directly north of the Willows Community School, which draws high traffic in the mornings and afternoons. Additionally the site abuts the pervasive railroad spur, which tends to be utilized by pedestrians as an access route.

The Parking Structure and Retail Project for 8511 Warner Drive will provide parking for new area businesses. The project will also serve the local residential and business community by providing retail and restaurant space, currently lacking in the area.

The conversion of the existing industrial buildings into bustling creative office space, as well as the addition of new office structures, requires a substantial increase in parking space. The new structure will supply 800 additional spaces.

In addition to the parking, 40,000 square feet (3716.1 square meters) of retail space and a 10,000-square-foot (929-square-meter) restaurant will be located on the interior perimeter of a five-sided, three-story, open courtyard space. The three floors of retail space and the three-story courtyard volume are positioned roughly in the center of the upper floors of the parking structure. Two full levels are filled with parking. Retail levels are directly accessible from cars parked on each floor, or from stairs and elevators that connect all garage floors to walks and bridges on all retail levels.

The courtyard is open to the south, and on the west, north, and east is surrounded by the inclined glass walls that enclose the retail space. An entry bridge on Warner Avenue allows pedestrians to enter the courtyard and proceed to the retail areas directly from the street. The garage is also entered directly from Warner.

The 2500-square-foot (232.3-square-meter) courtyard, 14 feet (4.3 meters) below the street, opens to bridges and walkways, a glass roof, and the sky above, and can be used for outdoor exhibitions and small-scale performances. The courtyard space and bridges are partially covered by a horizontal glass plane, supported by 18 trusses that span

COURTYARD STRUCTURE

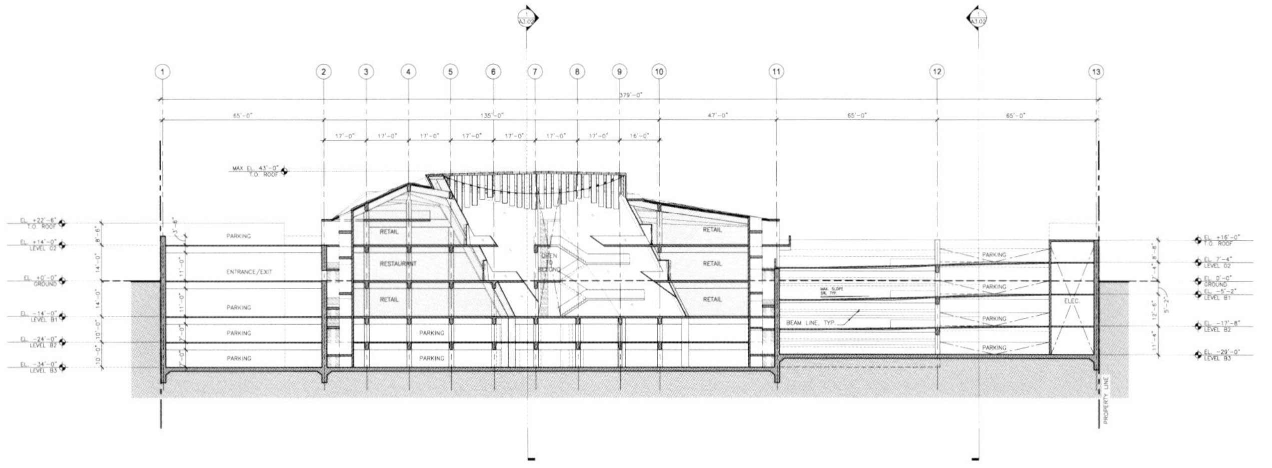

LONGITUDINAL SECTION

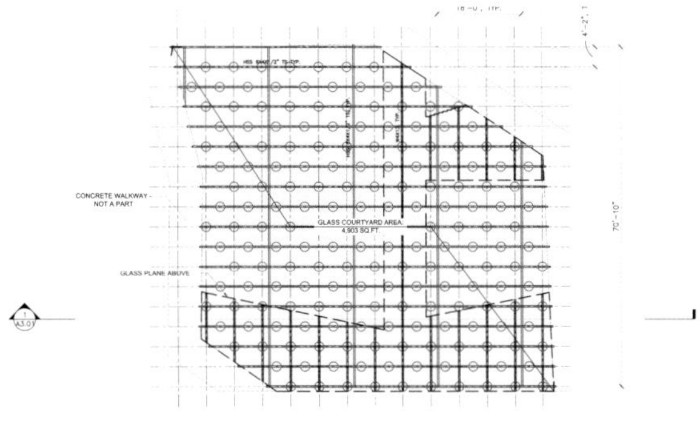

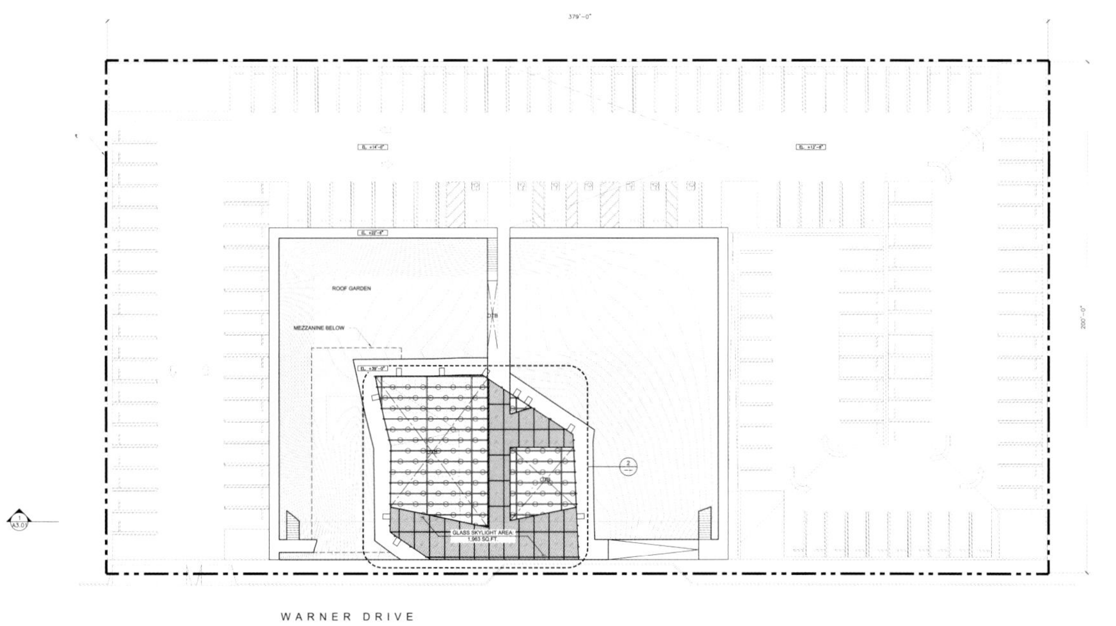

ROOF PLAN

0 15m

the courtyard below. The top chords of the trusses are steel tubes; the bottom chords are steel cables; and the vertical, compressive chords are cylinders of laminated structural glass. There are 196 glass cylinders extending below the cables, each 24 inches (610 millimeters) in diameter, and varying in length from five to 14 feet (1.5 to 4.3 meters), appearing as a field of transparent glass tubes suspended over the court.

A sod roof covers the top retail floor, reducing both heating and cooling loads, and serving as a small rooftop park.

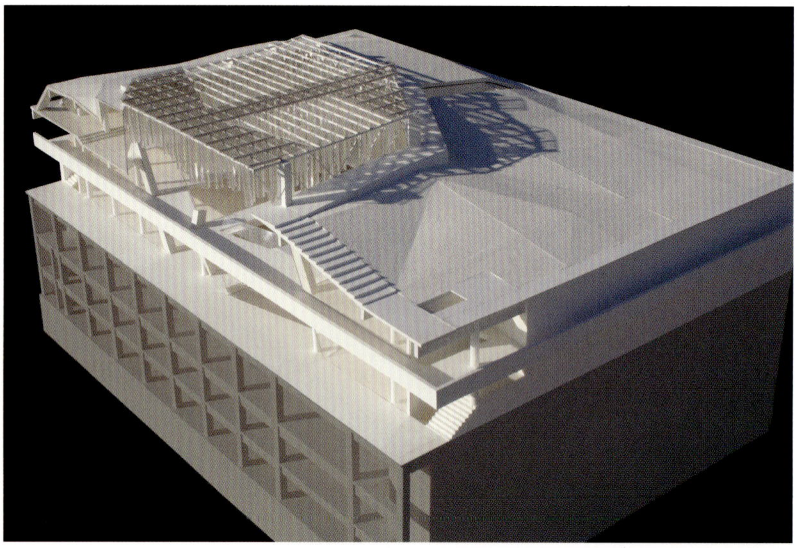

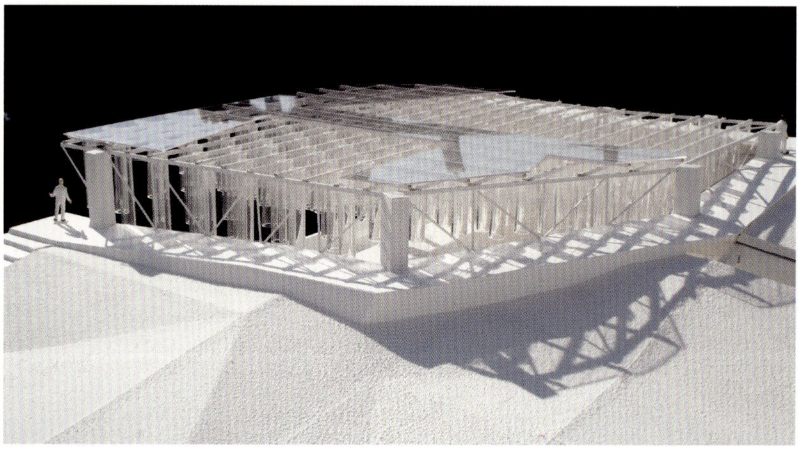

TÉRMICAS DEL BESÒS

A former power plant, built in 1976 and decommissioned in 2011, resides on the shore of the Mediterranean Sea, north of Barcelona's city center. The plant's three concrete smoke stacks and boiler building are slated for reuse while the rest of the facility will be demolished. At 656 feet (200 meters) each, the smoke stacks are the tallest structures in Barcelona.

The redesigned site will contain a variety of public uses including exhibition, theater, and observation decks, along with a hotel, restaurants, residential units, and office space.

Prompted by the city to reclaim and reuse these unique existing structures, this project envisions a new grand public gathering space. The original boiler building, an enormous shed once used to house heavy machinery, is stripped of its cladding and repurposed as a multilevel convention hall with a variety of exhibition and meeting spaces.

The three exhaust towers are connected to one another by large glass volumes, containing offices, residences, hotels and theaters. Observation decks at the top of the towers provide magnificent views of the city.

At ground level, existing coolant pools are extended from the coast and through the building to a new amphitheater. The rise and fall of the tide is harnessed by turbines set within the boiler building, which can hold the water in the amphitheater at a specific level, and generate energy when released. Existing cranes are repurposed as café platforms that travel across the site and over the water on extended tracks supported by a new breakwater. The amphitheater in the rear is shaped by the same concrete units as the breakwater, and bolstered by a built-up mound of earth that contains the theater lobby and concourse.

The grounds surrounding the plant are cleared and developed as multi-family housing served by existing mass transit lines that run along the northern edge of the site.

Location Barcelona, Spain
Client City of Barcelona
Size 1,955,910 ft^2 (181,710 m^2)
Date Under development

MODEL

SITE PLAN

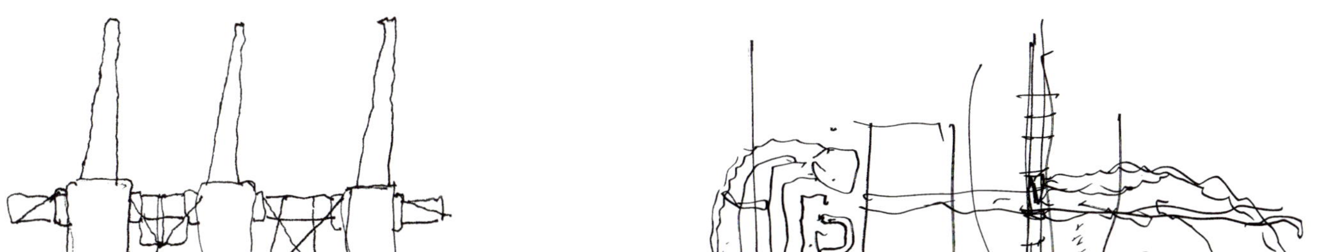

SKETCHES

S.P.A.R. CITY

Location Culver City, California, United States
Client Samitaur Constructs
Size 150,000 ft² (13,935.5 m²)
Date Under development

The former Southern Pacific Railway right-of-way spur that defines the S.P.A.R. City project begins on National Boulevard and loops counterclockwise through the development and out to Ballona Creek to the east. The distinctive shape of the spur is confirmed by the industrial buildings built up around it, many of which curve to avoid the setback.

The right-of-way branches south off National Boulevard just to the west of the intersection between National and Hayden Avenue. It begins as a large open space beside 3505 Hayden that tapers down as it continues south, parallel to Hayden Avenue, behind 3535 and 3555 Hayden. As it reaches the Hayden Tower Site, it makes a wide curve east. From here it crosses Hayden Avenue and continues, parallel to Warner Drive, behind the site of Warner Theater. East of this site, it momentarily spills perpendicularly into two alleys between buildings. It then begins to widely curve northward before it crosses over Eastham Drive, where it again overlaps its boundaries into a large lot along Eastham. The right-of-way terminates at the S.P.A.R. City Bridge, which crosses Ballona Creek and the Culver City/Los Angeles border.

The right-of-way, about 50 feet (15.2 meters) in width, stretches approximately half a mile from National Boulevard to Ballona Creek. The old tracks run through an area which for the past 50 years has been home to light industry and manufacturing. In the 1980s the industrial users relocated to overseas markets, where rent and labor costs are substantially less.

This area is perhaps a prototype for a number of dated industrial complexes, large and small, that must redefine or reinvent their urban purpose.

S.P.A.R. City's strategy is to redefine the area, increase its diversity, and reinforce and invigorate, where plausible, existing uses and activities. The project seeks both to begin again and to revive the existing context. These dual objectives are understood not as a conflict of intentions, but as mutually reinforcing goals.

The ground-level right-of-way itself will become a park and promenade accessing the adjacent buildings along the right-of-way and the vertical circulation to air-rights buildings and bridges above. Parking will be

MODEL

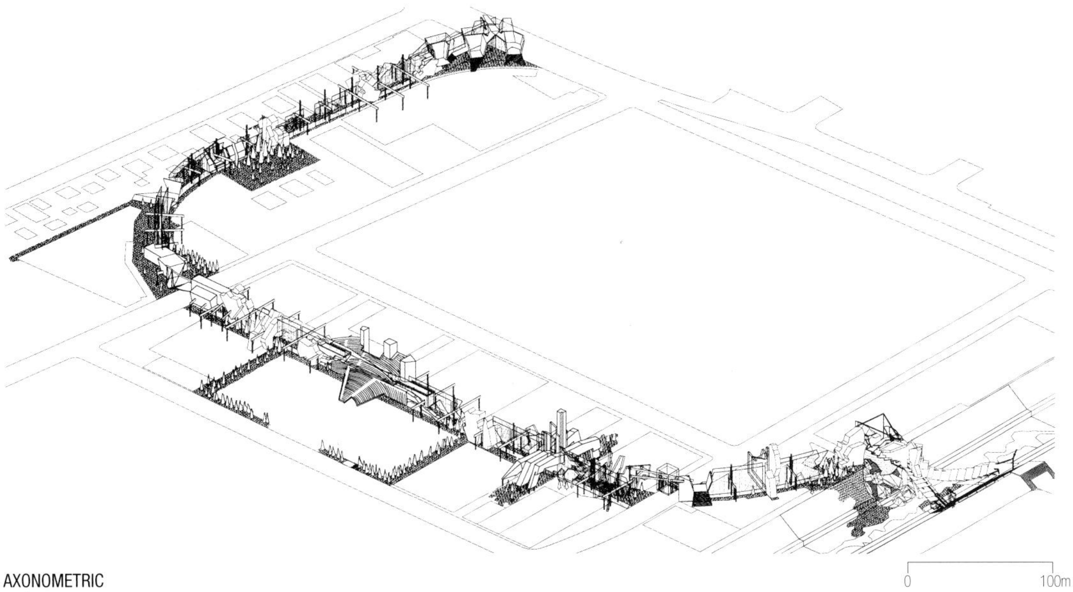

AXONOMETRIC

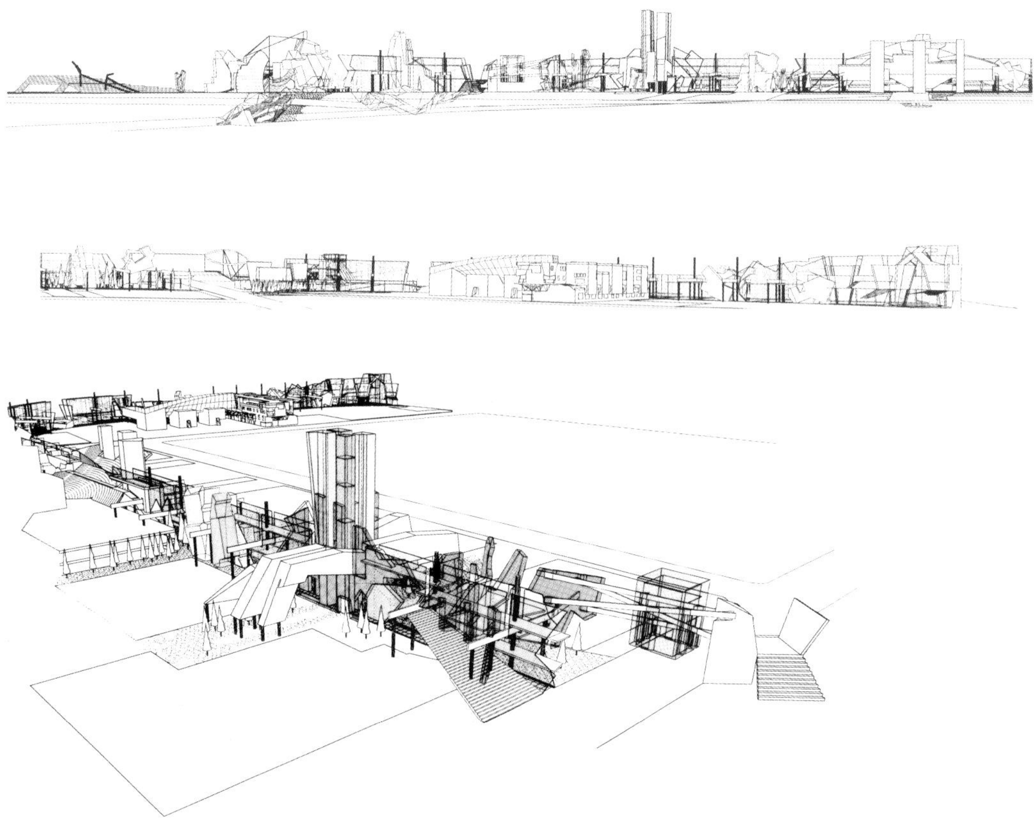

PERSPECTIVES

provided in city-owned lots, and shuttles (perhaps reusing the tracks) will deliver workers to their destinations along the route.

This plan is egalitarian and totalitarian. It adds to existing uses; it subtracts others; it entices; it compels; but doesn't demand that its neighbors join. It proposes to transform a debilitated area into a major civic component of the West Los Angeles area. And it will do this without public money.

S.P.A.R. City is a conceptual and formal hypothesis. In the end it may appear in pieces, all together, or in an altered, and as yet undetermined, form.

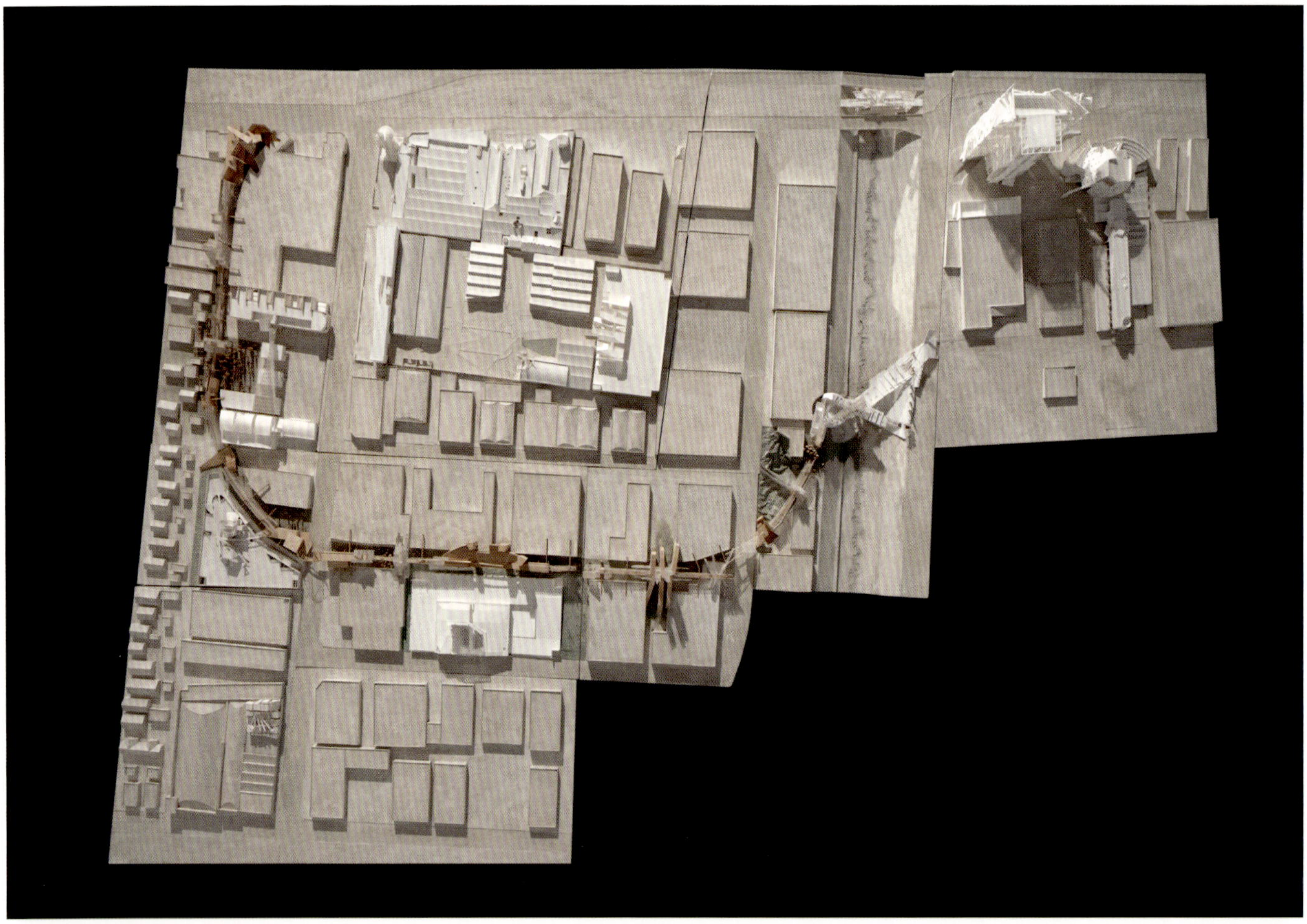

S.P.A.R. CITY BRIDGE

The terminus of the S.P.A.R. City project directly abuts Ballona Creek. Similar to the bridge along National Boulevard, the proposed S.P.A.R. City Bridge aspires to reconnect the east and west banks of the concrete river channel as the New City prepares to once again expand its reach to the Los Angeles side of the river.

Along the western riverbank the right-of-way expands in width and forms a large public park. The various components of the right-of-way zone (stilts, bridges, curtains) continue through the park and end with a large spherical volume at the edge of the river. The sphere is intersected by a glass tower volume that opens the sphere to the river. A series of pedestrian linkages draws people through the sphere out to sweeping views of the city.

At the point where the sphere rests on the western edge of the concrete channel, a large vomitory is opened to allow pedestrian travel down into the river channel to a proposed new river park and bike path access point. On the eastern slope of the channel, new amphitheater seating is provided for a variety of cultural events in the river park.

Two terraced suspension bridges span the river with a series of large activity decks and gardens over the concrete river channel. One leg of the bridge lands at grade along Jefferson Boulevard, and the other flies over Jefferson to connect to several future development sites in the area.

Location Culver City, California, United States
Client Samitaur Constructs
Size 20,000 ft^2 (1858.1 m^2)
Date Under development

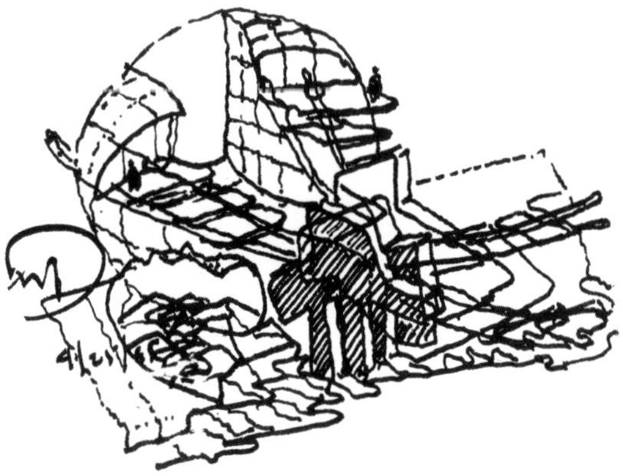

SKETCH

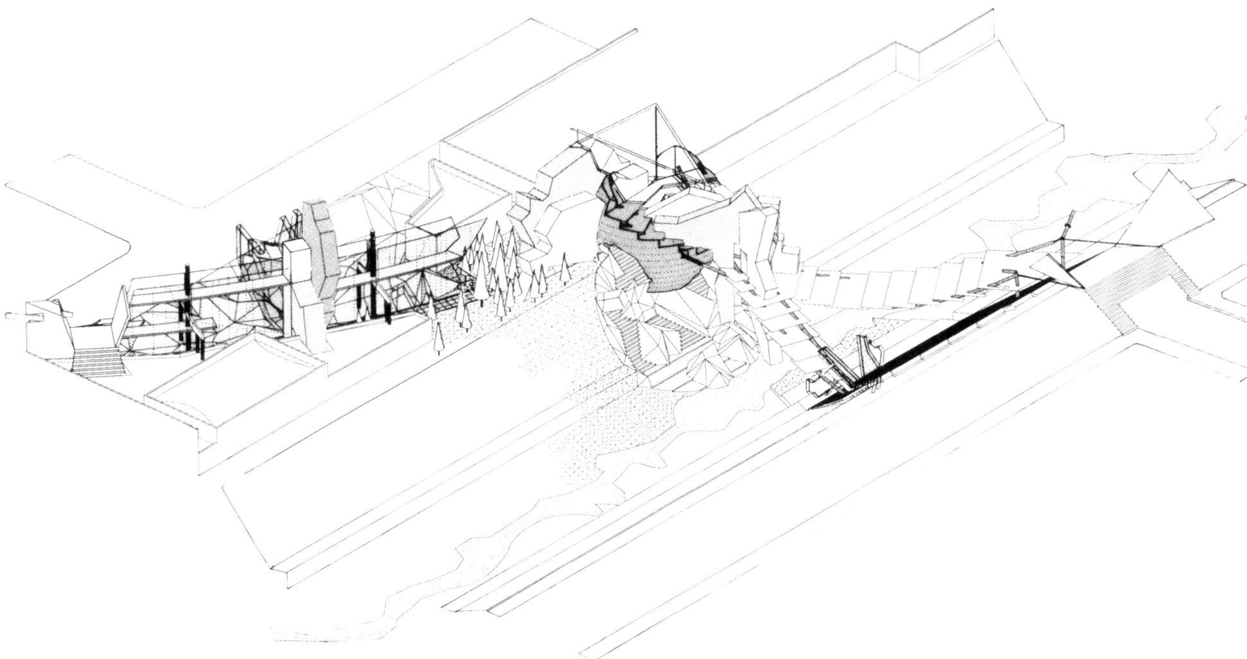

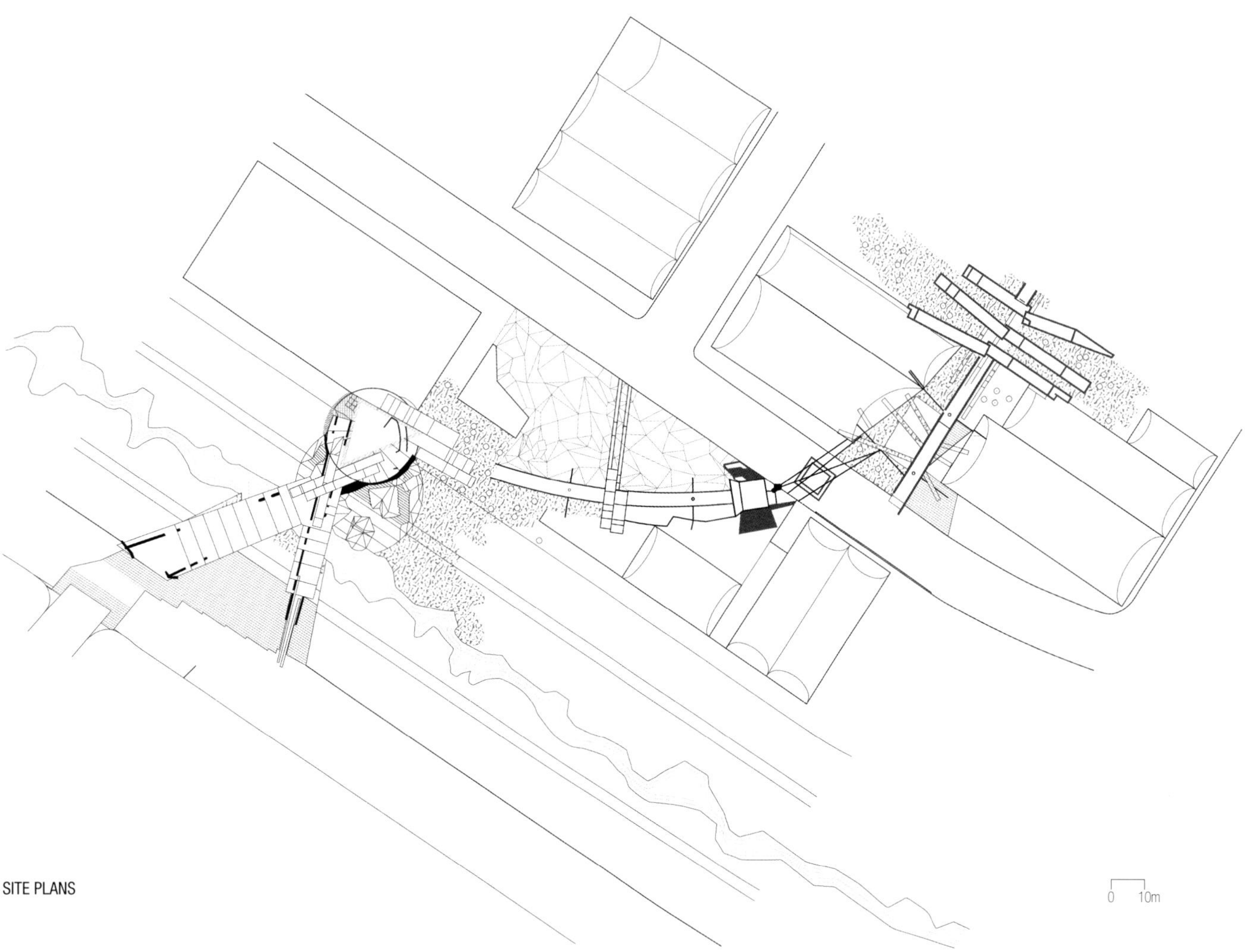

SITE PLANS

SMITHSONIAN PATENT OFFICE BUILDING

Location Washington, D.C., United States
Client Smithsonian Institution
Size 40,000 ft² (3716.1 m²)
Date Under development / 2004

The redesign of the Patent Office Building courtyard in Washington, D.C. was an opportunity for the Smithsonian Institution to confirm the building's unique institutional and architectural pedigree—'America's temple to the industrial arts'—by adding a contemporary design chapter to the building's history.

Fortuitously, the building's original purpose—the display of American inventors' models, submitted with patent applications—embodies a spirit of technical and artistic progress that the new courtyard inherited from the existing structure.

The roof design that encloses the Patent Office Building courtyard is technically unprecedented: a dense vertical amalgamation of glass rods of varying lengths offers an ever-changing vision of light and sky through a field of shimmering glass. The composite structure reaffirms the importance of the original courtyard in the Smithsonian program—the existing granite and sandstone walls that form the perimeter of the new 'great room' are now enclosed and covered with the glass tube array.

The field of rods is a courtyard enclosing a volume that adds interior, multi-purpose space to the Smithsonian program, and simultaneously provides structural, technical, and staging services for the many possible activities that take place in the great room.

As the lengths of the vertical glass rods vary from end to end and side to side across the courtyard, 827 proximate end points suggest a double-curving surface. The variable rod lengths and the intersection of two curving ceiling profiles (implied by the end points of the tubes) are determined by two hypothetical acoustic ceilings, positioned over the two preferred performance venues in the great room.

The hollow cylindrical shape of the glass rods enables a number of lighting opportunities. Natural light through the glass tubes varies over the course of the night and day as weather patterns and sun and moon shift in the surrounding sky. Electrically, lights at the top of the rods can be directed down; lights at the bottom of the rods can be directed up or down. Light can also be projected up from the rod tops, using the sky as a canvas, to produce a glowing field in the night sky.

The structural system consists of four steel Vierendeel truss frames, spanning in the short direction, that carry the primary loads.

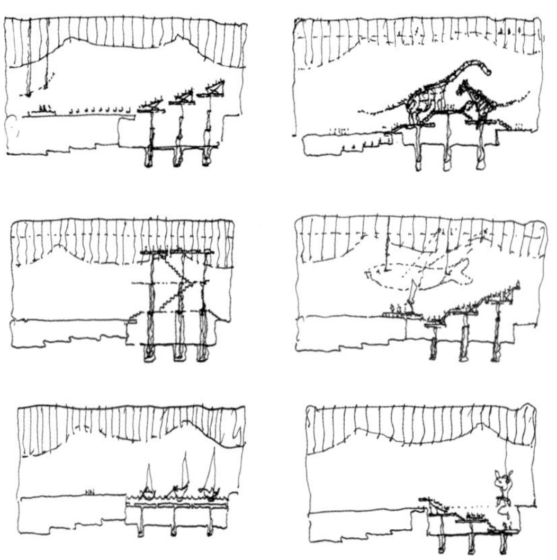

PERFORMANCE DIAGRAMS

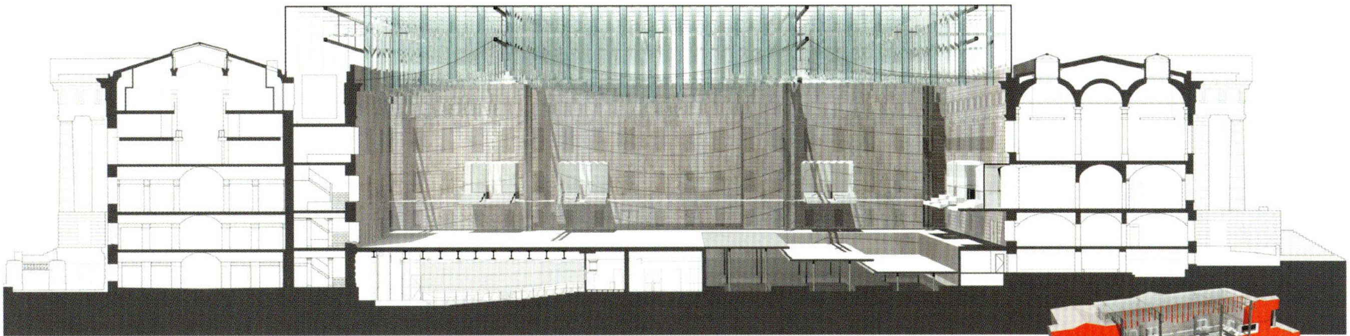

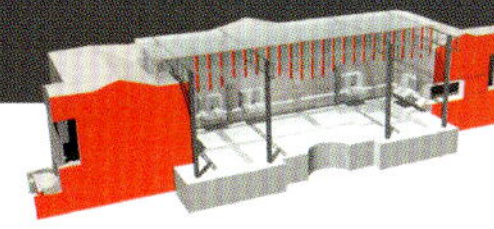

SECTION

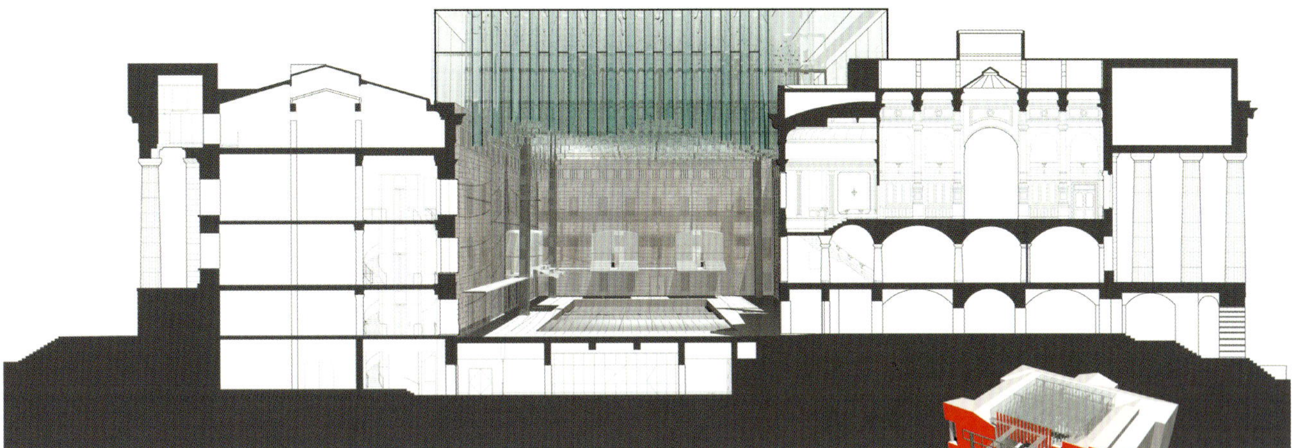

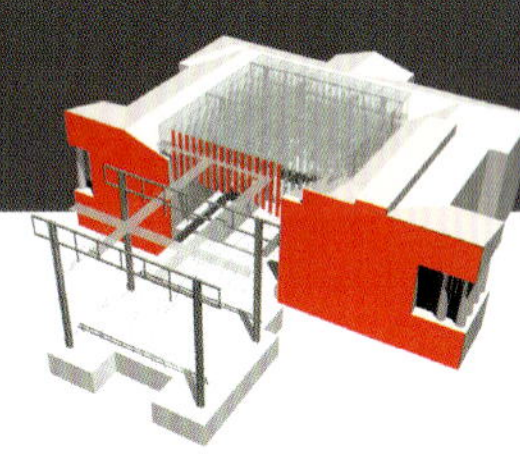

SECTION

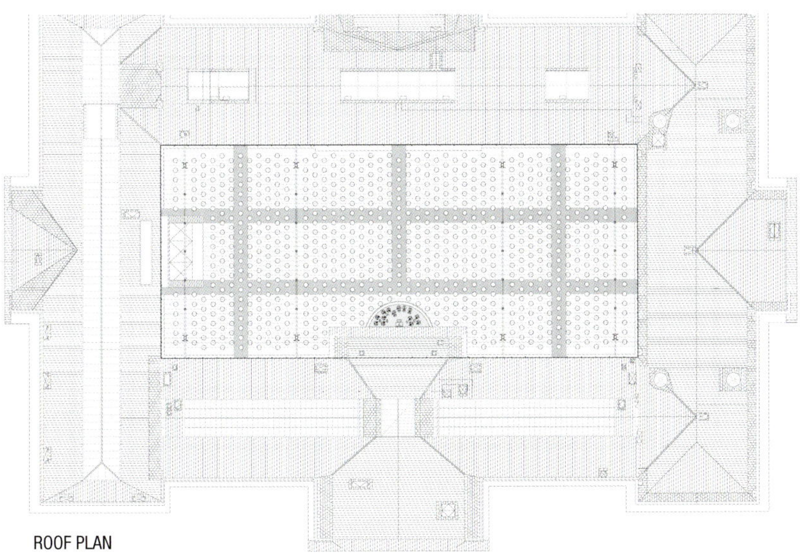

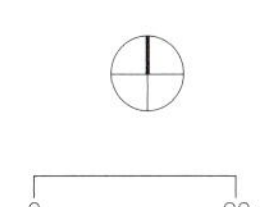

ROOF PLAN

Perpendicular to the primary truss structure is a second series of trusses, whose primary structural feature is the compressed, laminated glass tubes. The lower chord is a draped cable that passes through the cylinders that extend below the cable. The upper chords are steel tubes, which also support the mullions that carry the horizontal glass rooftop. The conceptual use of laminated glass as a compression strut in this project is unprecedented.

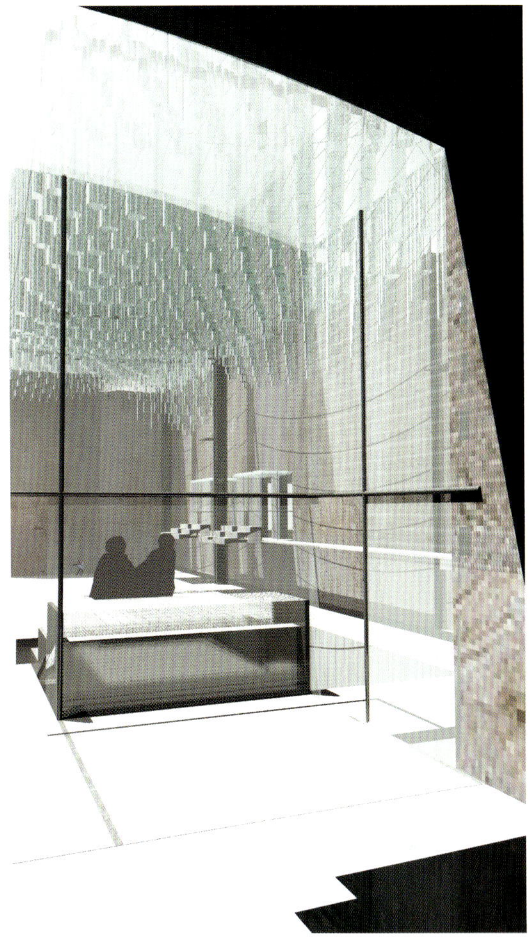

WEIHAI OBSERVATION TOWER

The Weihai Observation Tower is a key component of a new masterplan under development along the coastline of the Yellow Sea in Weihai, China. The site for the tower is atop a hill adjacent to a newly constructed harbor, and will serve as a beacon for the new development and an observation tower for viewing the city, the mountains, and the sea.

At the base of the tower the land is excavated to house new exhibition halls and retail to be located at the base of the 459-foot-tall (140-meter-tall) tower above. The roof of the exhibition hall is re-covered with the excavated soil to complete the hill, and provide a new outdoor performance venue above the exhibition area.

The tower is centered around concrete stair and elevator cores housed within a 39-foot-diameter (12-meter-diameter) structural 'mesh.' At the base, the cross-section of the tower widens and elongates to match the perimeter shape of the hilltop. The outside of the structural mesh is wrapped with a network of structural fins to reduce the sizes of the mesh components, and to stiffen the system against buckling.

Near the middle of the tower, five floors of office space are cantilevered toward the sea. The floors are connected back to the core, and braced around the structural fins. At the top of the tower, two floors accommodate observation decks as well as a skyline-view restaurant.

Location Weihai, Shandong, China
Client City of Weihai
Size 46,285 ft^2 (4300 m^2)
Date Under development

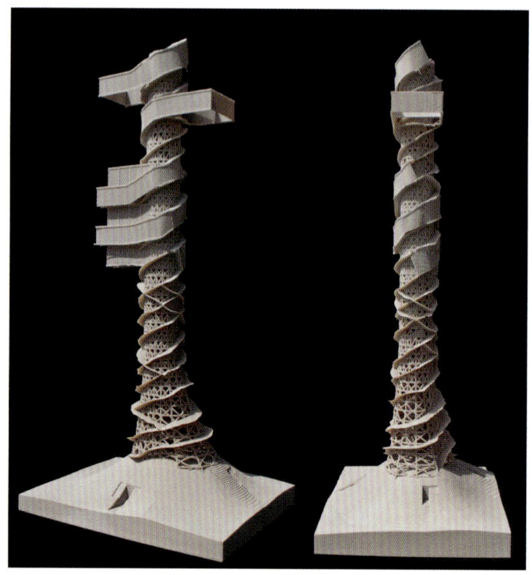
MODEL

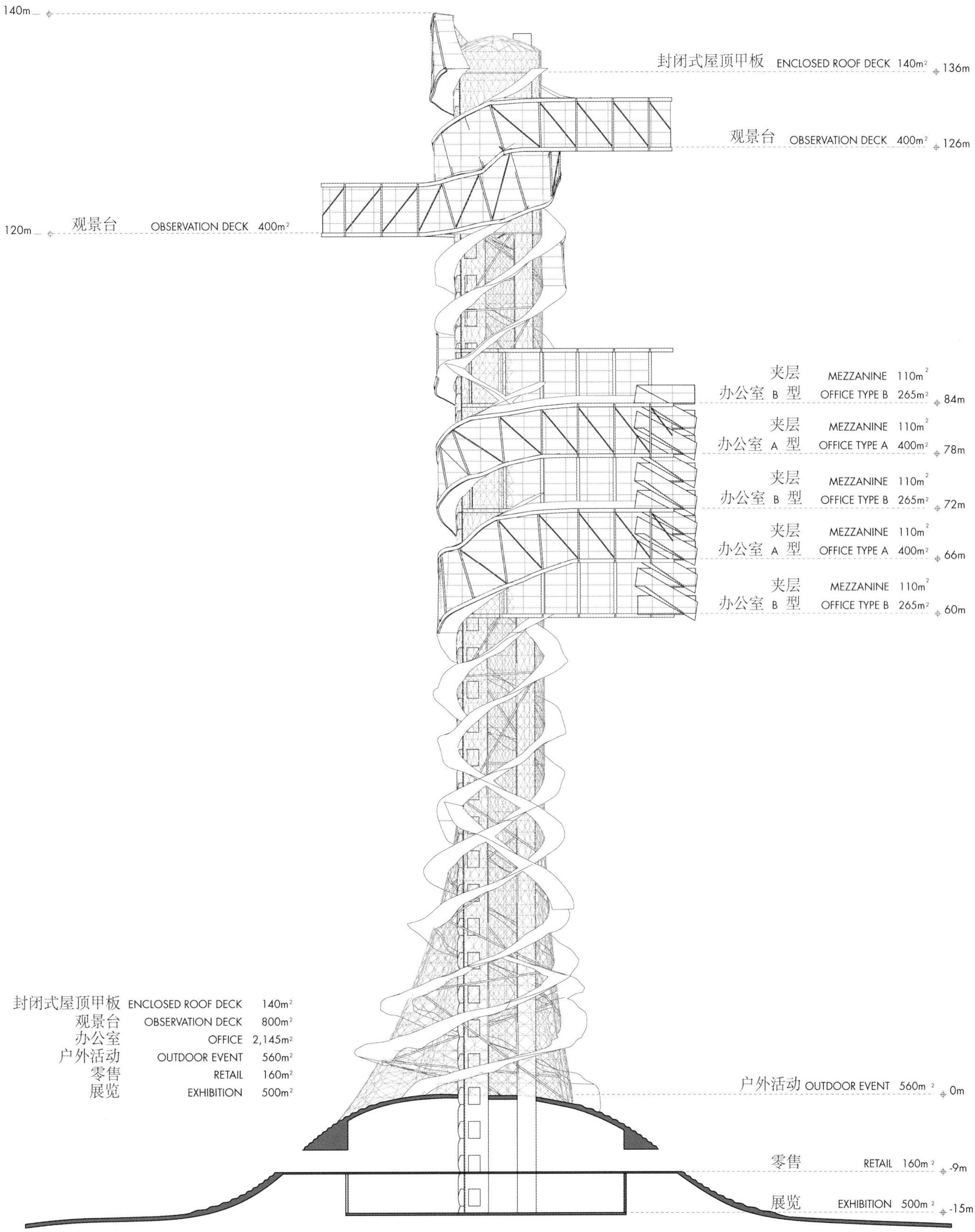

140m
封闭式屋顶甲板 ENCLOSED ROOF DECK 140m²
136m
观景台 OBSERVATION DECK 400m²
126m
120m
观景台 OBSERVATION DECK 400m²
夹层 MEZZANINE 110m²
办公室 B 型 OFFICE TYPE B 265m²
84m
夹层 MEZZANINE 110m²
办公室 A 型 OFFICE TYPE A 400m²
78m
夹层 MEZZANINE 110m²
办公室 B 型 OFFICE TYPE B 265m²
72m
夹层 MEZZANINE 110m²
办公室 A 型 OFFICE TYPE A 400m²
66m
夹层 MEZZANINE 110m²
办公室 B 型 OFFICE TYPE B 265m²
60m
封闭式屋顶甲板 ENCLOSED ROOF DECK 140m²
观景台 OBSERVATION DECK 800m²
办公室 OFFICE 2,145m²
户外活动 OUTDOOR EVENT 560m²
零售 RETAIL 160m²
展览 EXHIBITION 500m²
户外活动 OUTDOOR EVENT 560m²
0m
零售 RETAIL 160m²
-9m
展览 EXHIBITION 500m²
-15m
0
10m

ELEVATION

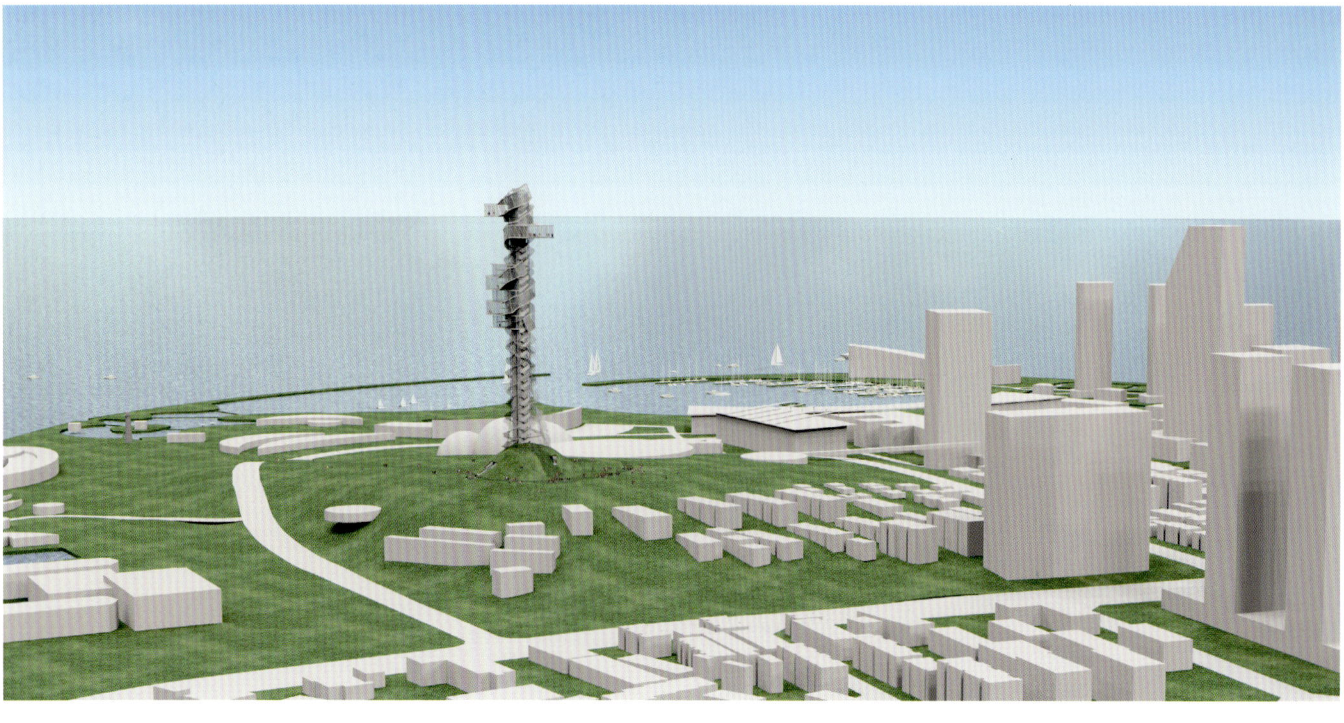

FIRST AND BROADWAY PARK

Location Los Angeles, California, United States
Client City of Los Angeles
Size 80,000 ft^2 (7432.2 m^2)
Date Under development

The park design has two essential land forms or topographies, one that conforms to the existing grade, a gradual slope from north to southeast. The first type, the exhibition zone, describes that portion of the site with direct pedestrian access from Spring, Broadway, and Grand Park. The surface is decomposed granite. The exhibit area accommodates the fabrication, assembly and viewing of cultural and educational installations, and pavilions of every sort.

The second topography is a planted landscape that departs from the natural grade, offering the visitor alternate landforms and use options. The exhibition area is a continuous material surface. The landscape area, in contrast, offers gradual slopes, horizontal plains, abrupt depressions, and terraced landforms—an adventure in land shaping. Pedestrian paths crisscross the landscape, not practiced and regularized patterns, but rather an exploratory journey across the site. Paths have a range of widths and directions, on a discovery journey as the land surface is explored over time. The rolling topography has a sense of unpredictability, less a park we know, more a park that invites us to discover.

There is a large restaurant beneath the landscape, with interior and courtyard dining options, accessible from First Street, or directly from the park.

Located on Spring Street, on the eastern edge of the site across from City Hall, is a large, covered exhibition gallery. Adjacent are multiple outdoor sequestered and partially enclosed exhibit spaces that accommodate assemblies and constructions of art and sculpture, connected by the continuous ground of decomposed granite.

The decomposed granite surface provides a flexible working area for exhibit production that facilitates truck delivery and service traffic, and permits the sort of wall- or site-mounted fabrication and assembly essential to building temporary installations. The multiple exhibition venues are available for a variety of topics and uses that park visitors will define over time.

A public event structure is positioned on the landscape at the south end of the site, framing the view north. The event structure can be used jointly with restaurant or exhibition programs to produce private

MODEL

SITE PLAN

0 30m

and public events. The event pavilion will be wrapped with a white projection screen. The taut, white surface will facilitate large-scale media projections for audiences standing or seated in the park and beyond.

The 'Hide-and-Seek Forest' is a combination of vertical poles mixed with small palm trees. The narrow admixture of poles and trees is placed roughly north–south, leading to Grand Park on the north side or to the restaurant on the south side. The juxtaposition of young palms with the fixed-length poles will allow visitors to measure the passage of time by comparing the heights of the palms over multiple park visits, against the constant heights of the poles.

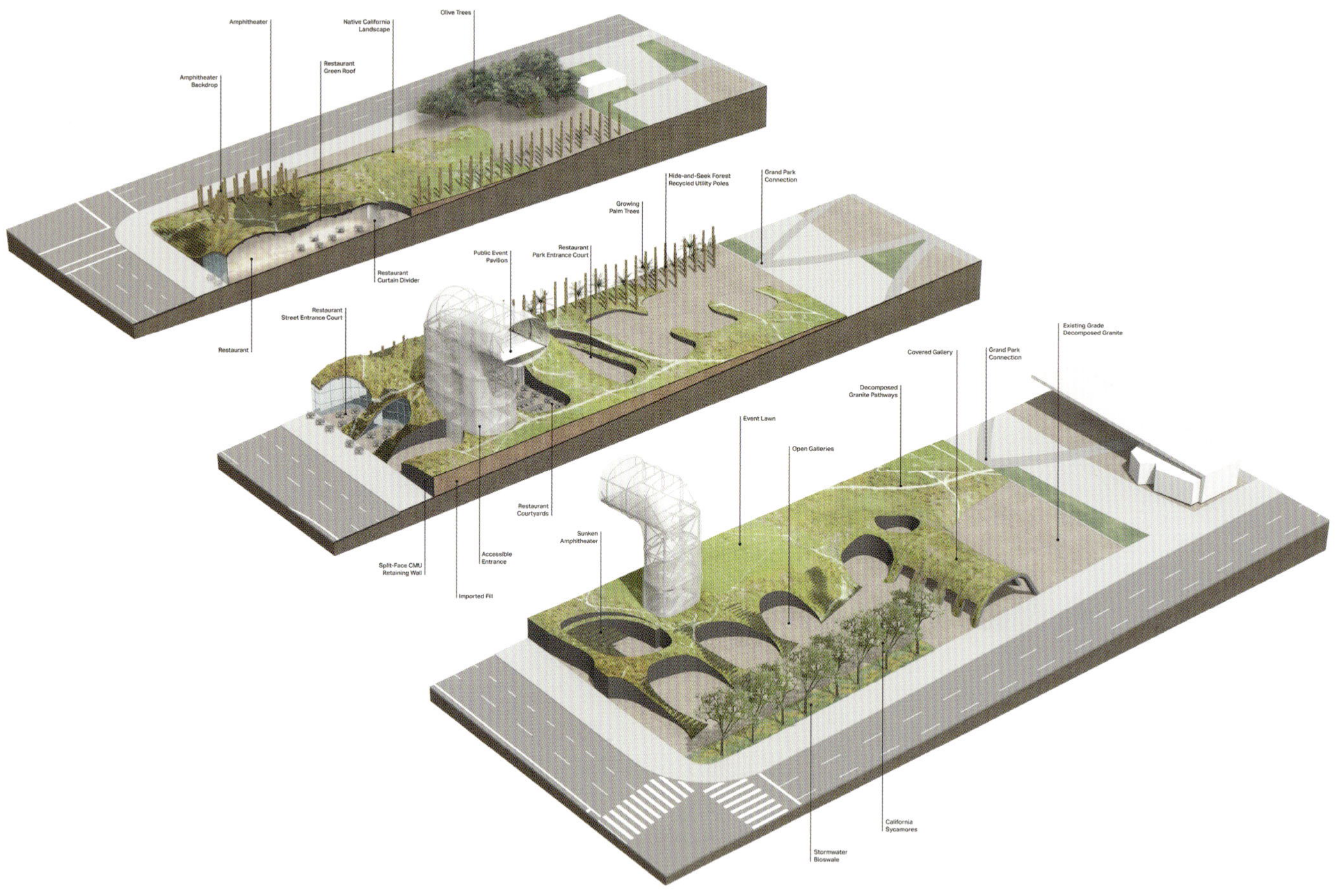
Amphitheater Backdrop
Amphitheater
Restaurant Green Roof
Native California Landscape
Olive Trees
Restaurant
Restaurant Curtain Divider
Hide-and-Seek Forest Recycled Utility Poles
Grand Park Connection
Growing Palm Trees
Restaurant Park Entrance Court
Public Event Pavilion
Restaurant Street Entrance Court
Restaurant Courtyards
Split-Face CMU Retaining Wall
Accessible Entrance
Imported Fill
Existing Grade Decomposed Granite
Covered Gallery
Grand Park Connection
Decomposed Granite Pathways
Event Lawn
Open Galleries
Sunken Amphitheater
California Sycamores
Stormwater Bioswale

Nightlife

Halloween

Sporting Events

New Year's
2016

SBERBANK TECHNOPARK

The Skolkovo Innovation Center is a new high technology business area currently under development in Moscow, Russia. The complex creates a community of international science and technology companies similar to Silicon Valley in the United States. The complex is organized as five distinct districts. The Sberbank Technopark will be located at the southern entrance to the park, and will become a landmark for the city of Moscow.

The project site is formed by two separate land parcels that are divided by a vehicular route for an electric shuttle service. The project massing will be distributed across the entire site, and subdivided into a series of connected units to reduce scale while maintaining a coherent organizational structure and pedestrian movement system on the site.

Visitors are welcomed by a series of media towers, a terraced landscape, and a clear pathway to the building lobby. Simplicity of movement is a key design element in the Technopark, to facilitate collaboration and the exchange of information between teams. Pedestrian traffic is prioritized and becomes the organizational driver for the project design. Outside transport streams connect to the Technopark in a variety of ways, but do not subdivide it.

The project is closely linked to nature. Gardens surround the exterior of the Technopark and serve both public spaces and office zones. The project perimeter is framed by a series of terraced plazas of stone and landscaping. This semi-public zone serves as a transition between the surrounding natural landscape and the Technopark. Open courtyards within the office area provide outdoor break areas and sport zones for worker recreation. Integration of landscape in and around the building allows the inhabitants and guests to expand their workplace by going outdoors, or in colder months, by establishing a visual connection with nature.

The internal building circulation is circumscribed across the entire site in a curving promenade that connects to office modules distributed throughout the project. The multistory volume is the primary public activity zone of the project and connects offices, display areas, conference rooms, vendors, negotiation rooms, and the rest of the major program elements both vertically and horizontally.

Location Skolkovo, Moscow, Russia
Size 1,624,059 ft^2 (150,880 m^2)
Date Unbuilt: competition entry

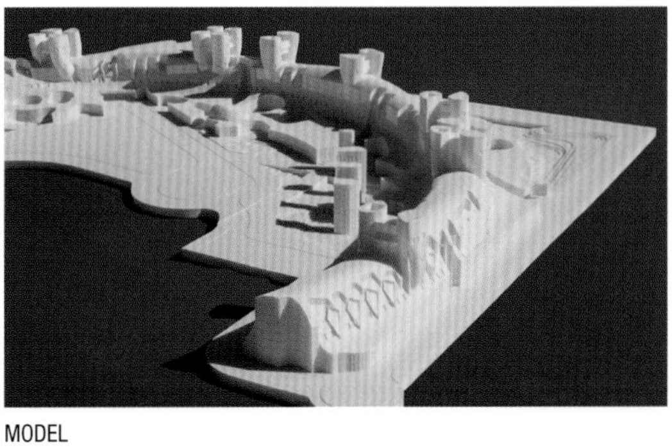

MODEL

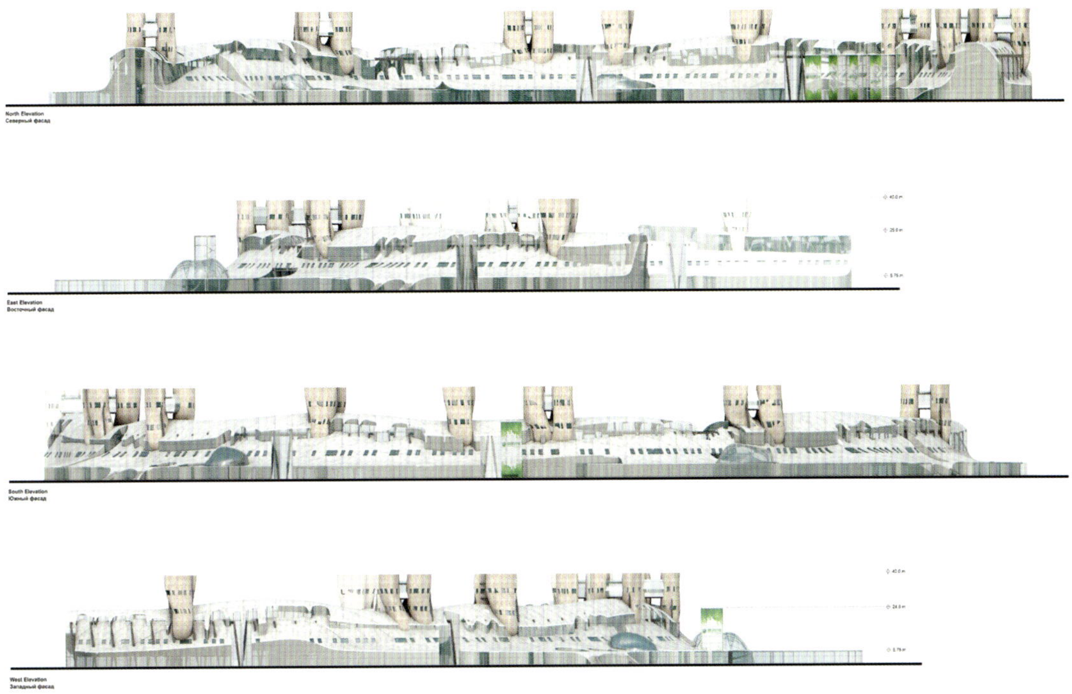

ELEVATIONS

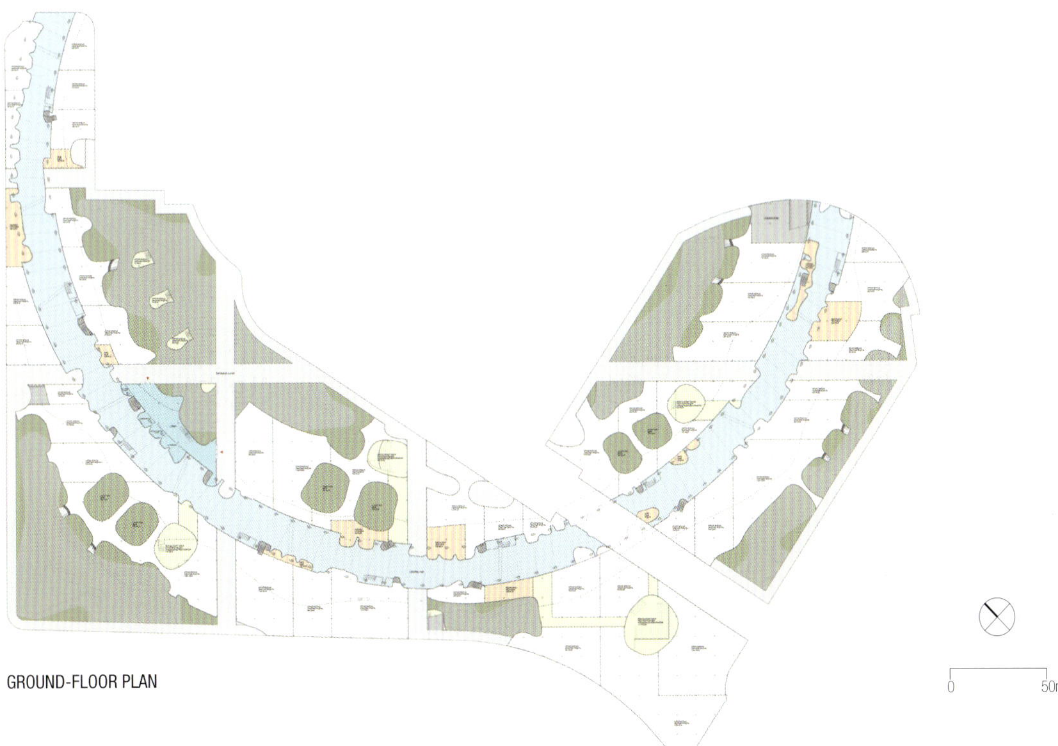

GROUND-FLOOR PLAN

Flexible and modular office bays may be easily reconfigured to accommodate changes in size or reorganization of project teams.

Every office area has an important and different view option. There are outdoor views from office areas via internal courtyards: the perimeter glazing; large windows on the mezzanine levels; and expansive elevated views from the conference towers. In addition, there are continuously variable views into the open Central Hub zone that provide natural light from the internal circulation zone. Above the office area and Central Hub, a series of Conference Towers extends upward to provide private conference and negation areas with expansive views of the surrounding park.

SBERBANK
By your side
SBERBANK
SBERBANK
By your side

REPUBLIC SQUARE

Republic Square is the ceremonial and organizational center of Almaty, the largest city in Kazakhstan. The competition site is located at the northwest of the square, surrounded by major public, institutional, and administrative buildings. Nominally, the project is a mix of commercial uses: luxury hotel and convention facilities, condominium housing, office space, retail and public space, and parking. By virtue of its enormous scale and prominent location, the project was intended as a constructed symbol of this newly affluent Central Asian nation.

Almaty's climate is one of extreme heat and cold. The conceptual solution connects Republic Square with a 'Great Hall' to the east, which increases the city's capacity for accommodating large public functions in inclement weather, and provides an indoor alternative to the square.

The program required a grouping of discrete high-rise structures, each defined by a different housing, office, hotel, or retail program. The design response is a single building which originates at the street as the Great Hall, and ascends as five separate components which merge to become a single structure. The vertical sequence: one building becomes five buildings become one building again.

Historically, Almaty is an area of sometimes violent seismic activity. The Great Hall is conceived as a sequence of arches, connected as a horizontal 'spring,' positioned to absorb lateral ground forces. To unify the action of the spring, a cable net ties the spring components together. Four braced 'light' net towers, roughly square in plan, each a different size, are supported on the 'net-springs.' They funnel seasonally varying patterns of sunlight through the tower interiors to the Great Hall below.

The topography rises gradually to the south toward the site of the National Art Museum. Four horizontal condominium housing blocks extend south from the Great Hall across the rising landscape. On the north side, public seating on a terraced earth mound abuts the Great Hall. Both the housing blocks and the earth mound provide lateral seismic resistance in the north–south direction.

The position of the primary structure maximizes twin spectacular views: south to the colossal Tian Shan mountain range, and north to the vast and austere Central Asian Plateau.

Location Almaty, Kazakhstan
Client TS Engineering
Size 861,113 ft^2 (80,000 m^2)
Date Unbuilt: competition entry

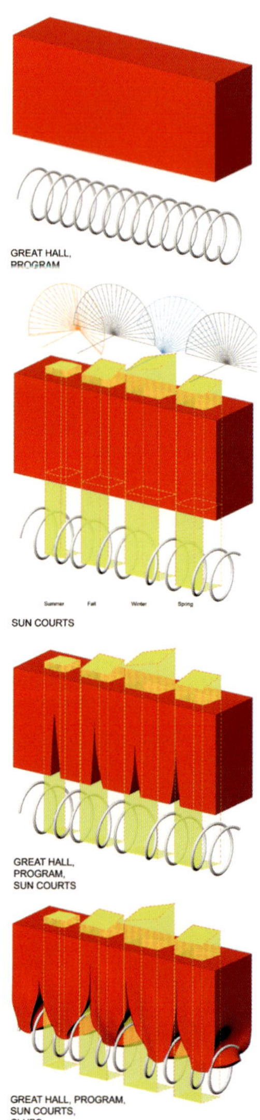

STRUCTURAL/MASSING DIAGRAM

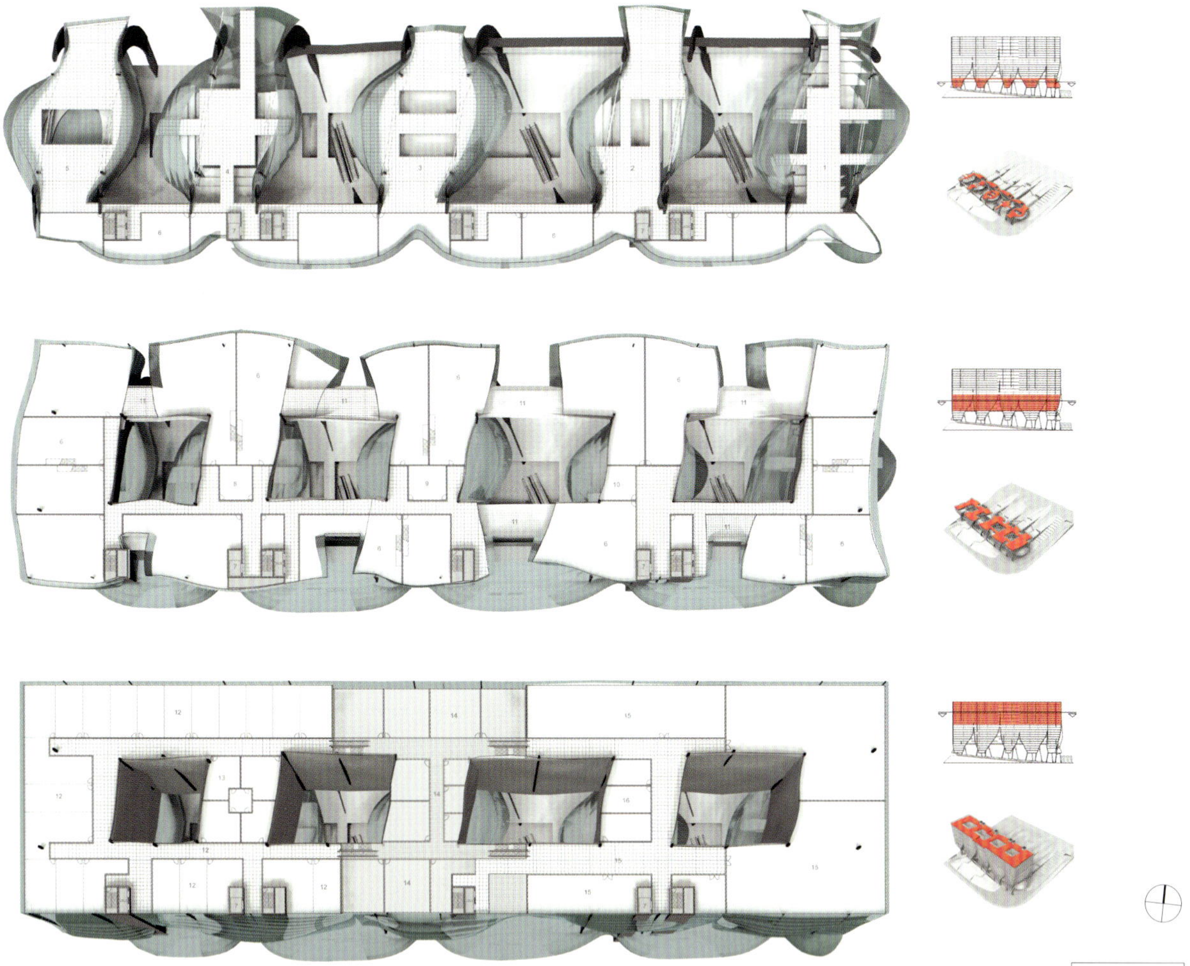

FLOOR PLANS

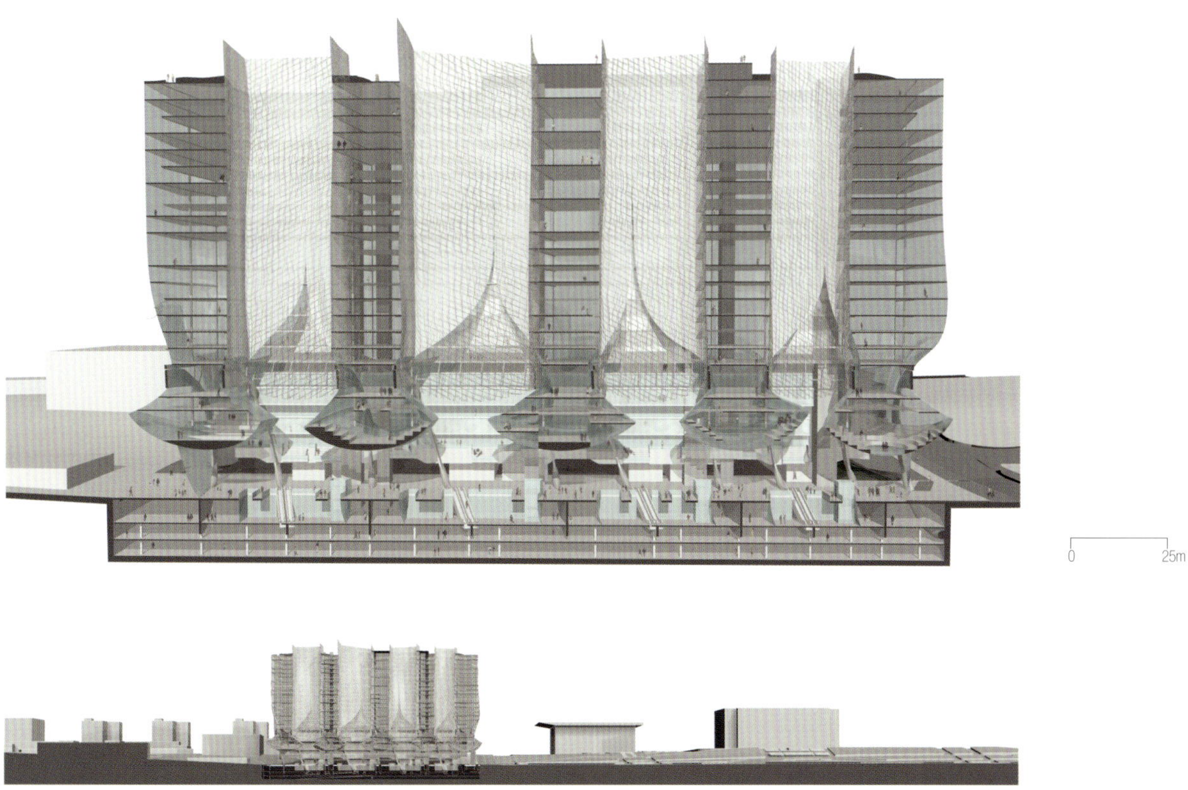

SECTIONS

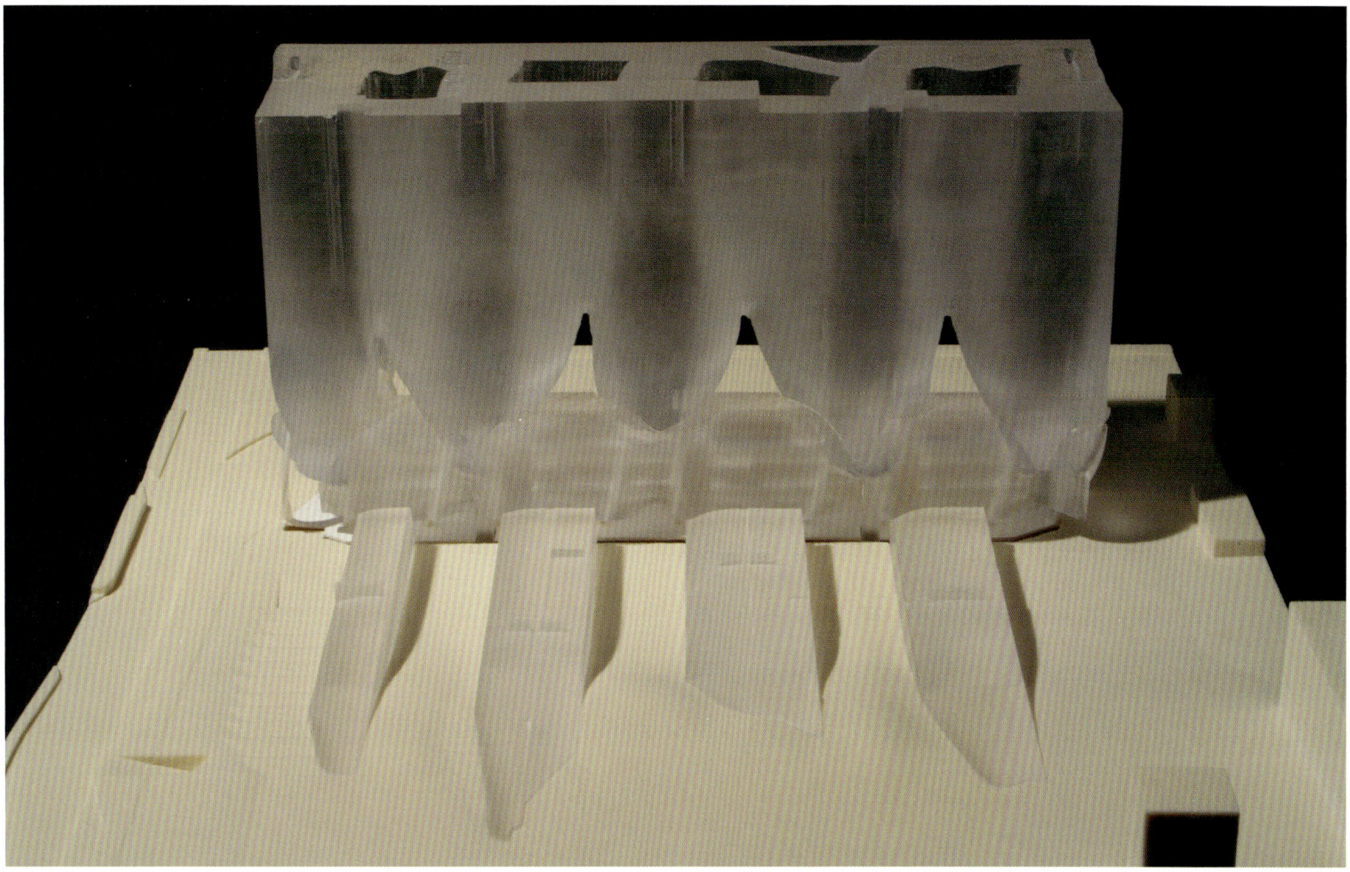

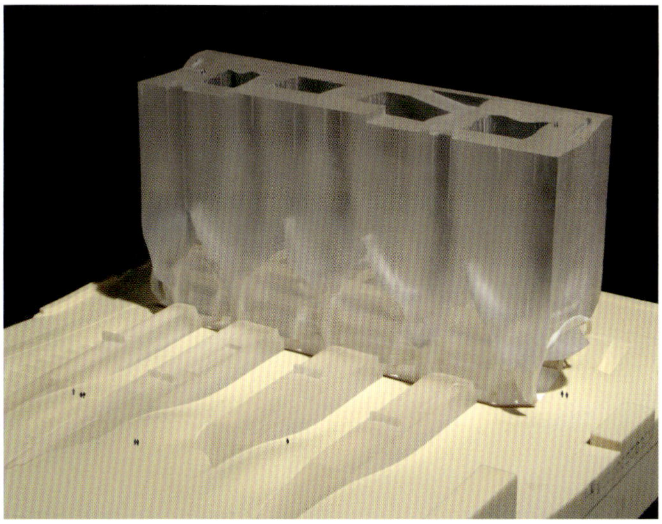

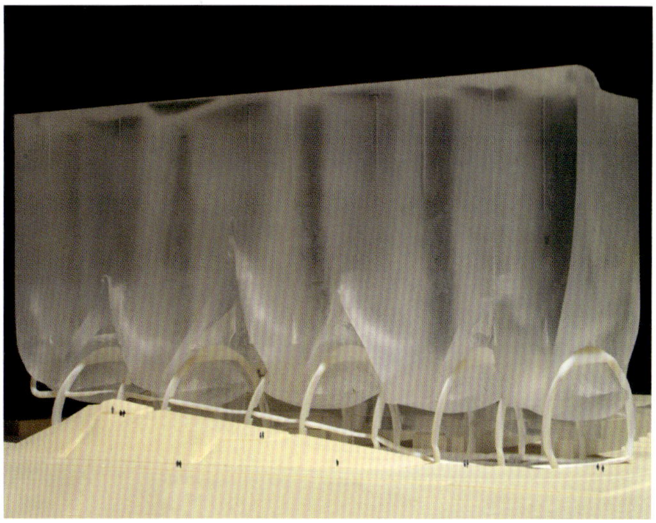

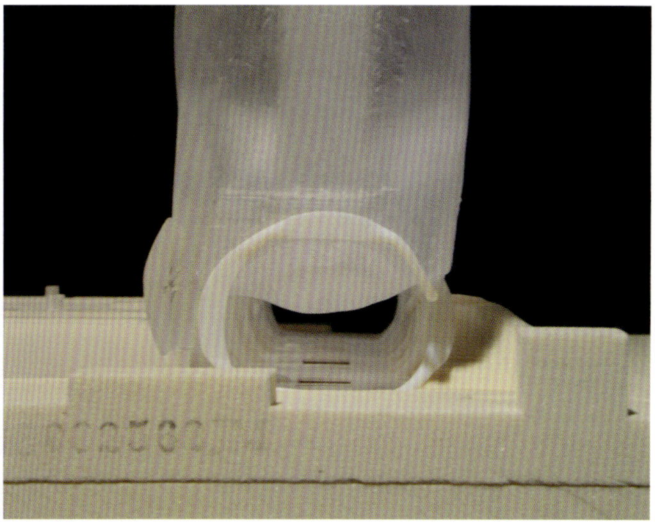

GUANGDONG PROVINCIAL MUSEUM

Location Guangzhou, China
Client City of Guangzhou
Size 430,556 ft^2 (40,000 m^2)
Date Unbuilt: competition entry

The site for the new Guangdong Provincial Museum and Opera House offered a unique planning opportunity to address rapid growth in the city while offering a unique experience of art and culture.

Two conceptual design metaphors were proposed—the Mountain with Four Peaks and the Glass Forest—to resolve the convergence of the expanding city, the Culture and Art Square, the Museum site, and the river.

Each collection in the Mountain with Four Peaks is housed in its own glass cube or tower. The Long Art March amidst the Glass Forest brings visitors to an open area at the center of the four glass towers with a large contemplation and seating space surrounding the walk and museum entrance. The sense of the commercial city dissipates and the museum's presence is primary.

Museum visitors enter from the contemplation area into the concourse level, a system of bridges and walkways above the Central Hall. The Central Hall is a flexible, multi-purpose area where huge, temporary exhibitions may be installed or bleachers set up for live performances.

Visitors can view collections from different perspectives, in different sequences. Exhibits may be examined individually, one tower at a time, by traveling vertically from floor to floor, or the collections can be studied by moving from one subject area to another, traveling horizontally on bridges that connect the glass towers. Each floor is divided into public circulation and gathering spaces, naturally lit exhibition areas, and a grouping of artificially lit interior galleries of varying size and number. The interior galleries are independent, variable concrete structures that extend vertically from the main gallery floor to the roof of the glass towers.

The public circulation floors provide a variety of spatial configurations that accommodate many forms of permanent displays, temporary installations and exhibits, and computer-guided monitors that are not compromised by natural light. The interior galleries are organized orthogonally which allows for the assembly and dismantling of temporary or permanent exhibits on the grid or off, and allow ceiling, wall, and floor lighting. The intermediate service zone is accessible from the public circulation side and the interior exhibit areas.

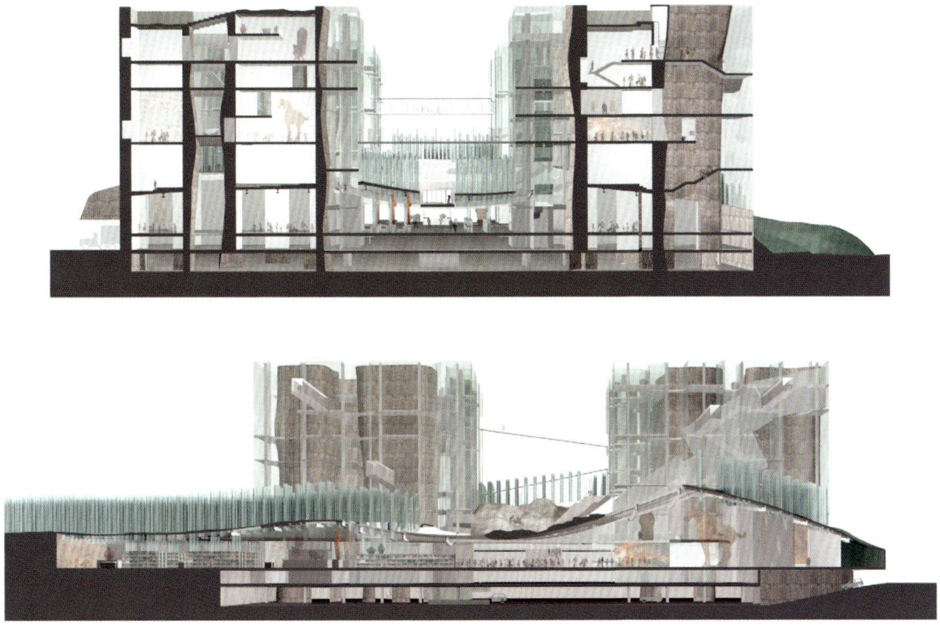

SECTIONS

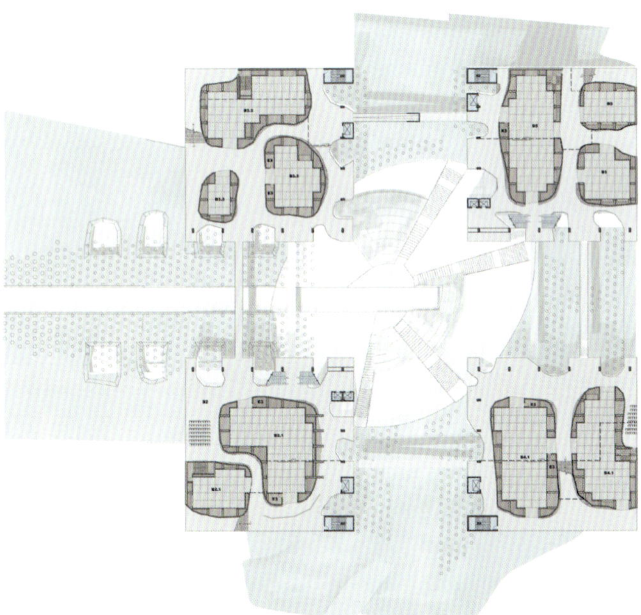

GALLERY-LEVEL PLAN

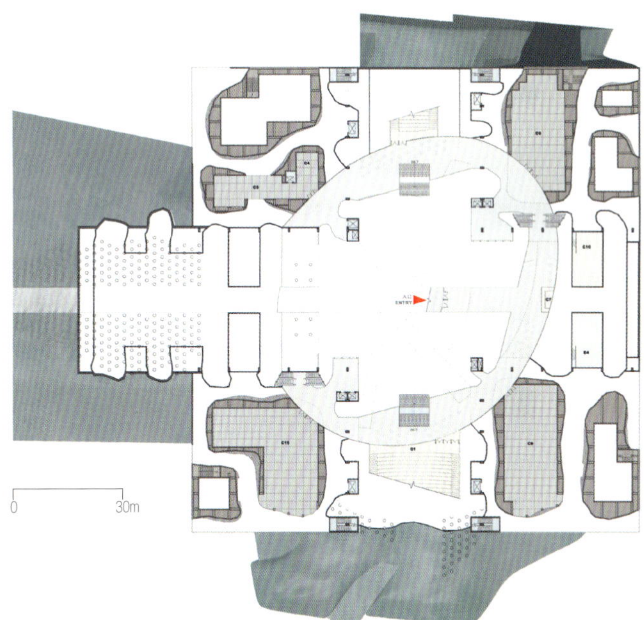

LOBBY PLAN

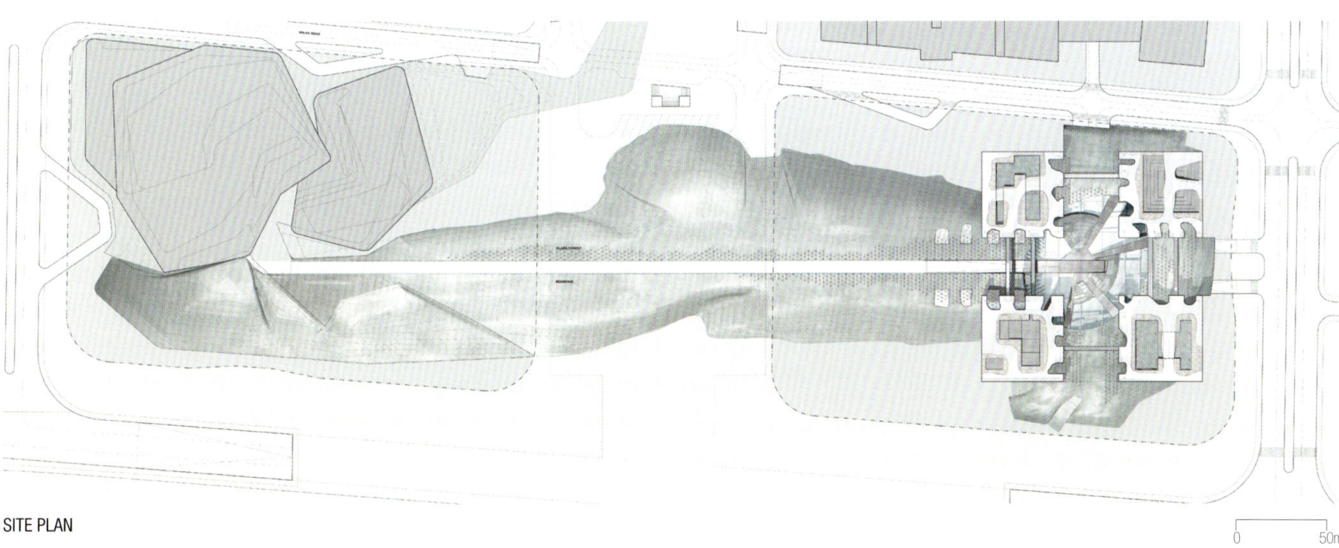

SITE PLAN

入口透视图
ENTRANCE PERSPECTIVE
透视图 PERSPECTIVES
中国广州 GUANGZHOU CHINA
广东省博物馆 GUANGDONG MUSEUM

JOSÉ VASCONCELOS LIBRARY

The design strategy for the Biblioteca de México extends the organizational systems of the surrounding neighborhood into the building, thus suggesting new prospects for public participation, interactive learning, and exhibition opportunities.

The site is first connected from north to south through the new 'Calle de los Libros.' The surrounding streets extend onto the site and intersect with this new street, forming the main organizational system for the new library.

The northern end of Calle de los Libros is excavated, leaving an amphitheater, gently sloping upward toward Buenavista Station. Temporary seating, oriented toward the new street, can be placed within the new amphitheater, or exhibits can be mounted over the sloping surface.

At the northern end of Calle de los Libros a portion of the generating station is extended over the railroad tracks to house a restaurant with broad views of the city.

The soil excavated to create the new amphitheater is reused and stacked as a linear, acoustic mountain along the western edge of the site. This provides a large, open, green space for library visitors to enjoy, and also shields noise from the adjacent Buenavista Train Station.

At each intersection of Calle de los Libros a courtyard is created demarcating an activity center within the library, and also serving as a large outdoor reading room. The walls of these courtyards slope southward to bring sunlight into the courtyard and the library.

The main entrance, located at the southern corner of the new library, is folded and lifted five stories vertically to create a new plaza that connects the Biblioteca de México to the Buenavista Train Station.

Location Mexico City, Mexico
Client Mexico City
Size 527,430 ft^2 (49,000 m^2)
Date Unbuilt: competition entry

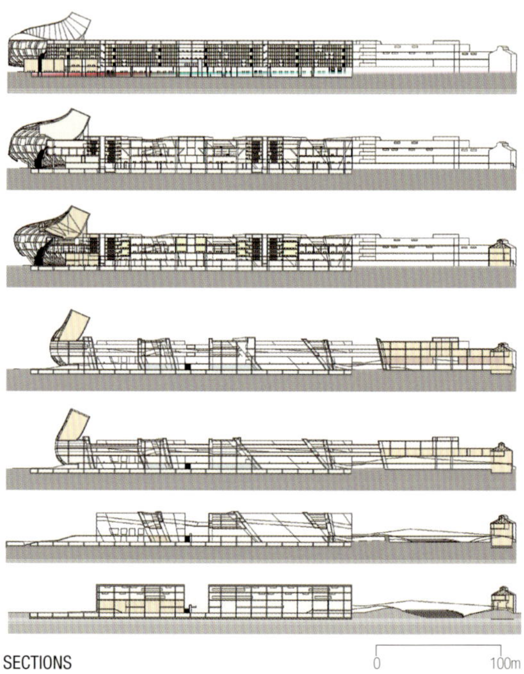

SECTIONS

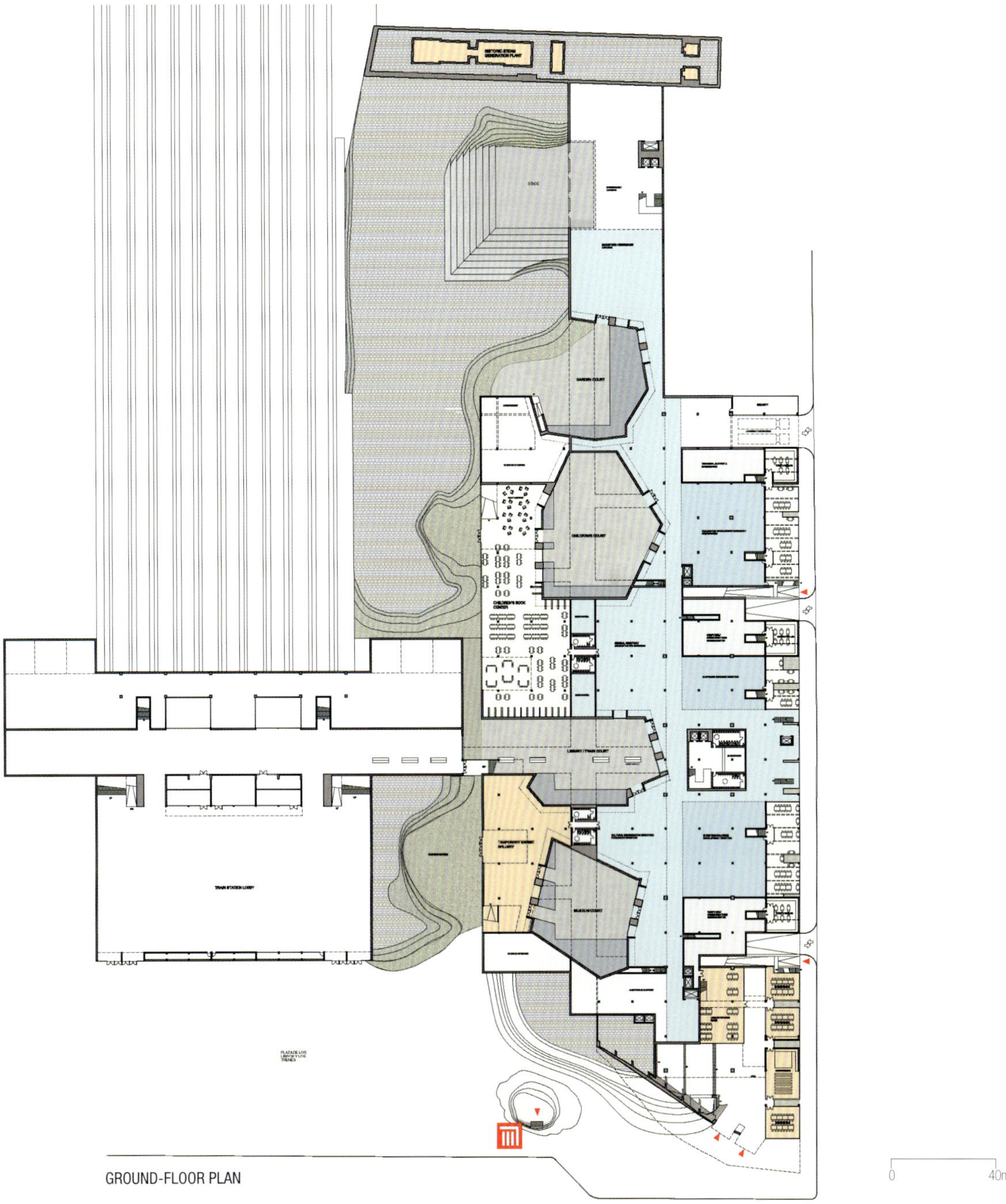

GROUND-FLOOR PLAN

SECTION

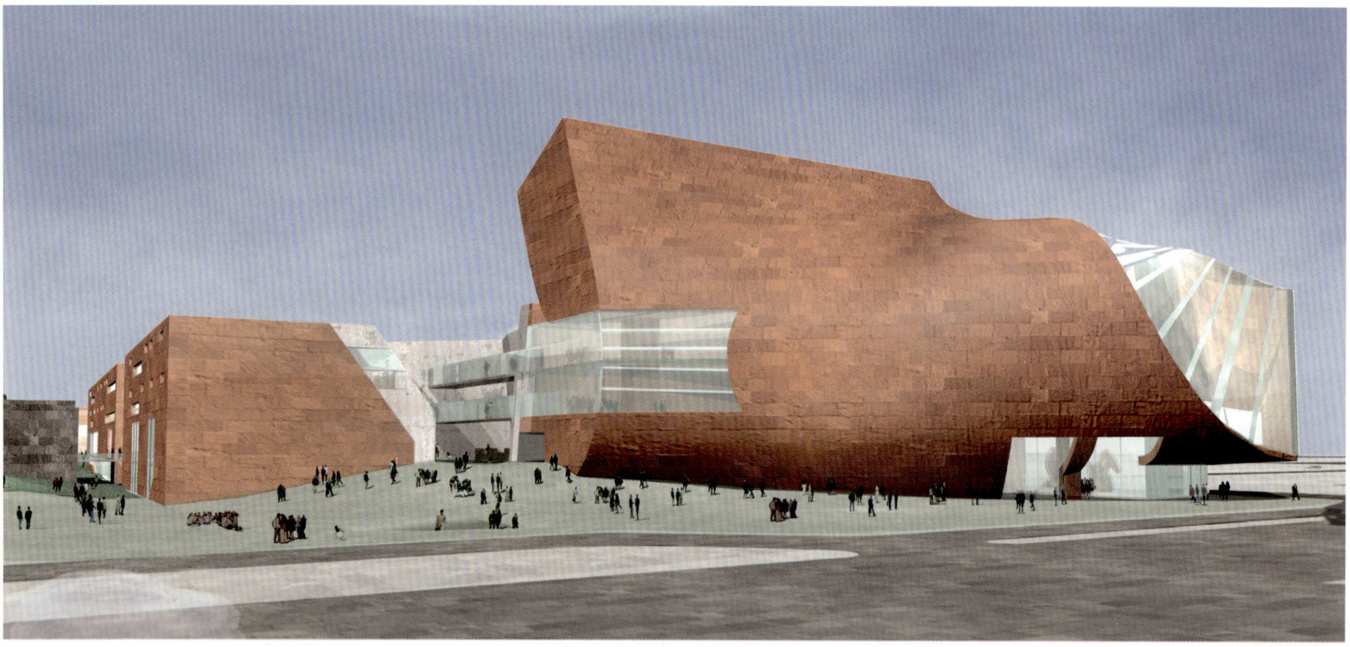

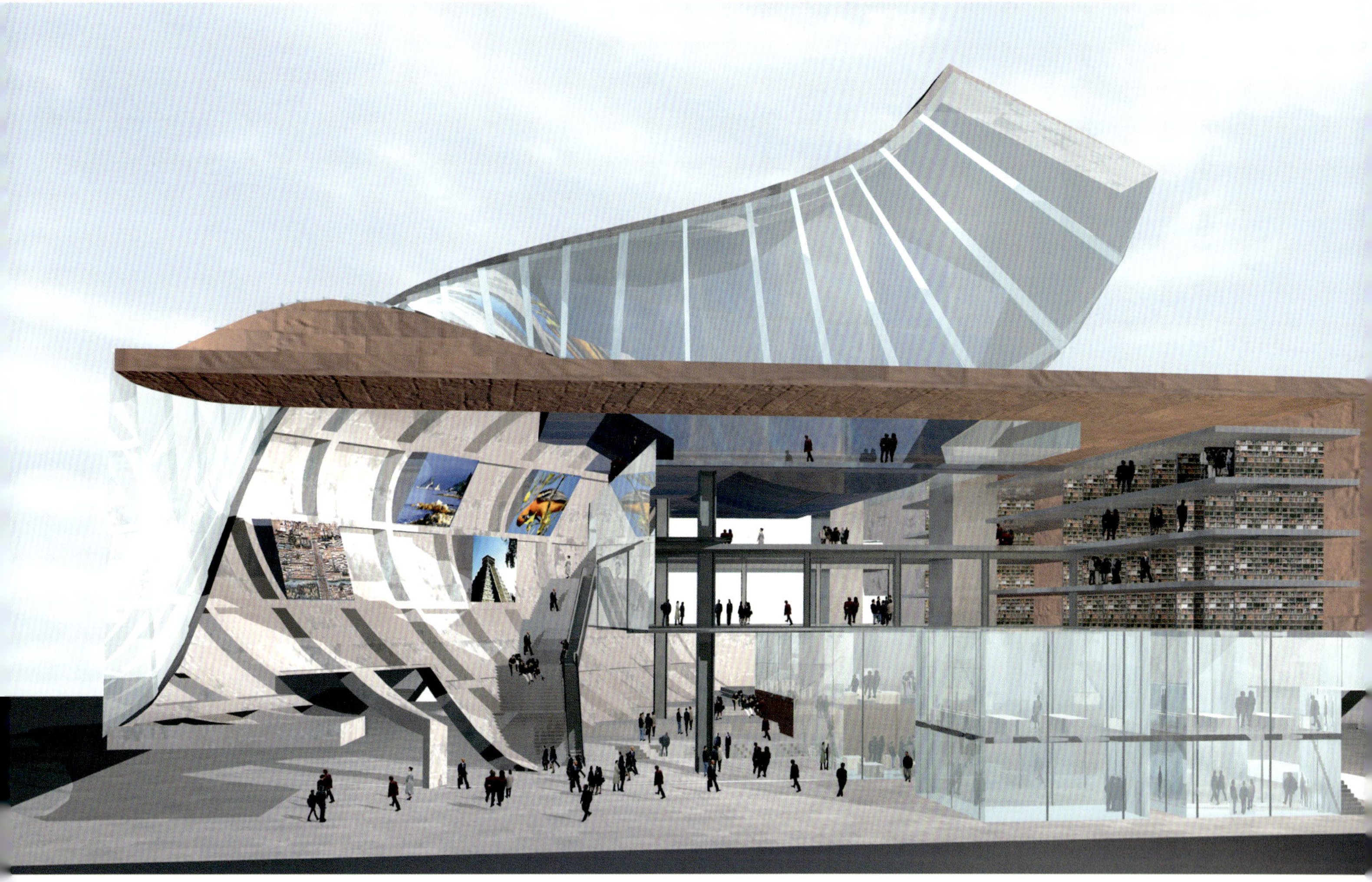

MARIINSKY THEATER I

Location St Petersburg, Russia
Client Mariinsky Theater
Size 750,000 ft^2 (69,677.3 m^2)
Date Unbuilt: competition entry

The Mariinsky and New Holland projects simultaneously reinforce existing relationships within St Petersburg as well as providing new connections that expand the operational understanding of the city. Two connections were developed—a cultural corridor and a religious corridor. These new urban relationships rely on the redevelopment of New Holland as a pivot point joining the cultural and religious areas of the city.

Two main cultural areas existed in St Petersburg—the Palace Square and surrounding buildings of the Winter Palace and the Hermitage, and the Admiralty—and a short distance away, the Mariinsky Theater and the Rimsky-Korsakov Conservatory. These two areas were linked through the development of the New Holland Cultural Center. Theoretically viewed as a pivot, the unique triangular shape of New Holland allows the corridor to change direction and connect both areas.

The religious corridor connects St Isaac's Cathedral to St Nicholas' Cathedral. Taking cues from the history of the city, the Blagoveschenskaya Church that used to stand near the New Holland site was reconstituted. The new church is located next to the intersection of axes drawn from St Isaac's Cathedral and St Nicholas' Cathedral. Consequently, it has become the terminus for the new axes and operates as the pivot point that connects the two cathedrals.

Along Glinka Street, the Mariinsky Theater is the anchor of the cultural corridor. Glinka Street was converted to a tree-lined boulevard to create a visual connection and continuation of Konnogvardeiskiy Boulevard. The Mariinsky was conserved and restored and a new larger-capacity Mariinsky Theater was built across the Kryukov Canal. Down the street, the Mariinsky Theater has become the anchor in the cultural corridor. The theaters are arranged back to back; the backstage of the Mariinsky connects to the backstage of the New Mariinsky. The plaza encompassing the Mariinsky, the New Mariinsky and the Rimsky-Korsakov Conservatory was redesigned to become a unified cultural site that promotes and enhances the urban and cultural importance of the complex.

The theater of the New Mariinsky is aligned on axis with the existing theater. The new theater is comprised of three modules that are barometers of the issues in the project. The design initially

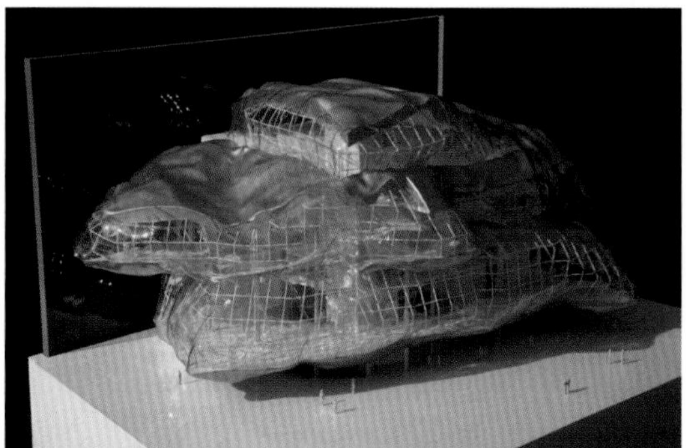

MODEL

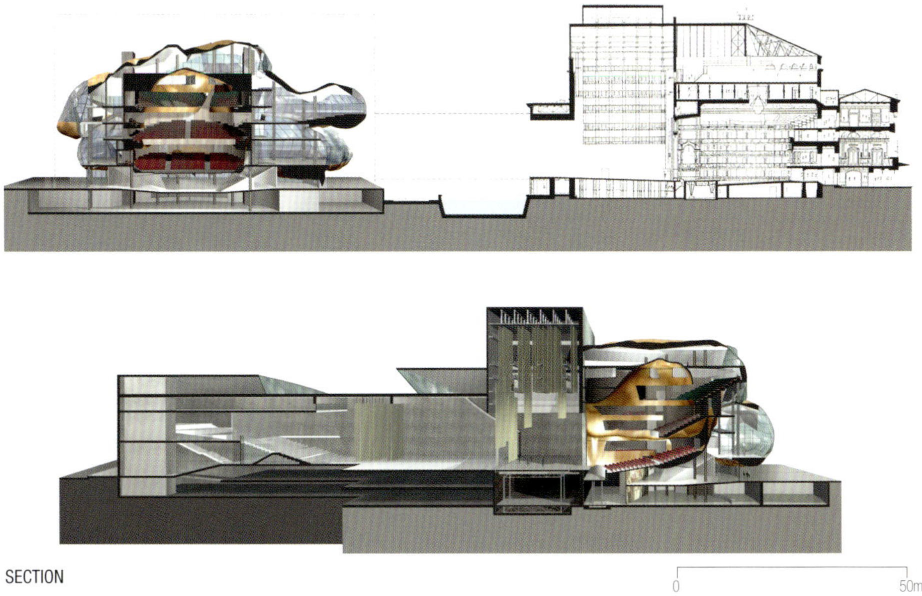

SECTION

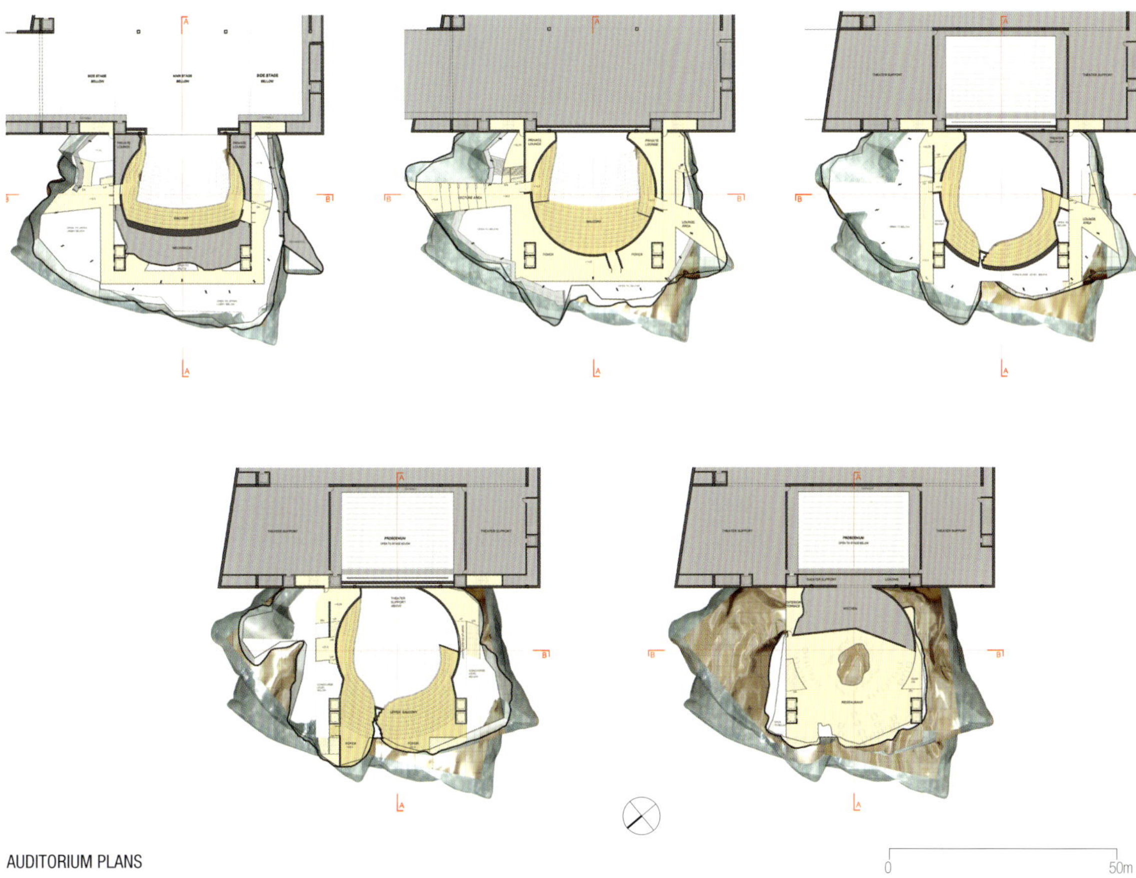

AUDITORIUM PLANS

accommodated the required number of stage-set modules and conventional theater dimensions. Due to the constraints of the site and the fixed dimension of the stage-set modules, the shape of the theater was compressed.

The majority of the square footage required for the support spaces for the theater occurs in a regularized block, providing a backdrop for the theater. The placement of the block and the theater creates two new exterior spaces—plaza and court. A glass-enclosed pedestrian street along the length of the site provides circulation/passage/access to the exterior plaza, main lobby and exterior court.

MARIINSKY THEATER II

The design strategy for Mariinsky II originates from two perspectives at two scales: the first defines the project as a new structure within an existing urban order, from the 'outside in'; the second originates from the performance hall itself, from the 'inside out.'

The new lobby, formed by the three contiguous glass modules, is metaphorically kinetic. It is simultaneously dependent on directional associations with key points in the city—the idea of the 'outside in'—and obligated by its internal program requirements like lobbies, walkways, lecture halls and gathering spaces—from the 'inside out.' The resulting interior space is a unique spatial and processional event. Its curving glass surfaces are climbing 141 feet (43 meters) through a shimmering volume whose dimensions continuously expand and contract as the space rises toward the light and the sky.

The curved glass panels of the outer skin provide a protective envelope for the building but do not seal the structure from the weather. The inner double-glazed façade is made of a series of flat plains that follow, by analogy, the shape of the exterior curves. Two semicircular truss rings soar through the lobby, and interrupt the curving exterior glazing. The two rings are pedestrian promenades, which can be used for strolls during intermissions much like the white hall of the original Mariinsky.

The theater entrance from the public plaza is demarcated by the raised glass canopy of the center façade module. The public passes into the grand foyer. This publicly accessible promenade is separated from the theater. The double lobby concept provides strict control of access to the theater, while allowing public circulation to the box office, below-grade retail and the Mariinsky gift shop.

The new theater hall is conceived metaphorically as 'inside the chandelier'—both a direct linkage with the shimmering glass prisms and interior design of the original Mariinsky, and a poetic spatial interpretation of the light and space of Mariinsky II. While the glass is most dominant in the aesthetic experience of the house, it also serves technical purposes. The undulating surface reproduces the acoustic diffusion quality of a highly ornamented classical opera house. The lobby concept of curving panels supported by a second, faceted plane, is reapplied in the interior. However, here the second surface becomes a second material—wood.

Location St Petersburg, Russia
Client Mariinsky Theater
Size 850,000 ft^2 (78,967.6 m^2)
Date 2004

MODEL

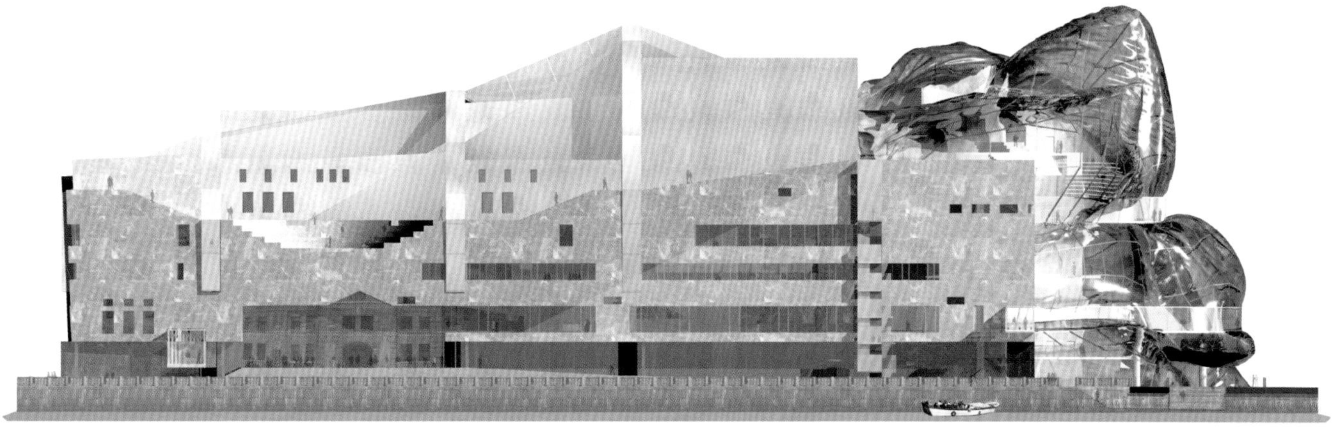

EAST ELEVATION

NORTH ELEVATION

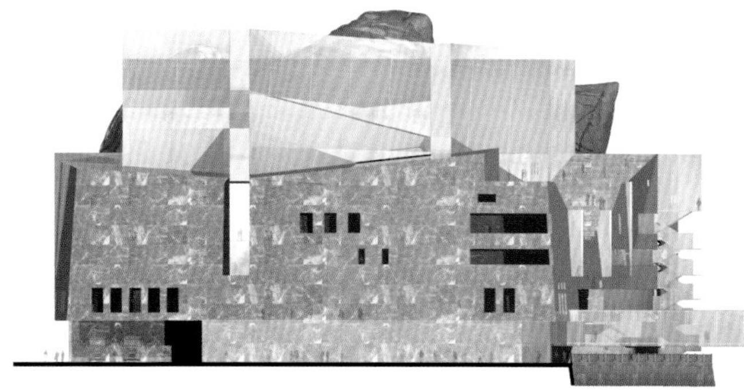

SOUTH ELEVATION

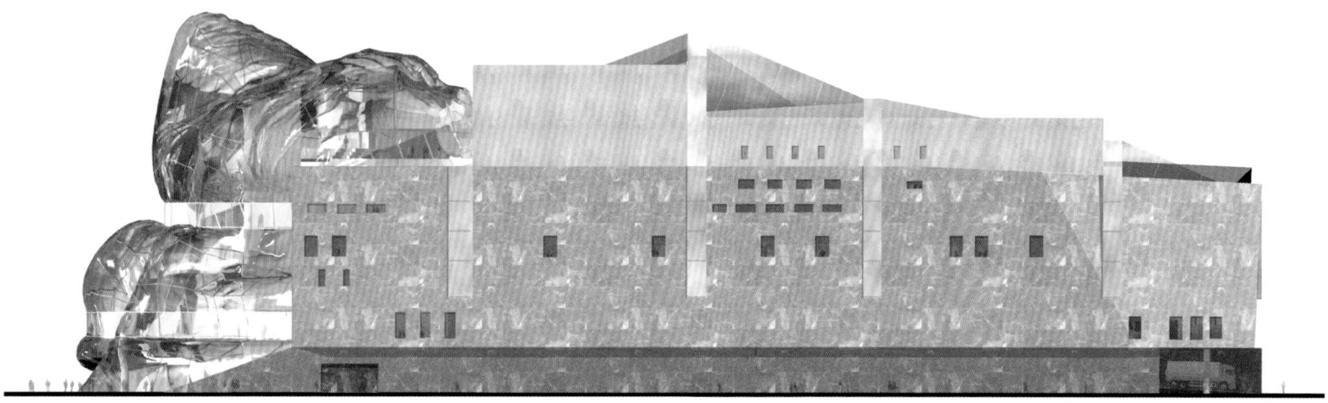

WEST ELEVATION

The ceiling is designed as an acoustically transparent glass grid with an opaque, moveable ceiling above, allowing optimal adjustments for opera, ballet, and symphonic music performances. Lighting is essential to this unique glass usage. The glass panels on the balcony faces will be backlit with their edges illuminated using fiber optics, producing a rich and sumptuous glow and a sparkle.

St Petersburg is known as Russia's 'window on the west.' The symbolic use of glass in the New Mariinsky project follows logically from the historic conception of the city as window. But this twenty-first-century 'window'—the public lobby and the performance hall of Mariinsky II—is no longer a simple east to west view. Rather, it has now become a metaphorical opening for multiple perspectives: from past to future and future to past; from outside in and inside out; from city to lobby to house and vice versa, from the first Mariinsky to the second, and the second to the first.

QUEENS MUSEUM OF ART

Location New York, United States
Client City of New York
Size 100,000 ft^2 (9290.3 m^2)
Date Unbuilt: competition entry

The design strategy for the Queens Museum of Art uncovers the organizational strengths of the original building and suggests new prospects for public participation, exhibition, and performance space.

The initial design gesture is surgical; the center portion of the building is removed, exposing the Panorama enclosure as a primary solid. Steel roof trusses remain and a re-enclosed central volume becomes the Main Event space.

The Main Event space is open and flexible. The original floor has been removed and the earth excavated, leaving a bowl, gently sloping toward a theoretical center at the base of the Panorama. Temporary seating can be placed within the bowl—an (almost) theater in the round. Exhibits can be mounted over the sloping surface or hung from the trusses above.

Connected to the Main Event space by a carefully orchestrated promenade are the bookstore and café, the Panorama, the World's Fair and Tiffany's permanent collections, and the temporary gallery spaces. A new public circulation ramp climbs the exterior wall of the Panorama enabling views of the Main Event from above. From the second floor, a second ramp up the face of the Panorama provides access to a glazed, multi-purpose space. Screens may be attached to the ramps so that film or video can be viewed in the space or projected through the glass to the park outside.

Unique among the temporary galleries is the double-height multi-purpose space. For the largest exhibits and performances, the main space and gallery can be used contiguously by opening the five glass doors that divide the space. Individual exhibits or performances can be segregated through the use of flexible and moving partitions. Spanning the double-height and Main Event spaces are two catwalks, facilitating object-hanging, projection and lighting.

Pedestrian circulation has been redirected from the Beaux Arts axis, affording the public the opportunity to pass by the perimeter of the Main Event space, viewing the exhibits without actually entering the galleries. This organizational 'short-cut' exposes the broader public to contemporary art.

The earth excavated from the bowl is re-used to form a linear mountain, creating a presence along the Grand Central Parkway. The

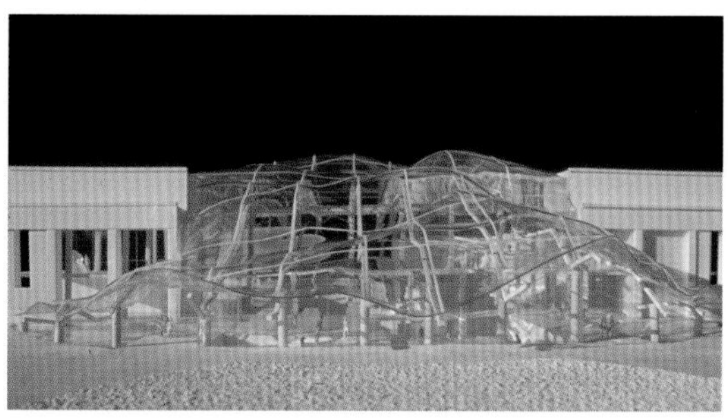

MODEL

SECTION

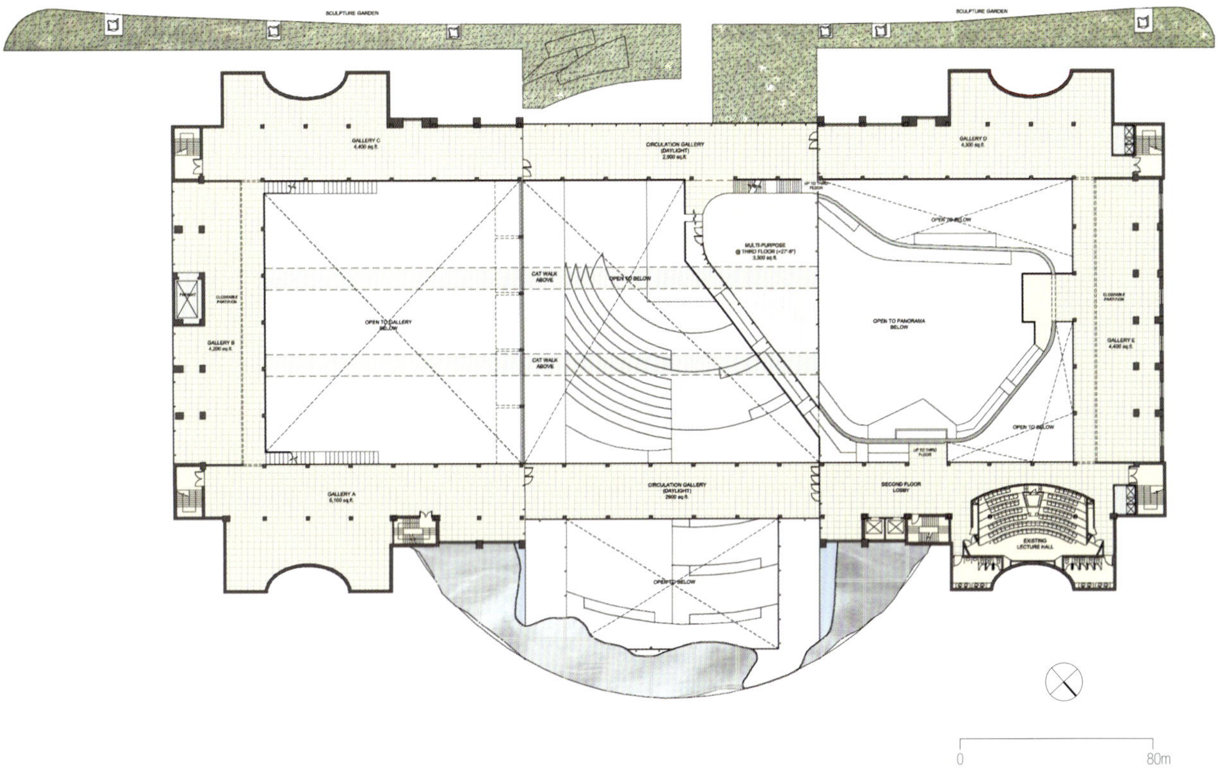

GALLERY CONFIGURATIONS

west end of the grass bowl extends, becoming a sculpture garden. Museum storage is placed within the mountain, beneath the sculpture garden. The grass embankment provides informal seating around an exterior exhibit/performance area.

A laminated glass 'drape' re-encloses the Main Event area. The glass can be made transparent, translucent, or opaque. Glass color is controlled by low-voltage wires, which alter the glass from clear to opaque milk-white. Water from the drape drains to two reflecting pools on either side of the east entrance. Seen at speed or on foot, the QMA communicates a powerful and intriguing long-distance profile.

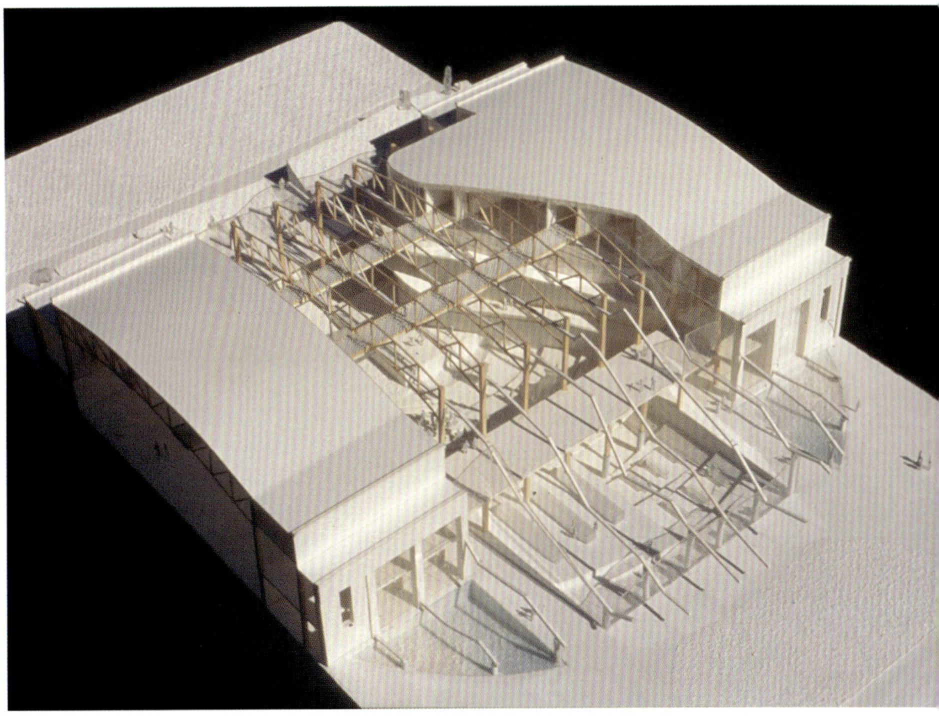
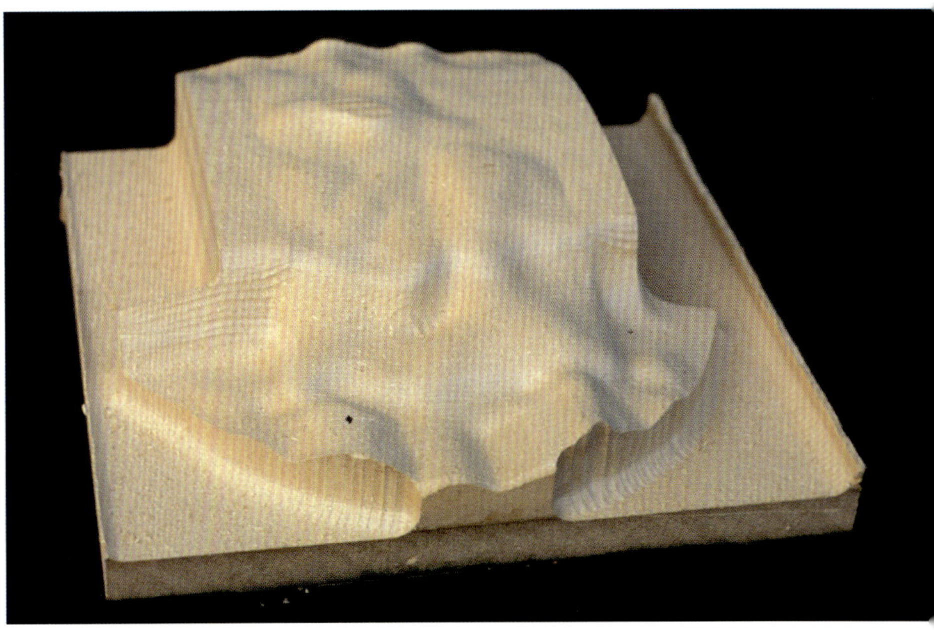

SELECTED EXHIBITIONS

2013 *Overdrive: L.A. Constructs the Future, 1940–1990*, J. Paul Getty Museum, Los Angeles, CA, United States

A New Sculpturalism: Contemporary Architecture from Southern California, The Museum of Contemporary Art, Los Angeles, CA, United States

Everything Loose Will Land, MAK Center for Art and Architecture, Los Angeles, CA, United States

A Confederacy of Heretics: The Architecture Gallery, Venice 1979, Southern California Institute of Architecture (SCI-Arc), Los Angeles, CA, United States

2010 *Under Construction—An Exhibition at the Austrian Pavilion,* 12th International Architecture Exhibition/ Biennale Architecttura 2010, Venice, Italy

2007 *Adventures in Kazakhstan—Eric Owen Moss Architects and Zaha Hadid Architects,* SCI-Arc Gallery, Los Angeles, CA, United States

Los Angeles: City of the Future, LACE Gallery, Los Angeles, CA, United States

Entropy—The Arts in Architects, Koplin Del Rio Gallery, Culver City, CA, United States

2006 *Royal Academy of Arts—Summer Exhibition 2006*, Guangdong Provincial Museum, Guangdong, China

London Architecture Biennale 2006, Clerkenwell, London, United Kingdom

Yildiz Exhibition 2006, Conjunctive Points Theater Complex, Culver City, CA, United States

2005 *Whatever Happened to LA?: Architectural and Urban Experiments, 1970–1990*, SCI-Arc Gallery, Los Angeles, CA, United States

2004 *Dedalo Minosse International Prize*, Palladian Basilica, Vicenza, Italy

La Biennale di Venezia, Metamorph, Giardini Arsenale, Venice, Italy

2003 *5th São Paulo International Biennale of Architecture and Design*, São Paulo, Brazil

Beyond Media/Oltre 1 Media 03, Florence, Italy

Mak Center/Schindler's Paradise Architectural Resistance 2003, MAK Center, Los Angeles, CA, United States

Architectures Experimentales, 1950–2000, Collection du Frac Centre, Orléans, France

GA Gallery, Tokyo, Japan

Westweek Exhibit

A New World Trade Center: Design Proposals, Cube Gallery, Manchester, United Kingdom; Deutsches Achitektur Museum, Frankfurt, Germany; Arkitekturmuseet, Stockholm, Sweden

2002 AIA/LA Design Awards

GA International 2002, GA Gallery, Tokyo, Japan

Top-Center Cultural Center, Taichung, Taiwan

Macau Museum of Art, Macau, China

Overseas Museum, Guangzhou, China

2002 Bass Museum of Art, Miami Beach, FL, United States

American Craft Museum, New York, United States

GA Gallery, Tokyo, Japan

Architecture for a New Millennium, Taipei, Taiwan

La Biennale di Venezia, Venice, Italy

Designing the Future, Queens Museum of Art, New York, NY, United States

A New World Trade Center: Design Proposals, Max Protetch Gallery, New York, NY, United States

National Building Museum, Washington, D.C., United States

What's Shakin': New Architecture in LA, Museum of Contemporary Art at The Geffen Contemporary, Los Angeles, CA, United States

Billiard Table—MAK Edition, MAK Center for Art and Architecture, Vienna, Austria

U.S. Design: 1975–2000, Denver Art Museum, Denver, CO, United States

Constructing California, SFMOMA, San Francisco, CA, United States

2001 *Seeing*, LACMA, Los Angeles, CA, United States

GA Gallery, Tokyo, Japan

Architectural Freehand Drawing Exhibition, New Opera House, Oslo, Norway

GA International 2001, Tokyo, Japan

2000 *GA Project 2000*, Tokyo, Japan

1999 *Recollecting Forward: 10 Years and the New City*, INMO Gallery, Los Angeles, CA, United States

Architettura in Vista, Ordine degli Architetti di Roma, Rome, Italy

American Academy, New York, United States

GA Houses 1999, Tokyo, Japan

Glasgow 1999, Glasgow, Scotland, United Kingdom

1998 *Architecture Again,* MAK, Vienna, Austria

Microspace/Global Times, Los Angeles, CA, United States

100 Years of Architecture, MOCA, Los Angeles, CA, United States

In the Tank, exhibit at UCLA, Los Angeles, CA, United States

8 Architects, exhibit at UC San Diego, San Diego, CA, United States

1997 *Fabrications*, Wexner Center, Columbus, OH, United States

GA International, Tokyo, Japan

Architect's Reflections of Chicago, The Art Institute of Chicago, Chicago, IL, United States

1996 *Paper Art 6*, Leopold-Hoesch-Museum der Stadt Düren, Düren, Germany

Green Umbrella, Havana, Cuba

La Biennale di Venezia, Venice, Italy

Present and Futures: Architecture in Cities, Centre de Cultura Contemporania, Barcelona, Spain

Artistes/Architectes, Le Centre Culturel de Belem, Lisbon, Portugal

Architecture Again, Los Angeles, CA, United States

1995 *Eric Owen Moss: Recent Work*, GA Gallery, Tokyo, Japan

Details, *Green Umbrella*, University of East London, London, United Kingdom

Artists/Architects, Institut d'Art Contemporain, Villeurbanne, France

Schindler House, Los Angeles, CA, United States

Wellington University, Wellington, New Zealand

GA International, Tokyo, Japan

GA International, Contemporary Art Center and Theater, Nueva Vieja, Havana, Cuba

School of Architecture, Princeton University, Princeton, NJ, United States

1993 *MANIFESTOS—International Exhibition of Contemporary Architecture*, Havana, Cuba

Concours pour l'Amenagement du Site Francis Poulenc, Contemporary Art Center, Tours, France

Philippe Uzzan Galerie, Paris, France

The Contemporary Arts Center, Cincinnati, OH, United States

Current Architecture and Furniture, Aspen Art Museum, Aspen, CO, United States

Fonds Regional d'Art Contemporain du Centre (FRAC), Orléans, France

Graduate School of Design, Harvard University, Cambridge, MA, United States

Angels & Franciscans: Innovative Architecture from Los Angeles and San Francisco, Santa Monica Museum of Art, Los Angeles, CA, United States

New Realities—Neue Wirklichkeiten II: Architektur—Animationen—Installationen, Museum fur Gestaltung Zürich, Zürich, Switzerland

1992 *Progressive Architecture 'New Public Realm'*, Washington, D.C.; New York, NY; Denver, CO; San Francisco, CA, United States; Toronto, Canada

Excavation, University of California, Los Angeles, CA, United States

Houses in Los Angeles, California, University of Zagreb, Zagreb, Croatia

Contemporary Architectural Freehand Drawing, GA Gallery, Tokyo, Japan

Angels and Franciscans: Innovative Architecture from Los Angeles and San Francisco, Gagosian/Castelli Gallery, New York, NY, United States

Theory and Experimentation, London, United Kingdom

Architects' Art 1992, Gallery of Functional Art, Santa Monica, CA, United States

1991 Bartlett School of Architecture and Urban Design, London, United Kingdom

Österreichisches Museum fur Angewandte Kunst, Vienna, Austria

1990 Salle des Tirages du Credit Foncier de France, Paris, France

Midnight at the Oasis, Harvard Graduate School of Design, Cambridge, MA, United States

Blueprints for Modern Living: History and Legacy of the Case Study Houses, Museum of Contemporary Art, Los Angeles, CA, United States

PHOTOGRAPHY CREDITS

Tom Bonner

Morgenstern Warehouse (30 below, 31 below)

Petal House (34 below)

UC Irvine Central Housing Office Building (42–47)

Lawson-Westen House (50–53)

Pterodactyl (56–61)

Umbrella (64–71)

Stealth (74–77)

Samitaur Tower (80–83)

Samitaur (86–89)

Box (92–95)

Beehive (98–101)

3555 Hayden (104–107)

3535 Hayden (110–113)

8522 National (116–119)

Cactus Tower (128–131)

What Wall? (134–137)

Paramount Laundry (140–143)

Gary Group (146–151)

If Not Now, When? (170–173)

Daniel Zimbaldi

Morgenstern Warehouse (26, 28–29, 30 above, 31 above)

Tim Street-Porter

Petal House (34 above left, above right, middle left, middle right, 35–39)

Piero Codato/Cameraphoto Arte, Venezia

Austria Under Construction (154)

All other drawings, diagrams, model images, and photographs courtesy Eric Owen Moss Architects

LIST OF PROJECTS